Sacred Music and Liturgy After Vatican II

Significant Works of
Monsignor Richard J. Schuler
in *Sacred Music*

Edited by

Virginia A. Schubert, PhD

AROUCA PRESS
WATERLOO, ONTARIO
2024

Sacred Music and Liturgy After Vatican II

Significant Works of Monsignor Richard J. Schuler in *Sacred Music*

Arouca Press
PO Box 55003
Bridgeport PO
Waterloo, ON N2J 0A5
Canada

www.aroucapress.com

Send inquiries to
info@aroucapress.com

ISBN: 978-1-990685-85-9 (pbk)

ISBN: 978-1-990685-86-6 (hc)

Copy Editor: Cindy Paslawski
Cover Art and Photograph: Christopher Foote
Design: Rhonda Klein, Evergreen Press, Ladysmith, WI

This volume is dedicated to Monsignor Richard J. Schuler, who founded the Twin Cities Catholic Chorale in 1955. This year we are celebrating the fiftieth season of the Chorale singing orchestra Masses at the Church of Saint Agnes.

Monsignor Richard J. Schuler
1920–2007

Photo by Virginia A. Schubert

CONTENTS

PREFACE

Sacrosanctum concilium (Constitution on the Sacred Liturgy), with a full chapter on sacred music, was published by the Vatican in December of 1963, the first of the documents resulting from the Second Vatican Council. An international church music congress, organized under the aegis of the International Society of Sacred Music – *Consociatio Internationalis Musicae Sacrae (CIMS)* – took place in Chicago and Milwaukee in August of 1966 with a two-fold purpose: in Chicago it was a meeting of scholars to discuss topics pertaining to Vatican II; and in Milwaukee, it was a working session designed to demonstrate how the ideas of the Council could be implemented. Monsignor Schuler, then Father Schuler, served on the international planning committee and was the general chairman of this music congress.

However, it soon became clear that there were two very different interpretations of *Sacrosanctum concilium*. The officers of the papal church music association *CIMS* saw the document as a continuation and flowering of previous papal documents. The other group, eager to find in the document a modernization of the liturgy and music, interpreted it in a much freer way which came to be known as the *Spirit of Vatican II*.

In 1975, Monsignor Richard J. Schuler became the editor of *Sacred Music*, the quarterly journal published by the Church Music Association of America. His tenure began with Volume 102, No. 3 (Fall 1975), and continued through Volume 125, Number 1 (Spring 1998), slightly over twenty years. When Monsignor Schuler took over as editor of *Sacred Music*, his task became that of a teacher. He brought his education and experience, his love of the liturgy and the Church to bear on what he wrote for every issue, always with the intent to make clear the directives of the Second Vatican Council. The purpose of this book is to bring Monsignor Schuler's most significant articles on sacred music, the liturgy and its practical implementation together in one place and in an easily accessible format, so others may benefit from his work.

What must never be forgotten is that Monsignor Schuler was a faithful son of the Church. He often said that it was possible to get off of a streetcar to the right or the left, but in either case, one was off of the streetcar. He *knew* that it was possible to carry out a sacred and reverent liturgy in Latin using the *Novus Ordo* with Gregorian chant and the Masses of the great composers like Mozart and Haydn with orchestra and organ. Thus, after the Council, there was a Latin High Mass in his parish, the Church of Saint Agnes in Saint Paul, Minnesota, every Sunday, using the *Novus Ordo*. This carried on the tradition of weekly Latin High Mass which had been established when the parish was founded in 1887. Several articles have been included in this book, either written by Monsignor Schuler or visitors, to demonstrate this practice which continues today. This is especially important as we enter the 50th season of the Twin Cities Catholic Chorale's presence at the Church of Saint Agnes in Saint Paul.[1]

When, at a gathering of priests with the Archbishop, a young priest asked Monsignor Schuler how he could have a Latin Mass, the Archbishop answered for him, by asking the questioner to explain why he was *not* having a Latin Mass in his parish.

Monsignor Schuler was often accused of being behind the times. To this, he answered that he was forty years ahead of the times. That is why I have included in this book, these many years later, contemporary commentaries on sacred music and the liturgy in the Catholic Church today with an eye toward the future.

Virginia A. Schubert, Ph.D.
Editor
Saint Paul, Minnesota

---

1. Monsignor Schuler, the Chorale's founder and longtime director, was succeeded by Dr. Robert Peterson. The current and third director of the Chorale is Dr. Marc Jaros.

Toward Continuity in Sacred Music

On December 22, 2005, Pope Benedict XVI gave a traditional Christmas greeting to the Roman Curia; this had previously been a simple formulaic occasion, but, typically, Benedict took the occasion for theological development. He spoke of the trends of development since the Second Vatican Council, distinguishing between a hermeneutic of *discontinuity* – which proposed to save only the innovations of the Council while disregarding the merely traditional elements articulated by its *Constitution* – and a hermeneutic of reform *in continuity* – which read the work of the Council in the light of tradition.

Monsignor Richard Schuler was an active proponent of the hermeneutic of reform in continuity; the work of the Council was to bring forward and perfect the traditions of liturgical reform. The *Constitution on the Sacred Liturgy, Sacrosanctum concilium* (1963) in its chapter on Sacred Music, summarizes the teachings of holy popes over centuries. It was the foundation of Monsignor Schuler's conduct of the liturgy at Saint Agnes with the Twin Cities Catholic Chorale. A key is paragraph 113:

> Liturgical worship is given a more noble form when the divine offices are celebrated solemnly in song, with the assistance of sacred ministers and the active participation of the people.

For the Fathers of the Council, "solemnly in song," and "sacred ministers" could have meant only one thing, the Solemn High Mass, whose strict convention was that practically everything to be said aloud is sung. This is not merely an archaic convention, but rather it expresses something essential to the sacred liturgy, that it be sung. Pope Benedict, when he was Joseph Cardinal Ratzinger, suggests this in his foundational work, *The Spirit of the Liturgy*. Here he articulates a principle evident in the liturgy for well over a millennium, that music is the essential means of addressing the most high God, the creator of the universe; Christ as *Logos* plays an essential role in creation, endowing the universe with principles of harmony, order, and purpose, and the highest kind of music reflects the same principles of harmony, order, and purpose. Thus,

> When man comes into contact with God, mere speech is not enough. Areas of his existence are awakened that spontaneously turn into song. Indeed, man's own being is insufficient for what he has to express, and so he invites the whole of creation to become a song (p. 136).

The function of sacred music is three-fold, "whether it adds delight to prayer, fosters unity of minds, or confers greater solemnity upon the sacred rites," with its purpose as "the glory of God and the sanctification of the faithful."

Gregorian chant is said, in the conventional English translation of the *Constitution on the Sacred Liturgy*, to have "pride of place in liturgical services." "Pride of place," may be a bit honorific and lead to place the chant on the shelf, but the Latin text says *"principem locum,"* "principal place." The normative liturgy is founded upon a completely sung Mass in Gregorian chant, with developments of polyphony and concerted music.

While the *Constitution* specifically mentions chant and polyphony, it admits other kinds of music, and those instruments particularly suited to the liturgy, such as string instruments. Moreover, it states a general principle: "The musical tradition of the universal Church is a treasure of inestimable value, greater even than that of any other art," and "the treasure of sacred music is to be preserved and fostered with great care." There could scarcely be a question that the Masses of the great classical masters should be included in this treasure. Monsignor Schuler's initiative to include the repertory of orchestral Masses, particularly those of Haydn, Mozart, Schubert, and others, links well with the status of the Church of Saint Agnes as a German nationality parish. Its architecture recalls the churches of southern Germany and Austria, and this music recalls the Masses still frequently celebrated in those countries.

Had the prescriptions of the chapter on sacred music been fulfilled completely, the work of centuries would have received a culmination with excellent musical liturgies celebrated in churches across the country. But the rest of the *Constitution* included little "time bombs," ambiguous statements which would reassure the Fathers of the Council of continuity with the tradition, but which, once the bishops returned to their dioceses, the experts could read the same statements in a sense of discontinuity. Thus, for example, even in churches with good musical establishments, the principle of a completely sung Mass, a *missa cantata,* has been replaced with a Mass which regularly alternates sung and spoken elements, breaking the continuity of sacred singing, in what I call a *missa mixta.*

Likewise, the Gregorian Propers of the Mass were substantially replaced. While the purpose of the Gradual is currently described as meditation, in my experience, a sung Gregorian Gradual can move a whole congregation to a state of recollection, something the trivial refrains of the "Responsorial Psalm" simply cannot do. The processional chants, Introit, Offertory, and Communion, were replaced wholesale with metric hymns, which, while they can be well-sung by a good congregation, their musical and textual substance does not reflect the liturgical action as the Gregorian chants do.

The hermeneutic of continuity disappeared completely with the incorporation of guitars and the styles of popular music, so that at one Mass I attended, when the combo struck up an introduction to the Gloria, I could not resist thinking, "Where's my martini?"

That sort of music is becoming passé, and more and more, churches are looking for music that best represents the essence of the liturgy in a hermeneutic of continuity. The Church Music Association of America and its journal *Sacred Music,* once popularly thought to be vestiges of the past, were for many years maintained heroically by Monsignor Schuler, who said, "Someday we will need these."

The need has now become evident, and the Association and its journal are thriving. Many churches are singing Gregorian chant again and even orchestral masses are performed in churches across the country. The example of the High Mass at Saint Agnes remains a paradigm now being followed more and more. This is thanks to the foresight of Monsignor Schuler and all the musicians of the Twin Cities Catholic Chorale, who stalwartly maintained the results of the hermeneutic of continuity.

In the nineteen-seventies, I was privileged to spend the Christmas octave in St. Paul, singing Mass and Vespers each day at Saint Agnes Church. Sometimes I stayed with a friend, but sometimes I stayed at the Saint Agnes rectory. This meant breakfast with Monsignor Schuler – a significant occasion, no chit-chat, just serious discussion of matters musical, liturgical, and theological. Everyone who knew him experienced the sharing of the depth of his commitment to the sacred liturgy. Now this book offers his wisdom to a much wider audience.

William Peter Mahrt, Ph.D.
Stanford University

PROLOGUE

Why the Church Needed the Second Vatican Council

In one of his last addresses as pope, Benedict XVI (Joseph Ratzinger) spoke to a group of Roman clergy. The German Pontiff spoke bluntly, perhaps even more bluntly than he had spoken on previous occasions about the Second Vatican Council. In the mid-1980s, the then-Cardinal Prefect for the Congregation for the Doctrine of the Faith sat for a book-length interview with Vittorio Messori which became known as *The Ratzinger Report*. There he was critical of the "spirit of the Council" which was (and in some quarters still is) taken to be a "hermeneutic of rupture" with the teaching of the Church prior to the Council. A whole host of issues is implicated by this approach, not least of which is the Church's moral teaching and the conviction that Jesus Christ and His Church are the only way to salvation for all of humanity. In the final days as he approached his resignation, Pope Benedict returned to the theme of the interpretation of the Second Vatican Council. In this, perhaps, he presciently anticipated the debates raging on the Council's meaning for individual Catholics today and during the pontificate of his successor, Francis. Indeed, the question persists: why did the Church need the Second Vatican Council?

Benedict XVI, in speaking to his priests, commented on the true Council and the "Council of the Media":

> The Council of journalists did not, naturally, take place within the world of faith but within the categories of the media of today, that is outside of the faith, with different hermeneutics...a hermeneutic of politics....The media saw the Council as a political struggle, a struggle for power between different currents within the Church. But it was obvious that the media would take the side of whatever faction best suited their world.[1]

While Benedict locates his criticism with the media, it seems that the "media" can be taken as a shorthand for those forces that had long circulated (and continue to circulate) throughout the centuries that echoed the ancient *non serviam* of the fallen angels to the order, design, and authority of God. Blessed Pius IX recognized some of the modern manifestations of revolt to God's order and called the First Vatican Council in the 19th century to reassert the prerogatives of God and His Church. Likewise, St. Pius X identified Modernism as the "synthesis of all heresies" as many from within and without the Church continued an assault on her doctrines and teaching.

While the Pian interventions shored up things for awhile within the Church, cultural currents continued to envelop the rest of the world in an anti-Gospel of a materialist, secularist, and atheist ethos. The rise of totalitarian states, the damage inflicted by the bloody World Wars, and what Pope St. John Paul II would later call "a loss of the sense of God" became the default position in the world of the mid-20th century. While the Church had seemed to be a bulwark of strength during the Pontificate of Pius XII, the evidence of subsequent decades would show that the world had infiltrated the sanctuary of God and many who should have guarded these sacred precincts had been asleep – content with appearances and trappings of strength, the equivalent of a flimsy, ecclesial "Beware of Dog" sign. But the dogs came in, and the Church was infested with fleas. It was in recognition of this reality, that Pope St. John XXIII called the Second Vatican Council.

In his recent book, *To Sanctify the World,* George Weigel summarizes the intellectual, political, and cultural currents of the roughly ninety years prior to the opening of the Council. He notes that there were two particular prophetic voices who saw what was coming: St. John Henry Newman and Joseph Ratzinger. Both, in Weigel's estimation, saw the need for the Church to respond to a new situation that emerged in the period since the end of Pius IX's reign. Newman, reflecting on challenges to the Church in 1873, commented "...Christianity has never yet had experience of a world simply irreligious." Eighty-five years later, a young professor Joseph Ratzinger, warned of the "new paganism...growing steadily in the heart of the Church." As these dark clouds were gathering, however, new light was dawning with a reappreciation of the wisdom of the Church Fathers of the first five centuries A.D. A dispassionate and honest look at the intellectual and cultural situation of the world and the Church prior to the Council is a powerful testimony of the wisdom of these two lodestars who, along with John XXIII, were convinced of the need of the Church to engage the world in a new way – *because it was a new world*. Thus, the pope's *raison d'être* and definition of the Council:

> ...[A]t issue is the response of the whole world to the testament of the Lord which He left us when He said, 'Go, teach all the nations...' The purpose of the Council is, therefore, evangelization.

This is why the Council was needed: *it was a new world*. Unfortunately, because of the power of the world and its preternatural influences, many took this to mean that it required *a new Church*. This was not, nor could ever be, possible. Every age since the time of the Apostles has seen the guardians of the tradition – the deposit of the faith left to the Church by Christ – preserve untouched Our Lord's teaching, but certainly clarifying or making more intelligible His teaching in light of new challenges or errors. Unfortunately, one of the unforeseen consequences of the heroic "opening of the windows" of the Church by John XXIII to address the prospect and reality of a world "simply irreligious," was the entrance of even more aforementioned dogs that furthered the supernatural war which had been raging since the fall of Lucifer and the seduction of our first parents.

In light of this, the Council has been a hotbed of controversy; and while the pontificates of Popes John Paul II and Benedict XVI seemed to serve as the prism through which the Council's authentic interpretation could be ascertained, some have taken advantage of the tenure of Pope Francis to renew and reinvigorate many of the confusions that were thought to have been settled. It is as if the "Council of the Media" has been given legitimacy by these same individuals; and indeed, the media, in promoting those causes *du jour*, is most willing to attempt an alignment of the Church with the standard of the world. This has, in turn, reignited controversies by so-called radical traditionalists and avowed modernists in the Church, who both claim that a new Church came into being with the Second Vatican Council. Both are wrong; both are in error; both are not *sentire cum Ecclesia* ("thinking with the Church").

There is one Church to which Christ calls all people. It is His

Church; in which, in light of a new world that doesn't recognize Him, He gives His grace to draw all to Himself – to save them from their sins, and to give them eternal beatitude, the fulfillment of every person's deepest longing. As a *kerygma* of sorts of the Second Vatican Council, let us let the Council Fathers speak for themselves in what is their ultimate message to the Church and the world:

> The Church, whose mystery is being set forth by this Sacred Synod, is believed to be indefectibly holy. Indeed Christ, the Son of God, who with the Father and the Spirit is praised as "uniquely holy" loved the Church as His bride, delivering Himself up for her. He did this that He might sanctify her. He united her to Himself as His own body and brought it to perfection by the gift of the Holy Spirit for God's glory. Therefore in the Church, everyone whether belonging to the hierarchy, or being cared for by it, is called to holiness, according to the saying of the Apostle: "For this is the will of God, your sanctification" (*Lumen gentium*, 39).

Which brings us to the volume you, dear reader, hold in your hands. An important front in the sanctification of individual souls and, therefore, the world is the promotion of an aesthetic that truly touches the innermost fibers of the human soul and puts one in touch with the divine. In his years as both pastor and musical scholar, Monsignor Richard Schuler has shown the way through a humble, persistent and attractive approach: *the way of beauty*. No radical traditionalist and most assuredly no modernist, Schuler was a son of the Church who understood better than most the need to cultivate holiness in souls through exposure to the beauty that is "ever ancient and ever new." His own scholarship and synthesis of magisterial teachings on sacred music and the liturgy was unrivalled. Such precision of thought, fidelity to the Church and her most recent ecumenical council, and greatness of soul was a comfort to Catholics across the United States and the world who were attempting to maintain their faith amidst the confusion of the 1960s through the 1990s. Likewise, he was a thorn in the side of and formidable opponent to those churchmen who promoted the notion that a new church came into being in 1965. These latter, perhaps exemplified best by the late Archbishop

Rembert Weakland, O.S.B., were fascinated with novelty and Sinatra-like, preferred to "do it their way," rather than be humble recipients of the wisdom of the ages. And, as pride goeth before the fall, the vacuousness of the Weakland approach has been soundly rejected, but for a few bureaucrats and several rather loud archbishops noted for their *blasé* commentary.

Monsignor Schuler knew the game from the beginning and aptly described the loss of the sacred in our lives with the resultant loss of the sacred in the practice of our faith. Heed well his words. His description of the chaos foisted on us also contains a response that includes the necessary infrastructure to make the liturgical life of the Church and the intent of the Second Vatican Council shine ever brighter: *Haec est voluntas Dei, sanctificatio vestra* ("This is the will of God, your sanctification").

John M. DeJak, J.D.
Front Royal, Virginia

1. https://www.vatican.va/content/benedict-xvi/en/speeches/2013/february/documents/hf_ben-xvi_spe_20130214_clero-roma.html

Section One

A CHRONICLE OF THE REFORM

Monsignor Schuler's own words, originally published in *Sacred Music*, Volumes 109 (1982) and 110 (1983), serve as the best introduction to this section.

> "This series of articles on the history of church music in the United States during this century is an attempt to recount the events that led up to the present state of the art in our times. It will cover the span from the *motu proprio, Tra le sollicitudini*, of Saint Pius X, through the encyclical, *Musicae sacrae disciplina*, of Pope Pius XII, and the *Constitution on the Sacred Liturgy (Sacrosanctum concilium)* of the Second Vatican Council and the documents that followed upon it. In knowing the course of development, musicians today may build on the accomplishments of the past and so fulfill the directives of the Church."

Virginia A. Schubert, Ph.D.

A CHRONICLE OF THE REFORM - PART I

Tra le sollicitudini

The *motu proprio, Tra le sollicitudini*, issued by Pope Pius X, November 22, 1903, shortly after he ascended the papal throne, marks the official beginning of the reform of the liturgy that has been so much a part of the life of the Church in this century. The liturgical reform began as a reform of church music. The *motu proprio* was a major document issued for the universal Church. Prior to that time, there had been some regulations promulgated by the Holy Father for his Diocese of Rome, and these *Instructions* were imitated in other dioceses by the local bishops. But Pope Pius' *motu proprio* of 1903 inaugurated a movement that would culminate in the action of the Second Vatican Council, which was the first ecumenical council to turn its attention to questions of church music so extensively, and in so doing, place the capstone on the reforms begun nearly a century before.

The *motu proprio* itself was the outcome of several decades of activity and study that had centered chiefly in Germany and France. Two movements flourished along separate but similar paths with the reform of liturgical music as their primary objective. One was the Caecilian movement in the German-speaking lands, centered in Regensburg in Bavaria. The other grew up around the Benedictine monastery at Solesmes in France. Roots of both movements can be traced to the romanticism of the nineteenth century with its interest in the culture of the Middle Ages, including the revival of Medieval music. Musicological research and interest in the discipline of history grew up in those years also. Efforts to study and perform Gregorian chant occupied both scholars and practical musicians, leading to the re-publication of the Medicean edition of 1614 (*Graduale* in 1871 and 1873, and *Antiphonale* in 1878) by the German firm of Pustet. Several volumes of chant were issued from the abbey of Solesmes too. An agreement with the Holy See granting Pustet exclusive rights for the sale of the chant books of the Church delayed the publication of the Solesmes editions which finally were adopted as the official texts and printed as the Vatican Edition in the first decade of the twentieth century.

Closely associated with the church music revival in Regensburg were Karl Proske, Franz X. Haberl and Franz X. Witt, founder of the Caecilian Society at Bamberg in 1868. Its journal, *Musica Sacra*, and the famous school of church music in Regensburg became the means of spreading their ideas throughout the German-speaking lands and even into Italy and the United States. Even the Pontifical Institute of Sacred Music, founded in Rome in 1911, and Italian musicians such as Licinio Refice, Raffaele Casimiri and Lorenzo Perosi had connections with the Caecilian activity at Regensburg. In the United States, the Caecilian ideals were promoted by John B. Singenberger, who came to this country at the invitation of Archbishop John Martin Henni of Milwaukee, and in 1873, founded the American Society of Saint Caecilia with its publication *Caecilia*.

While the Caecilians were interested in polyphonic music as well as Gregorian chant, the studies of the monks of Solesmes concentrated on chant under the direction of their abbot, Prosper Guéranger, who assigned Dom Paul Jausion, and later Dom Joseph Pothier, to the task of reconstructing the ancient melodies from manuscripts that were coming to light through interest in the monuments of the Middle Ages. Their work ultimately resulted in the Vatican Edition. Connected with its publication was the controversy stirred up between the proponents of the Medicean edition and the new Vatican books, repercussions of which were heard even in the United States and left their imprint, causing a decline in the Caecilian movement. Chant congresses which promoted the singing of the ancient melodies by vast congregations were promoted, especially in France. In the United States, the Gregorian congress in New York in 1920 was a great impetus in spreading the authentic melodies. It was attended by representatives from Solesmes and musicians from all parts of the world.

Although the Caecilian movement was active for nearly thirty years in the United States, particularly among German-speaking Catholics, the real catalyst for reform of church music in the United States came in 1903 with Pope Pius' *motu proprio*. Action did not begin immediately, but as the Caecilian movement ran into difficulties because of the suppression of the Regensburg Medicean edition of the chant, other efforts developed to carry out the papal *Instructions*. Just before the beginning of World War I, in June 1913, a meeting was held in Baltimore to organize a society that would implement the directives of the *motu proprio*. Father J. M. Petter of Saint Bernard's Seminary in Rochester, New York, with Monsignor Leo P. Manzetti of Saint Mary's Seminary in Baltimore and Nicola A. Montani of Philadelphia invited others to join them, and in the summer of 1914, a larger group of musicians met in Cliff Haven on Lake Champlain to draft the constitution of the Society of Saint Gregory of America. Their publication, *The Catholic Choirmaster*, appeared in 1915 with Montani as editor.

Important in the reform were the Catholic music publishing houses. In 1906, McLaughlin and Reilly was established in Boston, joining the older J. Fischer and Bro. of Dayton, Ohio, M.L. Nemmers Company of Milwaukee, and Pustet of Regensburg and Cincinnati. Their cooperation in bringing the compositions of the Caecilians of Europe and this country into print together with smaller editions of chants useful for parishes and schools provided the tools for choirmasters, teachers and pastors.

With the introduction of these materials it was hoped that the secular, cheap and sentimental music that was so prevalent in American churches would be eliminated. The chief thrust of the *motu proprio* was to demand a holiness and an artistic quality for all music used in the liturgy. The style held up as the best example of such sanctity and art was Gregorian chant. The polyphony of the Roman School of the sixteenth century as well as other polyphonists of the Renaissance period came second, and suitable compositions of modern writers that fulfilled the threefold requirement of sanctity, artistry and universality could also be allowed. The reformers were particularly concerned to eradicate music that came from the operatic literature, folk tunes, ballads and art songs. As in the application of any general principles to specific cases, judgments sometimes were not well-founded, and the interpretation of the *motu proprio* by some whose vision was too narrow often eliminated the good along with the bad and substituted music of no value.

The First World War had a great effect on church music in the United States. The roots of the Caecilian Society were German, and during the war, German culture in every aspect suffered from propaganda and prejudice. This contributed in a degree to the demise of the local Caecilian societies throughout the Midwest. By the same token, things French became very popular, and with that spirit in the land, the Solesmes chants found ready acceptance. A new era opened for the United States which brought in many European influences, not least a revival of interest in the liturgy with new ideas coming from Belgian, French, German and Austrian centers. Abbeys such as Maria Laach, Beuron, Maredsous, Mont-César and Kloster Neuburg were visited by Americans who brought back the research and new liturgical and theological thinking being done abroad. In this country, Saint John's Abbey in Collegeville, Minnesota, through the work of Dom Virgil Michel, became the center for a liturgical movement that published *Orate Fratres* (later *Worship*) to spread information and promote a renewed interest in the liturgy as the source of true spiritual life. Dom Gregory Huegle of Conception Abbey in Missouri and Dom Ermin Vitry, both of whom became editors of *Caecilia*, promoted Gregorian chant as part of the larger liturgical revival. The publication of *The Saint Gregory Hymnal and Catholic Choir Book* in 1921, under the editorship of Nicola A. Montani, marked a milestone in the reforms in both the United States and Canada. The *White List*, published by the Society of Saint Gregory, attempted to establish suitable repertory, both by suggesting and prohibiting certain compositions, although its restrictive stance and too-narrow standards reflected the poorer aspects of the Caecilian movement and led ultimately to its rejection. It did, however, accomplish a considerable amount by giving the clergy and musicians some definitive criteria for action on a practical level, while the theoretical aspects were promoted by the liturgical movement. Another publication that did much to improve architectural standards as well as artistic taste in vestments, chalices and other appurtenances of the church was *Liturgical Arts*, published by Maurice Lavanoux.

The reform was pushed forward by periodicals, new musical literature, congresses and various forms of legislation both universal and local. But the need for schools to train musicians was apparent very early. The Caecilians in Europe had their school in Regensburg. The Holy See established an international institute in Rome for students from all countries. The Institut Catholique in Paris did its part to prepare students according to the principles of Solesmes. In the United States, the Catholic Normal School in Milwaukee served the American

Society of Saint Caecilia and prepared many musicians to serve in the Midwest as teachers in the parochial schools and choirmasters in the parish churches. But the Solesmes chant also demanded a school for its study and the training of teachers to carry the new theories across the country. Such an institute was founded at Manhattanville College of the Sacred Heart in New York through the work of Mrs. Justine Ward and Mother Georgia Stevens who opened the Pius X School of Liturgical Music in 1916. It trained Sisters from many communities across the country who returned to train novices, who in turn took up the task of teaching Gregorian chant to the thousands of children in the growing parochial school system. Through the twenties and thirties, Gregorian chant became the music of the younger generations and in time as they entered monasteries, seminaries and convents, the chant there improved and flourished. By 1940, the implementation of the directives of the *motu proprio* on chant was well underway in the United States, but a restrictive, narrow reading of the document could be detected and this would ultimately lead to a negative force that deprived the movement of the freedom needed for any artistic development.

Part of the restrictive, legalistic attitude that grew during the years following World War I can be attributed to the efforts to dispose of poor and often offensive compositions that cluttered the repertory of most choirs. Unfortunately, along with the poor and secular and cheap, much that was good music, especially music of the classical period, was replaced by compositions judged to be safe and acceptable, but which were often insipid and characterless, music that was so innocuous that it could be said to be "seen but not heard." The supremacy of the text was so over-emphasized that melody and harmony were sometimes only tolerated and were thought to be most acceptable when they were hardly noticed. Repetition of the text was judged to be wrong, thus excluding much great music of the past from liturgical performance. A misunderstanding of the polyphony of the sixteenth century, including the work of Palestrina, deified the Roman School of composers, although their works were only rarely performed; but in fostering that style efforts to imitate it produced music of doubtful worth. Since the *motu proprio* had given chant a primacy of place among styles of music suitable for liturgical use, some thought that to imitate chant would produce the best contemporary music. But imitation and restriction have never produced true art, and so the period between the wars in this country saw the creation of a great bulk of mediocre music as well as the great progress that occurred in chant study and performance.

Parochial schools, seminaries, novitiates and abbeys were the scene of the greatest chant activity. Singing by even large congregations developed. The *Liber Usualis*, not an official book but a very useful one, served as the regular text for Mass, Vespers and other parts of the liturgy, and it gradually replaced the old Regensburg books that were still occasionally found, especially in German parishes. Unfortunately, the chant did not find as ready an acceptance in the parish choirs, many of which found it difficult to give up old repertory and to master the new theories of chant. A rigid insistence on the rhythmic theories of Solesmes in all performances of chant was a restrictive element, since most choirmasters had not been trained in it and thus were reluctant to try to teach it. Graduates of the Pius X School taught only the theories of Dom André Mocquereau and Dom Joseph Gajard to their students. These were very French in their approach to the Latin language, and often conflict developed in teaching the chant, especially among groups of German or other ethnic backgrounds. The chant became too precious and difficult to perform because of the theories of interpretation. Too often choirs imitated rather than learned the chants. School children in the Midwest sometimes sounded like members of a French choir instead of the children of immigrants from eastern Europe. Parish choirs found it too difficult to achieve the special effects demanded by the experts, and the result, unfortunately, was a reluctance to use chant, especially in parochial choirs and in congregations. The chant was intended to be the song of the people, but unfortunately it became an art form whose rendition was beyond the abilities of all except the specially trained.

The years following World War I saw also the establishment of departments of music in many Catholic colleges that were prospering in nearly every state. The women's colleges quite regularly promoted chant, because Pius X School trained nuns, and only later on allowed registration of male students. As a result, most men's colleges had very insignificant church music courses. This was caused also by the large number of colleges under Jesuit administration where courses in music were not usual. Seminaries did very little at first, since priests themselves were not trained to teach music. But little by little, seminary officials recognized the need of professional study for teachers of music, and as the Roman directives continued to insist on the training of seminarians in chant and music, such training was given to promising candidates who in time became the professors of music in seminaries, replacing many who had held the position, often without much training.

In 1943, even though the country and the world were at war, modest observances of the publication of the *motu proprio* were held in several parts of the United States. The question was always asked, "How much progress has been made in implementing the decrees of the Holy See?" Usually one could say that considerable work had been done. Seminary music courses had been established; departments of music that gave training in church music existed; religious orders of Sisters had prepared their members to teach the chant in the parochial schools; societies of church musicians continued to publish their journals; several firms made materials available for study and performance; many dioceses had issued regulations based on the Roman decrees; guilds of organists and choirmasters had been founded (Rochester in 1920, Newark in 1933, Saint Louis in 1933, Paterson in 1938, Saint Paul in 1939, Chicago in 1940, and San Francisco in 1941); many parishes had good choirs, and dedicated musicians worked hard to carry out the reforms.

If there was one single difficulty that surfaced as the main problem in this country in implementing fully the orders of the Church, it would be the lack of professional training of those who were trying to fulfill the decrees. This was caused chiefly by the lack of professional schools of music that taught anything about Catholic church music and the reluctance of church authorities to put adequate finances into the liturgical music programs. A few key positions were occupied by musicians trained in Europe, but the main body of choirmasters and organists lacked the training they needed to carry out what the Church was asking. As a result, the idea that one could be a "liturgical musician" without truly being a musician arose and did great damage by narrowing the scope of the reform and restricting the development of the musical art both in composition and in performance. A legalism and a false reading of the directives from Rome caused a restriction that kept the flowering of music in the liturgy from becoming a reality in every way.

Monsignor Richard J. Schuler
(*Sacred Music*, Vol. 109, no.1, Spring 1982, p.7-11)

<u>PART II</u>

Musicae sacrae disciplina

The nation went to war in December, 1941. Europe had already been embroiled in the conflict for two years. All things suffer in such global conflict, but the arts are particularly devastated, and not least of them, church music. Parish and cathedral choirs lost their male singers. Directors, composers and organists were called up to the various armed services. Only seminaries, abbeys and novitiates were able to maintain their regular programs since the law allowed for the exemption of the clergy from military conscription. A great deal of adaptation took place in most parishes as children's choirs and women's groups replaced the traditional adult mixed choirs. Congregational singing increased and the Gregorian melodies were found to be most useful as part-music became impossible because of the lack of tenors and basses.

The war years, 1939 to 1945, were years of great isolation for those who remained at home. Communication with Europe was cut off for the most part. Study abroad was not possible; new compositions and new publications were not available, not merely for lack of the possibility of importing them but because nothing was forthcoming from European countries engaged in total war. If the years between the First and Second World Wars are thought of as a period of isolation when the United States turned in upon itself, the actual years of the Second World War proved to be much more isolated and restricted. Nonetheless, the work of teaching the chant to the school children, seminarians and novices continued. The church music journals were published throughout the war. Parishes continued their regular services, and congregational singing, especially at the very popular novenas, spread and developed.

With peace in 1945, the men returned and choral organizations were reorganized. Interest in church music grew as returning soldiers told of what they had heard in the great cathedrals and churches in Europe. Prisoners of war told of the important role singing and especially sacred music played in their lives during captivity. European publishing houses, anxious to increase their markets and acquire some of the coveted American dollars, began to advertise their catalogs in the United States and open agencies to sell their publications in this country. Omer Westendorf of Cincinnati had observed the church music of several European capitals while in the armed service. On returning home he set up his World Library of Sacred Music to introduce to American choirmasters and organists the music he had experienced in Europe, particularly in the Netherlands. He brought to this country the compositions of Renaissance musicians in the Annie Bank editions, along with German, French, Belgian and Italian publishers' catalogs. With these new compositions came also various editions of Gregorian chant, some of which did not have the rhythmic markings of the Solesmes monks. The *Graduale Romanum* and the *Antiphonale Romanum* in the Vatican Polyglot Press printings, chant editions from Schwann-Verlag of Dusseldorf, from Dessaien in Mechlin in Belgium and other church music houses came to be known along with the more familiar *Liber Usualis,* which until the war, had been the exclusive volume for singing chant in this country. It came as a revelation to many that the Vatican Edition itself did not have the editorial markings of the Solesmes rhythmic theories, and in fact, many countries did not use them.

One of the greatest effects of the war and the anti-Catholic and anti-Jewish policies of the Nazi regimes in Europe was the influx into the United States of many important musicologists, especially from Germany. English joined German as a major language in the expanding discipline of musicology. Scholars from abroad took their places in American universities and began the training of young Americans in the history of music. Research, which blossomed into performances, left its mark on many Catholic church music organizations as interest in the compositions of the Middle Ages and the Renaissance grew. Programs for concerts, as well as for worship, often contained newly discovered and transcribed works from the fifteenth and sixteenth centuries. What the *motu proprio* of Pius X had praised so highly now became a possibility for practical use in this country. Opportunities for serious music study opened up for many young priests, Sisters and lay people in American universities as newly established chairs of musicology increased.

Enrollment in seminaries increased dramatically with the end of the war, and the teaching of chant and church music improved according to the directives from Rome. The position of professor of music was to be found in most major seminaries and regular courses in the theory and practice of liturgical singing were given. Among those occupying seminary music positions in the late forties and fifties were: Monsignor Richard B. Curtin in New York; Father Benedict Ehmann in Rochester; Father Francis V. Strahan in Boston; Father John Seiner, S.S., in Baltimore; Monsignor Joseph Kush in Chicago; Father Robert J. Stahl, S.M., in New Orleans; Father Francis A. Missia in Saint Paul; Father Elmer F. Pfeil in Milwaukee; Father Giles Pater in Cincinnati; Father John P. Cremins in Los Angeles; and Father Andrew A. Forster, S.S., in San Francisco. Programs in minor seminaries were improving, especially with the putting of emphasis on note reading and chant theory.

New developments in church music composition abroad reached this country shortly after the war. Noteworthy were the works of Netherlands composers: Hermann Strategier, Hendrik Andriessen, Jan Nieland; German composers: Theodor Propper, Heinrich Lemacher, Hermann Schroeder, Johann Nepomuk David, Georg Trexler; Belgian composers: Flor Peeters, Jules Van Nuffel; French composers: Jean Langlais, Olivier Messiaen, Maurice Duruflé; and Austrian composers: Ernst Tittel, Joseph Lechthaler, Herman and Joseph Kronsteiner and Anton Heiller. That new contemporary techniques of composition could be used in church music, involving dissonance, free rhythm and modal writing, was a surprise to many. The use of instruments in addition to the organ had not been common in the United States and usually required the permission of the local bishop, a remnant of the rigidity introduced by the misreading of Pius X's *motu proprio*. An interest in the new music was fostered through workshops in various parts of the country along with the journals, *Caecilia* and *The Catholic Choirmaster*, and many diocesan courses for organists and choirmasters.

In the Diocese of Pittsburgh, Father Carlo Rossini set up a system for training and evaluating church musicians. Guilds in many dioceses organized study courses that led to approbation and certification following testing for proficiency and knowledge of church music legislation. The Gregorian Institute of America under Clifford Bennett provided visiting faculties for sessions set up in various parts of the country, as well as a correspondence course through which church musicians in rural and remote areas could study privately and have their work corrected and evaluated, even making it possible to obtain a degree. The Archdiocese of Milwaukee under the direction of Father Elmer F. Pfeil and Sister Theophane, O.S.F., organized workshops that attracted students from all parts of the country, and at Boys Town, Nebraska, under the direction of Monsignor Francis P. Schmitt, workshops for church musicians were held in August beginning in 1953 and continuing through the 1960s.

The Boys Town events were a significant development of the post-war years, attracting faculty members of international reputation and students from all parts of the country. With a library of highest quality and facilities not equaled elsewhere, the workshops at Boys Town had a wide influence. Among those associated with the yearly events were Father Francis A. Brunner, C.S.R., Monsignor Richard J. Schuler, Dom Ermin Vitry, O.S.B., Marie Pierik, Flor Peeters, Anton Heiller, Jean Langlais, Paul Koch, Louise Cuyler, James Welch and Roger Wagner.

An outgrowth of the Boys Town workshops was the transfer of *Caecilia* to the revitalized Society of Saint Caecilia. With the cooperation of Arthur Reilly of the McLaughlin and Reilly music publishing firm, which had underwritten the magazine for many years, Monsignor Schmitt assumed the editorship of the journal which began then to reflect the policies and theories of the Boys Town associates. Interest in chant without the Solesmes rhythmic theories grew at Boys Town along with the introduction of contemporary compositions from this country and Europe. In a sense, the First World War had seen the decline in the Society of Saint Caecilia and the growth of the Society of Saint Gregory as the Solesmes editions replaced the Regensburg Medicaean books of chant. So did the Second World War and its aftermath witness a decline in the Society of Saint Gregory and its *White List* while the Society of Saint Caecilia revived with the introduction of new materials and ideas. Ultimately the two societies would combine.

In 1951, Pope Pius XII beatified Pope Pius X, and in 1954, he declared him to be a Saint of the Church. These events were widely celebrated by church musicians and gave a great impulse to efforts to implement the *motu proprio* of Pius X. But the most important event of the entire post-war period was the publication of the encyclical, *Musicae sacrae disciplina, On Sacred Music*, by Pope Pius XII, December 25, 1955. The first time a pope turned his attention in a major encyclical to questions of liturgical music, this document came in a logical and planned line of development that began with Pope Pius X's *motu proprio* of 1903 and was prepared for by the encyclical, *Mediator Dei, On the Sacred Liturgy*, of 1947. In adding yet another stone to the edifice of reform, Pius XII did not sound the negative note of excising decay that many thought they found in the *motu proprio* of Pius X. It is true that what is sensual and unchaste, illicit and extravagant and irreverent must be eliminated. But now the Holy See wished us rather to cultivate the great, the beautiful and the artistic. The valuable research of musicologists had opened the treasures of the past and new compositions of spiritual and artistic merit had appeared to adorn the liturgy. The developments of the fifty years since *Tra le sollicitudini* of Pius X were extensive and fruitful. All that is good and worthy, all that is true art and in conformity with the liturgical action could be employed as musical handmaiden of sacred liturgy. Pius XII wrote that music had progressed "from the simple and natural Gregorian modes, which are quite perfect in their kind, to great and even magnificent works of art which not only human voices, but also the organ and other musical instruments embellish, adorn and amplify almost endlessly."

Musicae sacrae disciplina brought a new freedom for the art of music that had been fettered, especially in the United States, by puritanical and rigid interpretations of Roman legislation. Music and all art needs freedom to flourish, even when its limitations as the handmaiden of the liturgy are clearly known and accepted by the artists. While the Church can clearly indicate what role music plays in worship, it is not legislation that produces art. Pope Pius XII discusses extensively the requirements for a true liturgical music: a God-given talent, properly trained, and the inspiration of the Holy Spirit who in a certain sense shares with the composer His role of creation. The theology of sacred music is beautifully developed in the encyclical which gave church musicians a sense of approbation for the success achieved in the first phase of the reform of liturgical music as well as a challenge to continue the work in a more constructive manner. Gregorian chant was reaffirmed as the music of the Church *par excellence*; the new researches in Medieval and Renaissance music were commended and approved for use; and new writing was encouraged with clear instructions given for composers and performers.

The encyclical was a great surprise to the church musicians of the United States, an almost totally unexpected Christmas present, since it came for the feast of the Nativity. The Holy Father encouraged choirs; he urged the professional training of those charged with the training of others, particularly seminary students; he permitted the use of other instruments in addition to the pipe organ; he ordered the congregations to participate in the liturgy through singing so they would not be "present at the Holy Sacrifice merely as dumb and inactive spectators." He commended the various musical societies and urged formation of diocesan commissions for music and art. Everything that had been stated before by his predecessors was confirmed and a new dimension of freedom and progress was added.

On September 3, 1958, the feast of Saint Pius X, the Sacred Congregation of Rites made specific the more general directions of the encyclical with the *Instruction, De musica sacra et sacra liturgia*. It was based solidly on the *motu proprio, Tra le sollicitudini*, of Pius X, the apostolic constitution, *Divini cultus* of Pius XI, the encyclical, *Mediator Dei* of Pius XII, and the encyclical, *Musicae sacrae disciplina*. It stated clearly a well-organized code of church music legislation. In 118 paragraphs, the church musician had his pattern for action. It set the direction for the continuing reform, protected the art of sacred music and determined its relationship with the liturgical action, both in general norms and in specific actions. It remains today the basis for much of the conciliar and post-conciliar directives, and just as truly, many of the abuses afflicting the Church today were condemned and prohibited by the *Instruction* which preceded the Vatican Council by ten years. Anyone truly wishing to understand such conciliar directives as *actuosa participatio populi* [active participation of the people] must read the 1958 *Instruction* in which participation of the faithful is clearly spelled out. Use of instruments, questions of radio and television broadcasts, remuneration of professional musicians, establishment of schools of music and diocesan commissions are explained. What the

Constitution on the Sacred Liturgy of the Second Vatican Council as well as the various *Instructions* that followed after the Council had to say on sacred music could be found almost in detail in the 1958 *Instruction*.

In those areas of the United States where serious efforts had been made to implement the reforms of Saint Pius X, the new encyclical and the *Instruction* came as confirmation of work accomplished and direction for future activity. Where nothing had been done about the *motu proprio*, either nothing was done about the encyclical or the task of initiating the reform, fifty years late, had to be begun. But the 1950s saw continuing progress musically in the reform. Guilds of organists and choirmasters were organized in many more dioceses with courses of instruction scheduled, festivals for parish choirs arranged, efforts made to give church musicians a fair remuneration, and diocesan legislation echoing the papal decrees promulgated. The National Catholic Music Educators Association (NCMEA), while primarily organized for teachers of classroom music, turned its attention to church music. In Minnesota, the NCMEA sponsored annual state-wide festivals for boys choirs. Seminary professors in the Midwest met under the auspices of NCMEA to plan courses for both major and minor seminary music programs. National conventions of most Catholic societies were planned with good liturgical music. National Liturgical Weeks were scheduled to promote interest among clergy and laity in the new liturgical reforms. There was a conscious effort in most parts of the land to carry out the wishes of the Holy Father in *Musicae sacrae disciplina*.

In Saint Louis, Mario Salvador had his choir of boys at the cathedral; in New Orleans, Elise Cambon specialized in Renaissance polyphony; Monsignor Charles N. Meter directed the choirboys at Holy Name Cathedral in Chicago; James Welch's chorale sang at Saint Philip Neri in the Bronx; and Father Joseph R. Foley, C.S.P., carried on the traditions of Father Finn's Paulist Choir. Richard Keys Biggs composed and directed at Blessed Sacrament Church in Hollywood and Roger Wagner gained international acclaim with his chorale and his performances of Catholic music. Monsignor Francis P. Schmitt, in addition to his national tours, conducted his Boys Town choir each Sunday at the solemn Mass, presenting a repertory of wide variety. In Saint Paul, Monsignor Richard J. Schuler organized the Twin Cities Catholic Chorale in addition to his Nativity Choir. Paul Koch worked at the cathedral in Pittsburgh and Theodore Marier founded his choir school in Boston. In Dallas, Father Ralph S. March, O.Cist. organized and directed the Dallas Catholic Choir, and in Saint Paul, Richard Proulx conducted the Holy Childhood *Schola Cantorum*, founded by Father John Buchanan. Monsignor Robert F. Hayburn worked in San Francisco; C. Alexander Peloquin, in Providence; Frank Campbell-Watson in New York City and Philip G. Kreckel in Rochester. The pages of *Caecilia* and *The Catholic Choirmaster* record their programs and many others.

In Europe in the years following World War II, musicians felt the need for international consultation and discussion among themselves. As a part of the Holy Year of 1950, the Pontifical Institute of Sacred Music in Rome, under the direction of Monsignor Iginio Anglès, set up a series of conferences on sacred music which came to be the First International Congress of Church Music. Later ones were held in Vienna in 1954, Paris in 1957, Cologne in 1961, Chicago-Milwaukee in 1966, Salzburg in 1974, Cologne again in 1980. The leadership of the Pontifical Institute was felt in these international gatherings with the papal directives forming the basis of discussion and the resolutions adopted. Action at the 1961 Cologne congress led to the establishment of the Consociatio Internationalis Musicae Sacrae (CIMS) by Pope Paul VI in 1963, with the responsibility of organizing succeeding international gatherings, the first of which was held in Chicago and Milwaukee under the auspices of the newly organized Church Music Association of America.

In late summer of 1964, at the close of the twelfth annual liturgical music workshop, members of the Society of Saint Gregory of America and the American Society of Saint Caecilia and other interested church musicians met at Boys Town in Nebraska, at the invitation of Monsignor Francis P. Schmitt, to consider the possibilities of uniting the two organizations into a single society for church musicians in the United States. In the friendly hospitality of Father Flanagan's Boys' Home and its president, Monsignor Nicholas J. Wegner, the procedures for forming the Church Music Association of America moved along smoothly, and the new society was born.

Representation at the meeting was truly nationwide and well-divided among clerical and lay persons. Among those present were the members of the board of directors of the Society of Saint Gregory:

Monsignor Richard B. Curtin, Reverend Benedict Ehmann, Reverend Joseph F. Mytych, Reverend Cletus Madsen, Reverend Joseph R. Foley, C.S.P., J. Vincent Higginson and Ralph Jusko. Representing the Society of Saint Caecilia were Monsignor Francis P. Schmitt, Reverend Richard J. Schuler, Reverend Francis A. Brunner, C.Ss.R., Sister M. Theophane, O.S.F., Archabbot Rembert Weakland, O.S.B., Paul Koch, Alexander Peloquin, Lavern Wagner, Roger Wagner, James Welch, James Keenan, Frank Szynskie, Norbert Letter and Mrs. Winifred Flanagan. Reverend Elmer Pfeil was a member of both boards. Monsignor Curtin, who represented Father John Selner, S.S., president of the Society of Saint Gregory, and Monsignor Schmitt acted as co-chairmen of the meetings.

A provisional constitution was drafted and officers were chosen for one year. Archabbot Weakland was named president; Father Madsen, vice-president; Father Schuler, secretary; and Frank Szynskie, treasurer. Various committees and a board of directors were selected. Two resolutions, submitted by Father Brunner, Father Robert Skeris and Father Schuler, were adopted by the new society:

> 1) We pledge ourselves to maintain the highest artistic standards in church music;
> 2) We pledge ourselves to preserve the treasury of sacred music, especially Gregorian chant, at the same time encouraging composers to write artistically fine music, especially for more active participation of the people.

At subsequent meetings, a permanent constitution was drafted, submitted to the membership and adopted. *The Catholic Choirmaster*, begun in 1915 and published through fifty volumes by the Society of Saint Gregory, merged with *Caecilia*, then in its ninety-fourth volume and published by the Society of Saint Caecilia. The journal of the new Church Music Association of America, continuing the volume numbers of *Caecilia*, was named *Sacred Music*. Coadjutor Archabbot Rembert Weakland, O.S.B., became editor.

The calling of the Second Vatican Council and the publication of its first document, the *Constitution on the Sacred Liturgy*, marked the closing of an era and the opening of another. So did the founding of the Church Music Association of America signal the end of the age when church music was fostered and regulated by the two

American societies, Saint Gregory and Saint Caecilia. The new society inaugurated the conciliar and post-conciliar period with all the challenges and problems that it brought to the church musician in the ongoing task of reform. In 1964, the future still looked bright and the challenge of the conciliar decrees attracted the American church musicians. The foundations had been laid over the past sixty years, and now the crowning stones were to be put in place. Little did anyone know what lay ahead.

Monsignor Richard J. Schuler
(*Sacred Music*, Vol. 109, no. 2, Summer 1982, p. 7-12)

PART III

Sacrosanctum concilium

On December 4, 1963, the first document to be issued by the Second Vatican Council was officially promulgated. With the title, *Sacrosanctum concilium*, it was the *Constitution on the Sacred Liturgy*. Its sixth chapter was dedicated to sacred music, the first time an ecumenical council had turned its attention so extensively to the subject of music in liturgy. It was the capstone placed on all the official pronouncements made over the past sixty years by Roman authority in the ongoing reform of church music, begun by Pope Pius X with his *motu proprio* of 1903.

For church musicians around the world, two principal challenges stood out in the Council's document: the permission for the use of the vernacular in certain parts of the liturgy; and the continuing insistence on *actuosa participatio populi* (the active participation of the people), an idea clearly enunciated by Pope Pius X and often repeated through the intervening years, especially in the *Instruction* of 1958. Both challenges were welcomed with joy and in anticipation of the rich possibilities that the vernacular languages and the singing of the people promised for new compositions and in revitalized performance practices. A sense of freedom for artistic development with new avenues of expression was clearly foreseen by those who commented on the conciliar *Constitution*. Truly, *Sacrosanctum concilium* was a *magna carta* for the church musician, re-enforcing the historical developments of liturgical music from the Gregorian chant to modern works, openly allowing all styles of sacred music as long as they were appropriate to the occasion, encouraging and even demanding new works, both in the vernacular and in Latin, both for choirs and for congregations, permitting the use of various instruments but insuring the honored position of the pipe organ.

The sections of the *Constitution* that dealt with sacred music had been studied and debated by the pre-conciliar committees and, once the Council opened, developed further by the conciliar committee. As early as 1960, Monsignor lginio Anglès, rector of the Pontifical Institute of Sacred Music in Rome, was appointed a member of the preparatory commission on sacred liturgy. Others among the consultors to the preparatory commission were: Father Eugène Cardine of Solesmes Abbey; Father Frederick D. McManus of the Catholic University in Washington; Father Godfrey Diekmann, O.S.B., editor of *Worship*; Monsignor Johannes Wagner of the Liturgical Institute in Trier, Germany; and Canon George A. Martimort of the Liturgical Center in France. Secretary of the commission was Father Annibale Bugnini, C.M., of the Lateran University in Rome. Records of the discussions and proposals of this commission may some day be the subject of considerable study, together with the deliberations of the conciliar committees and the interventions of the Fathers of the Council during their meetings in Saint Peter's Basilica. The exact intentions of the Fathers will be known only through the careful study of their deliberations, since the published conciliar documents themselves are only the distillation of many hours of study, discussion and argument. An interesting proposal, for example, to permit the vernacular languages in all spoken liturgy, while retaining Latin for the solemn, sung Masses and offices, would have allowed for the free exchange of musical compositions among the nations, giving the countries without a strong musical establishment opportunities to use music from other lands, and at the same time strengthening the universality of the Church through such exchange. But the proposal, unfortunately, was not approved for the final draft, and thus much of the difficulty provoked by the sudden introduction of vernacular singing into the solemn liturgy resulted.

With the announcement of the appointment of the conciliar commissions in 1962, Archbishop Paul Hallinan of Atlanta, Georgia, was the sole American listed on the liturgy commission. Among the *periti*, or consultors, were Monsignor Anglès, Father Bugnini, Father Frederick McManus, Monsignor Johannes Overath, Monsignor Fiorenza Romita, Canon Martimort and Monsignor Johannes Wagner. Reorganization of the schema developed by the pre-conciliar commission changed the decrees on sacred music into the sixth chapter, which was finally approved as we have it today. The records of the meetings of the members of the commission on sacred liturgy, together with the suggestions of *periti* and the final discussion of the document in Saint Peter's, form the foundation for future study of what was exactly the intention of those who gave us *Sacrosanctum concilium*. Several things concerning sacred music were crystal clear: Gregorian chant is the special music of the Church and must be given primacy of place; the long tradition of sacred music in all styles must be fostered and used; the purpose of music in the liturgy remains the glory of God and the sanctification of the faithful; the reforms begun by Pius X must continue and grow, especially the active participation of the people. The Council clearly re-affirmed the musical traditions of the Church and at the same time gave ample challenge to musicians to continue and enlarge their work in the service of God's worship.

It was with the Council's directives in mind that the Fifth International Church Music Congress, under the sponsorship of the newly organized Consociatio Internationalis Musicae Sacrae and with the Church Music Association of America as host, met in Chicago and Milwaukee, August 21 through 28, 1966. Father Richard J. Schuler was chairman of the event, together with Father Elmer F. Pfeil and Father Robert A. Skeris. This was the first international meeting of church musicians since the close of the Second Vatican Council, December 8, 1965. Present were world-renowned musicians and scholars from fifteen nations on five continents.[1] Proceedings were divided into study days at Rosary College in Chicago and a public Congress in Milwaukee for which special music was composed and performed, specifically to display the intentions of the conciliar reforms. The purpose of the assembly was to begin the work asked for by the Council, and the musicians eagerly came to Milwaukee in great numbers from all parts of the country to learn and to put into practice what were the wishes of the Council. There had never been in this country before, nor has there been since, so distinguished a gathering of nationally and internationally famous church musicians. Many had themselves been the *periti* responsible for drafting the *Constitution on the Sacred Liturgy*.

However, all was not harmonious when the Fifth International Congress opened its study days in Chicago. Father C. J. McNaspy, S.J., who was himself never present at any part of the Congress, wrote in *America* about "secret meetings," "planned exclusion of important liturgists," and "reactionary attitudes in liturgical thinking."[2] Others joined in this vein, including persons belonging to a group called Universa Laus, organized under Father Joseph Gelineau, S.J. Archabbot Rembert Weakland, O.S.B., who was president of the Church Music Association of America, the host of the Congress, was unfortunately very outspoken in his criticisms, saying that the Congress was "negative and restrictive." He, too, was present only for the last day of the Chicago sessions and was apparently unaware of the procedures established long before, governing the discussions during the study days. He and others wished to introduce many subjects to the floor for discussion that were not a part of the announced theme, which was *actuosa participatio populi* and its relation to sacred music. This theme had been approved by the Holy See as the only subject matter for discussion. In an interview with the Milwaukee press, the archabbot alluded to the Congress as a kind of legislative body with the task of acting for the universal Church in order to exclude modern music and among other things, dancing. The Congress, of course, had no legislative authority, nor had its organizers thought of it as having such a role. Nevertheless, a small group tried to subvert the work of the Congress.[3] This group was responsible for the false criticism of the Congress printed and reprinted in the American press after the close of the meeting. This was the beginning of efforts that have continued over the past twenty years to undermine the intentions of the Council Fathers and the work of the Consociatio Internationalis Musicae Sacrae, founded by Pope Paul VI for the express purpose of implementing the directives of the Vatican Council in matters of liturgical music. Those who were unhappy with the role given to sacred music in the sixth chapter of the *Constitution on the Sacred Liturgy* have never ceased to oppose what the Church has ordered for sacred music in its liturgy.[4] They have, by their actions, set church music back to a state far worse than when Pope St. Pius X began the work of reform in 1903. They have promoted their own ideas of what music and liturgy should be, but these fail to correspond to the decrees of the Council or the documents that followed after the close of the Council. A careful analysis of the legislation given for the universal Church and the reality as it is presently promoted in the United States exposes a considerable divergence between the two.

Far from being the springboard from which a great development in church music would be launched, the Fifth International Church Music Congress marks the end of progress in the reform begun in the time of Pius X and continuing until 1966. At the Congress, new compositions, employing the vernacular and engaging the congregation as well as choral and instrumental forces, written in contemporary idiom and demonstrating that the art of music could indeed be employed for the glory of God and the edification of the faithful, filled four days of liturgical worship. Papers prepared by experts on the theological basis for liturgical music and the use of art in worship showed how necessary both the inspiration of the Holy Spirit and adequate training in the musical art are to create music that is worthy of its exalted purpose in the liturgy. That the quality of music for church would in a few years be lowered to the banality and profanity of some liturgical developments was beyond the imagination of most of those who participated in the events in Chicago and Milwaukee in the late summer of 1966.

One might well ask the source of the attacks leveled against the Congress.[5] Opposition was apparent against Latin, the preservation and use of Gregorian chant, the right of the Roman See to regulate the liturgy and the music that is an integral part of the liturgy, and even against the very use of music as an art in God's service. Father Joseph Gelineau, a French Jesuit and himself a pastoral theologian but an amateur in music, in his book, *Voices and Instruments in Christian Worship*, clearly wrote against striving for excellence in music for worship.[6] The long tradition of the *Missa Romana* and its accompanying *Cantilena Romana* was pushed aside, along with the treasury of composition from nearly every school of writers, despite the demand of the Council Fathers that those very works be fostered and employed. The impression could not but be detected that the opposition was against the Roman authority. The attack that began in the field of liturgy and church music within a few years advanced to the doctrines of the Faith and the actions governed by Christian morality. In 1966, the initial disturbance caused waves on the surface of the ecclesiastical scene, but great rumblings and churning lay beneath the troubled surface waters. Within a few years, the reality became visible. Every area of the life of the Church was infected: the religious orders, the Catholic press, Catholic schools of every level, the clergy, catechetics, vocations. The authority of the Holy Father was openly challenged without reprimand by American clerics who refused to accept the encyclical, *Humanae vitae;* incredible denials of Catholic truth and Catholic morality by word and ad became commonplace; the press, both religious and secular, has recorded the disintegration of the Church in the United States during the two decades following the bright days of the Music Congress of 1966.

It became clear that the problem was a theological one, not a musical one. Those who analyzed the decrees of the Vatican Council on sacred music could see that the musicians were capable of doing what was asked. They could provide what was ordered, but the problems lay in the theology of worship, indeed in the very fundamental concepts of the sacraments, the priesthood and the Church itself. It was apparent to those who had a Catholic sense of history that the Church was in the last throes of the heresy of Modernism, the malady that Pius X called the "synthesis of all heresies." It is interesting that the pope, who in 1903 launched the liturgical renewal, was the same pope who undertook to exterminate Modernism. He drove it underground, but it resurfaced with the Second Vatican Council, and with the speed characteristic of the communications of our day, it spread throughout the world, transported to every continent by many of the participants in the Council who became infected. Since liturgy expresses belief, the importance of using it to diffuse errors is clear. Most Catholics know their Church and their faith chiefly through the Sunday Mass. When their worship is turned about, so will their very religion follow. When liturgy becomes entertainment, secularized and profaned, then its role as the expression of Catholic dogma is weakened and even lost for those who look to it for their spiritual sustenance, the "primary source of Catholic life," as Pope Pius X called it.

The resurgence of Modernism or Neo-Modernism was well organized all over the world. It spread with incredible velocity and efficiency. Indeed, there are those who think that an international conspiracy was operating.[7] An agency called the International Center of Information and Documentation concerning the Conciliar Church (IDOC) promoted the tenets of Neo-Modernism and functioned on an international level with associates in every country. All areas of Catholic life came under its scrutiny, and the names of those working under its direction included some of the best known scholars, religious and clergy of this country.[8] Their aim was the same in liturgy, catechetics, religious life, education, the press, social action and even church music. What was happening was not without direction and purpose. To counter required equal if not greater organization, and such was not at hand. The results of the greatly advertised "changes" introduced into the post-conciliar Church by the modernist camp can be seen in the catastrophe we have witnessed in the closed schools, defections from the clergy, decayed religious life, fewer converts, a substantial drop in attendance at Sunday Mass, theologians who defy the *Magisterium*, fewer vocations to the priesthood, and the banality, profanity and ineptitude of what is now promoted as liturgical music.

Who is responsible? In the field of liturgical music, those who voiced their opposition to the conciliar directives at the Congress in Chicago and Milwaukee were associated with the National Liturgical Conference, Universa Laus, the Bishops' Committee on the Liturgy and the Music Advisory Board organized under that committee. The activities of these groups in the years following the Fifth International Church Music Congress provide the answers to many of the questions asked by Catholics who wonder what has become of their musical heritage, what has happened to deprive them of the sacred worship of God that the liturgy should be. They wonder, in a word, why the clear orders of the Second Vatican Council on the reform of sacred music, set out in the sixth chapter of the *Constitution on the Sacred Liturgy*, have not been heeded and implemented in the United States.

Monsignor Richard J. Schuler
(*Sacred Music*, Vol. 109, no. 3, Fall 1982, p.7-10)

NOTES

1. For a list of participants and speakers at the Chicago sessions, see *Sacred Music and Liturgy Reform after Vatican II* (Rome: Consociatio Internationalis Musicae Sacrae, 1969) p. 197-201.

2. *Ibid.*, p. 283-288.

3. On August 24, 1966, a meeting of Americans was held at Rosary College during the Congress. At it, Archabbot Weakland complained about the Congress, saying that those present were being brainwashed by papers which were filled with recurring incompetency and lack of artistic direction. He accused the *praesidium* of the Consociatio of employing undemocratic procedures, saying that he stood for liberty, pluralism and humanism since the Church in America has its own physiognomy.

4. A meeting was sponsored in Kansas City, Missouri, December 1-2, 1966, by the American Liturgical Conference. Opposition to the sixth chapter of the *Constitution on the Sacred Liturgy* was voiced by Archabbot Weakland, who said that "false liturgical orientation gave birth to what we call the treasury of sacred music, and false judgments perpetuated it." Those "false judgments" seem to have been made by the Fathers of the Council who ordered that the treasury of sacred music be preserved and fostered. At the same meeting, Theodore Marier, president of the Church Music Association of America, was unable to get an indication from the assembled liturgists that they accepted the *Constitution*, including the sixth chapter.

5. For an account of the maneuvering that went on to impose the liturgical "reforms" on the Church in the United States, see Gary K. Potter, "The Liturgy Club," *Triumph*, Vol. 3 (May 1968), p. 10-14, 37. For similar activity in the area of liturgical music, see Richard J. Schuler, "Who Killed Sacred Music?" *Triumph*, Vol. 4 (March 1969), p. 21-23.

6. "We must give up the idea that liturgical celebrations, in the performance of their music, ought to rival the standards of the concert hall, the radio, the theater, and the achievements of professional composers and performers. Their art is too equivocal in spirit, too different in plan, too heterogeneous in its productions to be directly allied to the requirements of a worship celebrated in spirit and in truth" (*Voices and Instruments in Christian Worship*, Collegeville, Minnesota: The Liturgical Press, 1964), p. 141.

7. Even Pope Paul VI spoke of the attack of Satan on the Church, saying that the smoke of hell could be detected.

8. For a list of those from various nations including the United States, see "Dossier on IDO-C," *Approaches*, No. 10-11, (January, 1968), p. 30-95. Among those listed for liturgical action in the United States are Reverend Godfrey Diekmann, O.S.B., Reverend Frederick McManus and Jack Mannion. Cf. John Leo, "The Catholic Establishment," *The Critic* (December 1966-January 1967).

PART IV

Musicam sacram

With the close of the Second Vatican Council in December of 1965, church musicians began the work of implementing the decrees on music promulgated in the *Constitution on the Sacred Liturgy*. The first international effort was organized by the Consociatio Internationalis Musicae Sacrae and the Church Music Association of America. The Congress held in Chicago and Milwaukee, August 21 to 28, 1966, undertook to implement the two major challenges given musicians by the Council Fathers: *actuosa participatio populi* and the permission for an extended use of the vernacular languages. Pope Paul VI had erected the Consociatio in his chirograph of November 22, 1963, *Nobile subsidium liturgiae*, giving it the express mission of implementing the decrees of the Council and furthering international meetings and discussions of developments in sacred music. With a roster of scholars, composers and practicing musicians of international reputation, the Consociatio had the potential to solve the problems presented by the introduction of the vernacular languages, the more extensive involvement of the congregation in singing, the employment of modern techniques of composition, the use of various instruments and the need for maintaining a truly sacred character in all music used in divine worship.

However, opposition to the Consociatio and its efforts was manifest very early. On an international level, Universa Laus, an organization led by Father Joseph Gelineau, S.J., openly worked against the Consociatio and its leaders. On the American scene, the American Liturgical Conference was the chief opponent. It worked through groups within the Church Music Association of America led by Archabbot Rembert G. Weakland, O.S.B., and through persons associated with the Bishops' Committee on the Liturgy which was directed by Father Frederick R. McManus. The editor of *Worship*,

Father Godfrey Diekmann, O.S.B., also played a leading role along with other journalists in fostering the tenets of Universa Laus. In time, the Music Advisory Board, set up under the Bishops' Committee on the Liturgy, became a tool for these groups in their efforts to oppose the Consociatio and its program to implement the decrees of the Council on sacred music. The common denominator of the struggle was soon seen to be the conflict between the liturgists and the church musicians. The battle was fought in Europe and in the United States.

Universa Laus had its origin at an assembly of liturgists and musicians that met in Lugano, Switzerland, April 20 to 22, 1966, with the encouragement of Abbot Raimund Tschudy of Einsiedeln and Bishop A. Jelmini, president of the Swiss conference of bishops. Previous sessions of a similar kind had been held in Cresus in 1962, at Essen in 1963, at Taizé in 1964, and in Freiburg in Switzerland in 1965. The announced purpose of the gatherings was to study chant and music in their place in liturgical celebrations. At the Freiburg meeting, nearly three hundred participants came from thirty-two countries, and at Lugano a selected group of seventy came from sixteen countries including America and Australia. Historical, liturgical, pastoral and technical studies were presented by Helmut Hucke, H. Leel, Bernard Hujbers, Luigi Agustoni, G. Stefani, Lucian Deiss, Joseph Gelineau, and Abbot Raimund Tschudy.

Favorable comments on the activities of Universa Laus were printed in *Musik und Altar*, published in Freiburg in Breisgau, in *De Linie* from Holland, in *Herder Korrespondenz*, and in *Notitiae*, the organ of the newly created Consilium for the Implementation of the *Constitution on the Sacred Liturgy*. An article in *Notitiae* noted the Holy Father's reply to a letter sent to the Vatican by the assembly at Lugano:

> ...the association has received the praise and the felicitations of the Secretary of State: "The sovereign Pontiff has accepted with benevolence the letter addressed to him by both of you, Don Luigi Agustoni and Erhard Quack, informing him of the results of the assembly of Lugano, and also of the foundation of an international group for the study of chant and music in the liturgy, under the name of Universa Laus. This initiative has appeared opportune to His Holiness in this special period

in which the development of the various directions in the department of liturgical chant and music has led to so many delicate problems. Therefore he has been pleased to invoke God's blessing on the newborn association and sends to the three chairmen and to all the members the Apostolic Blessing asked for."

This letter was sent on May 11 by Monsignor Angelo Dell'Acqua, *substitutus* to Father Joseph Gelineau, S. J., who together with Dr. Erhard Quack and Don Luigi Agustoni form the *praesidium* of the new association.[1] When it became clear that Universa Laus was promoting opposition to the Consociatio Internationalis Musicae Sacrae, which had been officially erected by Pope Paul VI, another letter was issued by Monsignor Dell'Acqua, July 16, 1966, addressed to Monsignor Johannes Overath, president of the Consociatio, and to Father Joseph Gelineau, a director of Universa Laus.

> As you are aware, there was established with the pontifical chirograph, *Nobile subsidium liturgiae*, of November 22, 1963, the Consociatio Internationalis Musicae Sacrae, which is the only international association of sacred music approved by the Holy See; moreover, any eventual duplication is useless and harmful.[2]

Another letter concerning Universa Laus from the Secretariat of State, dated July 29, 1966, was addressed to Monsignor Overath saying that the Holy Father is of the opinion "that the matter involves a superfluous duplication (*inutile duplicato*), and this group should either place itself under the Consociatio or dissolve itself." Much of the conflict surfaced in Chicago and Milwaukee during the Fifth International Church Music Congress.

While the battle raged around the official status of the two groups and what kind of approbation could be obtained from the Holy See, the real conflict lay in the place of sacred music in the liturgy and the implementing of the directives of the Council. The position of Universa Laus was clearly stated in Father Gelineau's *Voices and Instruments in Christian Worship*,[3] a volume that received strong criticisms in many languages.[4] The position of the Consociatio was clearly outlined in the papers delivered at the Chicago-Milwaukee Congress.[5]

The final clash would occur over the publication of the 1967 *Instruction, Musicam sacram,* issued jointly by the Consilium for the Implementation of the *Constitution on the Sacred Liturgy* and the Sacred Congregation of Rites. Monsignor Iginio Anglès said of the preparation of the *Instruction:*

> As you know we had to fight many a battle over this *Instruction,* as the liturgists did not want to hear about the true value of good church music in the liturgy. They tried to destroy everything that belonged to the old Roman rite. The Holy Father showed much personal interest in this *Instruction.* Sometimes he accepted an article composed by the liturgists, though we were against it. But in spite of this, the fundamental principles of church music were preserved.[6]

In the United States, during the 1966 Congress and following it, the battle developed along similar lines to those in Europe. The Church Music Association was affiliated with the Consociatio and (with the exception of its president, Archabbot Weakland) stood in support of the principles outlined by the papal international association. On the opposite side, supporting Universa Laus, were the liturgists as represented by the Liturgical Conference and many members of the official bodies set up by the American bishops and dominated by Father Frederick McManus. These were the Bishops' Committee on the Liturgy and its Music Advisory Board.

Father McManus was in close relationship with Father Annibale Bugnini, secretary of the Consilium for the Implementation of the *Constitution on the Sacred Liturgy* in Rome. Together with Father Johannes Wagner of Trier and Canon George A. Martimort of Paris, they promoted the liturgical innovations that were so devastating to church music both in Europe and in America. The resistance of the church musicians to the activities of these liturgists, and even efforts at discussions about the disagreements, were characterized by Father Bugnini, speaking at an Italian liturgical convention on January 4, 1968, as "four years of musical polemics."[7] Controversy was noted even in Rome between the Congregation of Rites, long the authority in liturgical and musical matters for the universal Church, and the newly established Consilium for the Implementation of the *Constitution on the*

Sacred Liturgy, of which Father Bugnini was secretary.

As Father Bugnini used the Consilium, so in the United States the liturgical revolution against the Roman rite and its treasury of sacred music was led by Archabbot Weakland as chairman of the Music Advisory Board of the Bishops' Committee on the Liturgy. He and Father McManus achieved the ends set forth by Universa Laus through the official American agencies organized to fulfill the directives of the Council. Since Father McManus was a part of the Consilium and also the International Committee for English in the Liturgy (ICEL), he was the key man in introducing into the United States all the plans of Universa Laus.[8] He worked through the Bishops' Committee on the Liturgy, the Liturgical Conference, *Worship*, and the Music Advisory Board.

The Music Advisory Board was set up in 1965 to assist the Bishops' Committee on the Liturgy in musical matters. It had been the proposal of the Church Music Association of America that, as in England and in Germany, such advice be sought from the existing national association of musicians instead of organizing still another group, but the suggestion was not taken. With the introduction of the vernacular into the sung liturgy, questions of chants for both priest and people had to be solved. Other problems concerning the education of church musicians for the vernacular changes, professional training for church musicians and teachers of church music, new hymnals, the position of the pipe organ in new churches and many other matters were to be brought to the attention of the experts appointed to the board.

According to Archbishop Paul Hallinan, secretary of the Bishops' Committee on the Liturgy, the new board was to be made up of "musicians, music critics and authorities in pastoral liturgy."[9] He further stated that the bishops were seeking advice about a broad statement on the principles of sacred music, the selection of a musical setting for the Our Father, and help for seminaries. Members appointed to the board in 1965 were: J. Robert Carroll, Monsignor Richard B. Curtin, Louise Cuyler, Reverend Francis J. Guentner, S.J., Paul Hume, Theodore Marier, C. Alexander Peloquin, Reverend Richard J. Schuler, Robert Snow, Reverend Eugene Walsh, S.S., and Archabbot Rembert G. Weakland, O.S.B. The first meeting was in Detroit, Michigan, May 4 and 5, 1965. Archabbot Weakland was elected chairman and Father Schuler, secretary. Father McManus announced that he was the liaison with the bishops and spoke about sacred music in the new liturgical legislation. Archbishop Dearden, chairman of the bishops' committee, and other members of that committee, welcomed the members. Although it was not as yet obvious, the stage was now set to accomplish in sacred music what the Liturgical Conference had achieved in the renovation of the rites and ceremonies. The plans of Universa Laus could now be implemented despite the wishes of the Consociatio or the Church Music Association of America. In fact, some members of those organizations would even be involved in carrying out the work. In a word, the Music Advisory Board was intended to become a rubber stamp in the United States for the proposals from Universa Laus as presented to it by Father McManus. The Benedictines, Father Godfrey Diekmann and Father Rembert Weakland, were cooperators, one as editor of the liturgy magazine, *Worship*, the other as chairman of the Music Advisory Board. A few musicians on the board fought against the introduction of the plans of Universa Laus, but they were outnumbered and were eventually replaced on the board by more cooperative advisors.[10]

Typical and perhaps most interesting of the innovations engineered through the Music Advisory Board by Father McManus, Father Diekmann and Father Weakland was the "hootenanny Mass." The scenario began in April 1965, when Father Diekmann delivered an address entitled "Liturgical Renewal and the Student Mass" at the convention of the National Catholic Educational Association in New York. In his speech, he called for the use of the "hootenanny Mass" as a means of worship for high school students. This was the kick-off of a determined campaign on the part of the Liturgical Conference to establish the use of profane music in the liturgy celebrated in the United States. Universa Laus had already begun a similar effort in Europe.[11]

In September 1965, the Catholic press began to carry reports of the use of hootenanny music by those in charge of college and high school student worship. In February 1966, the Music Advisory Board was called to meet in Chicago, with an agenda that included a proposal for the use of guitars and so-called "folk music" in the liturgy. It was clear at the meeting that both Fr. McManus and Archabbot Weakland were most anxious to obtain the board's approval. The Archabbot told of the success of such "experiments" at his college in Latrobe, Pennsylvania, where, during Mass, the students enthusiastically had sung, "He's got the Archabbot in the palm of His hand." Vigorous debate considerably altered the original proposal, and a much modified statement about "music for special groups" was finally approved by a majority of one, late in the day when many members already had left. But once the rubber stamp had been applied, the intensity of the debate and the narrow margin of the vote were immediately forgotten. The Music Advisory Board had fulfilled its function; it had been used.

The press took over. American newspapers, both secular and ecclesiastical, announced that the American bishops had approved of the use of guitars, folk music and the hootenanny Mass. Despite repeated statements from the Holy See prohibiting the use of secular music and words in the liturgy, the movement continued to be promoted in the United States and in Europe.[12] Deception played a part, since American priests were allowed to think that the decision of the Music Advisory Board was an order from the bishops themselves. In reality, an advisory board has no legislative authority, nor does a committee of bishops have such authority. Decisions on liturgical matters need the approval of the entire body of bishops after a committee has received the report of its advisors and submitted its own recommendations to the full body.[13]

The hootenanny Mass never came to the full body of bishops; it did not have to. The intended effect had been achieved through the announcement of the action of the Music Advisory Board and the publicity given to it by the national press. It was not honest, and further, it was against the expressed wishes and legislation of the Church.[14] There are other examples of the introduction of the ideas of Universa Laus and the progressive liturgists that involved confusion and even deceit. The gullibility of the American clergy and their willingness to obey was used. A confusion was fostered in the minds of priests between the Bishops' Committee on the Liturgy and the Liturgical Conference, which indeed had interlocking directorates. As anticipated, most American priests failed to distinguish between the releases that came from them, taking the proclamations of both as being the will of their bishops. Meanwhile, the official directives of the post-conciliar commissions in Rome rarely reached most American priests. They knew only the commentaries on them provided by the liturgists both nationally and on the diocesan level. As a result, the altars of most American churches were turned *versus populum*; choirs were disbanded; Gregorian chant was prohibited; Latin was forbidden for celebration of the Mass in many dioceses; church furniture and statuary were discarded. These innovations which distressed untold numbers of Catholics were thought to be the orders of the Second Vatican Council. Rather, they were the results of a conspiracy whose foundations and intentions have yet to be completely discovered and revealed.

The Church is clear in what is its liturgical reform. The documents for an ongoing work, begun by Pius X and slowly developed through several pontificates, reached their fullness in the Council and the later *Instruction*s that undertook to implement the will of the Council Fathers. Formulating the specific details of the liturgical renewal fell to the pontificate of Pope Paul VI. In the area of sacred music, the most significant document was the *Instruction on Sacred Music in the Liturgy* of March 15, 1967, *Musicam sacram*.[15]

The text of the *Instruction* was bitterly fought over, and both sides, liturgists and musicians, ultimately came away with less than they were expecting. Monsignor Anglès and Monsignor Overath presented the scholarly and practical positions of the church musicians in face of pressure for experimentation and triviality that would lead to the destruction of art, reverence and the treasury of sacred music, the heritage of the Roman Church through fifteen centuries. Their chief opponent was Father Bugnini. Pope Paul VI himself took an active part in determining the final draft.[16] In the final analysis, the church musicians were satisfied at having saved the Church's musical heritage and were ready to carry out the requirements of the *Instruction*, but what was ordered by the authority of the Church has not yet been achieved, chiefly because the liturgists wanted even further innovations. They were not ready to have the liturgy determined by an *Instruction*; they were not yet finished with their experimentation and innovation. Even another *Instruction* of September 5, 1970, has not succeeded in putting an end to innovations and so-called experimenting, now rechristened "creativity."[17]

Musicam sacram clearly presumes the use of the ancient form of the *Missa Romana cantata* (*Kyrie, Gloria, Credo, Sanctus-Benedictus, Agnus Dei*) in its thousand-year development musically, and gives detailed directions for using it involving the participation of the congregation.

But that traditional structure, the Ordinary and Proper parts of the Mass, has ceased to be a vital entity to contemporary liturgists. Further, *Musicam sacram* clearly states that the distinction between solemn, sung and read Masses is to be retained; but the liturgists from the beginning have refused to accept that order. Again, *Musicam sacram* has a detailed listing of the various degrees of participation by singing, but the liturgists have never observed the order of priority established by the *Instruction*. Also, the "treasury of sacred music," mentioned in the *Constitution on the Sacred Liturgy* of the Second Vatican Council, is carefully guarded and its use commanded, including the polyphonic settings of the Ordinary of the Mass produced over the past six centuries by the greatest composers of every age; but the liturgists have all but eliminated this heritage as a reality in worship.

Not the least important point made by *Musicam sacram* is found in its very title, "Sacred Music." This reaffirms the statement of the Council that the purpose of church music is the "glory of God and the sanctification of the faithful." Some were trying to assert that all things are sacred, and thus all music was suitable for the liturgy. They were in fact saying that nothing is "sacred," and the result was a desacralization. The *Instruction* reaffirms the ongoing tradition that begins with the patristic age.[18] Pope Paul VI himself spoke several times on the subject of sacred music. On April 15, 1971, he addressed a thousand religious dedicated to the work of liturgical music at a national convention of the Italian Society of Saint Cecilia held in Rome, repeating the admonition that "all is not valid; all is not licit; all is not good." The secular, the cheap, the inferior and the inartistic "are not meant to cross the threshold of God's temple."[19] *Musicam sacram*, in its nine chapters and preface, lays down general norms about sacred music, directives about musical personnel, orders about the Mass, the Divine Office and other rites; it treats of the use of Latin and the vernacular; it promotes congregational singing and fosters the creation of new music; it gives instruction about the use of instruments, directives for composers and for establishing music commissions. The always present question of a sound education for performing musicians and composers is emphasized along with the musical training of those preparing for the priesthood. Appreciation of what is "sacred" and what is "beautiful" in music demands long and well-directed study.

What had been the principal problem preventing the reforms of Pius X from being fully implemented in the United States – inadequate musical and liturgical formation – now was compounded as total amateurs invaded the areas of composition and performance, contrary to the directives of *Musicam sacram* and against the warnings of professional church musicians. Encouraged by liturgists who lacked musical learning, many amateurs began to sing, play and compose under the false idea that they were fulfilling the commands of the Council for active participation. They were, in fact, breaking the rules of the highest authority in the Church. Texts to be sung in church are to be taken from the Holy Scriptures or liturgical sources,[20] but all kinds of secular ballads and songs have become commonplace. A *sensus ecclesiae* should determine the fittingness of musical forms and techniques for use in divine worship, but without proper training such a sense is not present or operative, even with all the good will and good intentions of many amateurs. What Pope Paul VI called "liturgical taste, sensitiveness, study and education," were demanded to carry out the directives of the 1967 *Instruction*. Since they have been lacking in most of those who have assumed the church music positions in this country, the *Instruction*, *Musicam sacram*, was never truly put into effect. It was obscured by a document prepared by the Music Advisory Board of the Bishops' Committee on the Liturgy, entitled *The Place of Music in Eucharistic Celebrations*, which has done untold harm.

Monsignor Richard J. Schuler
(*Sacred Music*, Vol. 109, No. 3, Winter 1982, p.15-21)

NOTES

1. *Notitiae*, Vol. II (1966), p. 198-199.

2. Secretariate of State, Dispatch N. 74270. Printed in *Musicae Sacrae Ministerium*, Anno III, N. 2-3 (Summer-Autumn 1966), p. 29.

3. Joseph Gelineau, *Voices and Instruments in Christian Worship* (Collegeville, Minnesota: The Liturgical Press, 1964).

4. Cf. *Response*, Vol. VII, No. 2 (1965), p. 104-107 (Reprinted in *Sacred Music*, Vol. 92, No. 3 (Autumn 1965), p. 83-88; *Musicae Sacrae Ministerium*, Vol. III, No. 1 (Spring 1966), p. 14-20.

5. Johannes Overath, ed., *Sacred Music and Liturgy Reform after Vatican II*. (Rome: Consociatio Internationalis Musicae Sacrae, 1969). English edition available from Church Music Association of America, 548 Lafond Avenue, Saint Paul, Minnesota 55103.)

6. Quoted from a personal letter sent to the author.

7. Cf. *Sacred Music and Liturgy Reform after Vatican II*, p. 17 (footnote).

8. Cf. Gary K. Potter, "The Liturgy Club," *Triumph*, May 1968, p. 10-14f.

9. Unpublished minutes of the meeting.

10. At its meeting, December 1 and 2, 1966, in Kansas City, Missouri, under the leadership of Archbishop Hallinan and Father McManus, the following were retired from the Music Advisory Board: Monsignor Curtin, Father Schuler, Father McNaspy, Louise Cuyler, Alexander Peloquin and Paul Hume. In their places, the Archbishop appointed Reverend Paul Byron, Reverend John Cannon and Reverend Robert Leodogar. Also added were Dennis Fitzpatrick, Haldan Tompkins and Richard Felciano.

11. At the Chicago Congress, the Allgemeiner Cäcilein-Verband of the German-speaking nations had introduced a resolution against such profane music which had already begun to appear in Europe (See *Sacred Music and Liturgy Reform after Vatican II*, p. 182-185); news reports from Europe, including the city of Rome, report the use of beat music, youth combos and folk music; the reaction from the Vatican was also reported calling for an end to such abuses *(Minneapolis Star,* January 4, 1967) with Father Bugnini himself explaining that "everything profane and worldly must be excluded from church services."

12. Cf. *"Declaratio Sacrae Rituum Congregationis et Consilii ad exsequendam Constitutionem de sacra Liturgia,"* *Notitiae,* Vol. III (1967), p. 37-38. The text of Father Bugnini's meeting with journalists clarifies the official declaration. It is appended on p. 39-46. Some discrepancy appears in that what Fr. McManus is promoting in the United States is apparently contradicted by Fr. Bugnini in Rome.

13. Cf. *Acta Apostolicae Sedis,* Vol. LX, N. 6 (June 28, 1968), p. 361.

14. For a more extensive discussion of the hootenanny Mass, see Richard J. Schuler, "Who Killed Sacred Music," *Triumph*, March 1969, p. 21-23.

15. Cf. *Sacred Music,* Vol. 94, No. I (Spring, 1967), p. 7-21. The Latin text can be found in *Musicae Sacrae Ministerium,* Vol. IV (Special number 1967), p. 1-16, and in *Notitiae,* Vol. III (March 1967), p. 87-108.

16. It is said that Pope Paul, in his own hand, wrote that he saw no reason why a polyphonic *Sanctus* could not be sung, thus correcting the false claim of the liturgists who wished to make that hymn into an acclamation always to be sung by the congregation. The Pope preserved the integrity of the *Missa Romana Cantata.*

17. Cf. Robert A. Skeris, "The *Third Instruction,"* *Sacred Music,* Vol. 98, No. I (Spring 1971), p. 3-8. The Latin text of the *Instruction* may be found in *Acta Apostolicae Sedis,* LXII (1970), p. 692-704. Several criticisms have been made of the English translation that was widely circulated in this country. For an assessment of the implementation of the *Instruction,* see Richard J. Schuler, "1967 *Instruction* - Ten Years Later," *Sacred Music,* Vol. 104, No. 3, Fall 1977, p. 3-12.

18. The problem of the "sacred" is basic to the entire liturgical reform; violation of the "sacred" has been the chief scandal for most people. For literature on this subject, see "Pope Paul on Sacred Music" *Sacred Music,* Vol. 96, No. 2 (Summer 1969), p. 3-6; John Buchanan, "The Subject is Worship," *Sacred Music,* Vol. 96, No. 3 (Fall 1969), p. 3-11; Richard J. Schuler, "Humanism and the Sacred," *Sacred Music,* Vol. 96, No. 4 (Winter 1969), p. 3-6; Richard J. Schuler, "Pope Paul on Sacred Music," *Sacred Music,* Vol. 98, No. 2 (Summer 1971), p. 3-5; James Hitchcock, "The Decline of the Sacred," *Sacred Music,* Vol. 100, No. 4 (Winter 1973), p. 3-9; Deryck Hanshall, "Resacralization," *Sacred Music,* Vol. 103, No. 4 (Winter 1976), p. 3-12; Richard J. Schuler, "Sacred Music and Contemplation," *Sacred Music,* Vol. 106, No. 1 (Spring 1979), p. 23-26; Richard J. Schuler, "The Sacred," *Sacred Music,* Vol. 107, No. 3 (Fall 1980), p. 21-27.

19. Cf. *Sacred Music,* Vol. 98, No. 2 (Summer 1971), p. 3-5.

20. The *Constitution on the Sacred Liturgy,* Art. 121.

PART V

The Place of Music in Eucharistic Celebrations

The enormous task of implementing in the practical order the wishes of the Council Fathers as expressed in the *Constitution on the Sacred Liturgy* occupied the attention of the Roman authorities for nearly ten years. Two official bodies were involved in the process, the Consilium for the Implementation of the *Constitution on the Sacred Liturgy* and the Sacred Congregation of Rites. Difficulties between the two groups were many, but they were eventually solved by the establishment of the Sacred Congregation of Divine Worship to replace the old Congregation of Rites and the reorganization of the Consilium as a special commission dedicated to completing the liturgical reform.[1] Many conflicts of personalities and problems between the liturgists and the musicians continued to trouble the work of implementing the reforms called for by the Council.

For church musicians, the most important events of the decade following the close of the Council were the publication of the new liturgical books as well as the various *Instructions* and decrees of the Consilium and the Congregation of Rites and later, the new Congregation of Divine Worship. Fundamental to the entire reform was the new Order of the Mass which was finalized with the appearance of the *Missale Romanum* in 1969. Controversy over the introduction to the 1969 edition led to the issuing of another *Institutio Generalis Missalis Romani* in 1970. The Latin text of the *Missal* remains the basis for all vernacular sacramentaries that have been published throughout the world.[2]

The new Order of the Mass brought new texts for which musical settings were wanting, particularly the responsorial psalms. The rearrangement of Introits and Communions, different from the old Order, as well as the three-year cycle of scripture readings, presented some difficulties at first. The new calendar impinged more closely on the church musician, because of the suppression of some feasts and a revised positioning of others. A new system of classification of liturgical celebrations according to importance brought a new vocabulary with "memorials," "solemnities," "ordinary time," etc. The old octaves were gone for the most part, and the familiar Sequences were no longer obligatory.

Publication of a new *Graduale Romanum* followed shortly. Based on scholarly research and sound methodology, the chants for the Mass were made available in an edition prepared by the monks of Solesmes.[3] According to the principles enunciated in the preface to the volume, only authentic chants were included, eliminating many pieces that had cluttered the earlier 1908 edition. New feasts introduced into the calendar with texts lacking in authentic chant settings would have to be provided with music written in the idiom of our day, since Gregorian chant is no longer the style of contemporary composition and the process of producing an ersatz chant has been discredited. Music for newly introduced responsorial psalms would have to be newly composed. The challenge of the Council Fathers to musicians was seen to be an ongoing one.

The new *Missal* contains eighty-seven different preface texts. To provide musical settings for use at the altar, the monks of Solesmes edited a volume called *Ordo Missae in cantu*. Settings for the prefaces in both solemn and simple tones, as well as musical notation for the singing of the four Eucharistic prayers, and the various introductory rites made up this most useful volume.[4] Together with the *Graduale Romanum* and the *Missale Romanum*, the *Ordo Missae in Cantu* provided the clergy and the musicians with all the books needed to celebrate the sung liturgy in Latin.

An effort to introduce a simpler chant for the Mass produced a *Graduale Simplex*, which was a failure from the beginning. It pleased neither the progressive liturgists, who wanted only the vernacular, nor the musicians who pointed out that it was a mutilation of Gregorian chant as well as a misunderstanding of the relationship between text and musical setting with reference to form. They objected to the use of antiphon melodies from the Office as settings for texts of the Mass. An effort at an English vernacular version proved to be even a greater disaster.

The revision of the Office and the ritual had less impact on the ordinary church musician, although it caused grave changes in monastic communities.[5] No new official books in Latin with musical notation have been forthcoming as yet for the universal Church for the singing of the Hours, although attempts to set the vernacular texts can be found. The official *Liturgia Horarum* has no musical settings.

While the Holy See published the official revised liturgical books in the Latin language and spread them around the world, in the United States these books remained almost totally unknown, and in fact, in some dioceses, their use was prohibited by local legislation that forbade the use of Latin.[6] To a great degree, the American clergy still do not know the *Missale Romanum*, the new *Graduale Romanum* or the *Ordo Missae in Cantu*. They continue to co-relate the use of Latin with the old rite and the vernacular with the reformed rite. When asked to sing a Mass in Latin, they frequently resort to the old editions which are no longer in use. The confusion spread in the sixties concerning the use of Latin still continues.

Thus, with the virtual demise of Latin and with it, the repertory of Gregorian chant and polyphonic music, church musicians turned their efforts to music for the new vernacular liturgy. Among the early problems was the instability of the translations, which were changed a number of times during the period of experimentation, which produced many temporary versions. Choirs were discouraged by the assertion that there was no longer a placc for them, and they regretted the loss of familiar repertory. New music was not quickly forthcoming, although publishers rushed to sell compositions, many the work of total amateurs. It soon became apparent that the congregations that were expected to sing psalms and responsories and lengthy antiphons and parts of the Mass, were only capable of mastering a few hymns and not much more. The vernacular liturgy did not generate a "nest of singing birds" in the United States, and with choirs disorganized, the combo of a few instruments with various types of so-called folk music became the musical ensemble in many churches. The organ was replaced by the guitar, the choir by the vocal combo, the professional musician by the amateur, the sacred by the secular. The hoped-for flowering of the privilege of the vernacular did not mature. Rather, the speed of the disintegration of all that had been worked for during the years since Pius X amazed serious musicians. The decay was incredible.

In asking the question why, musically speaking, the reforms of the Council were not a success, one must always arrive at the same answer: the wishes of the Council Fathers were not carried out. The Council documents are clear; the *Instructions* that followed are detailed and understandable; the official liturgical books leave no doubt about their use. But why have they not been put into effect in the United States? An important reason lies in the issuing of a document by the Bishops' Committee on the Liturgy, prepared by the Music Advisory Board and entitled *The Place of Music in Eucharistic Celebrations*.[7]

While claiming to be an American interpretation of the Roman *Instruction, Musicam sacram*, this statement is based on principles quite contrary to the expression of liturgical theology continuing through the past one hundred years. It is confused and even erroneous in doctrinal, musical and legal aspects. One wonders why the Roman *Instruction* was not allowed to stand on its own and why an American statement was necessary at all, unless perhaps to prevent the Roman directions from becoming known and implemented in the United States.

Three years before the appearance of *The Place of Music in Eucharistic Celebrations*, Pope Paul VI issued his encyclical on the Holy Eucharist, *Mysterium fidei*, September 3, 1965. Strangely, the American document has no reference to the encyclical even though its chief concern is with the Mass. In fact, it contains several statements quite contrary to the clear teaching of the encyclical. Pope Paul wrote in *Mysterium fidei*:

> Having safeguarded the integrity of the faith, it is necessary to safeguard also its proper mode of expression, lest by the careless use of words, we occasion (God forbid) the rise of false opinions regarding faith in the most sublime of mysteries. St. Augustine gives a stern warning about this in his consideration of the way of speaking employed by the philosophers and of that which must be used by Christians. "The philosophers," he says, "who use words loosely and in matters very difficult to understand have no great fear of offending a religious audience. We religious, however, have the obligation of speaking according to a definite norm lest the license of our words give rise to an impious opinion about the matters which are signified by these words."

The norm, therefore, of speaking which the Church after centuries of toil and under the protection of the Holy Spirit has established and confirmed by the authority of Councils, and which has become more than once the watchword and standard of correct belief is to be religiously preserved and let no one at his own good pleasure or under the pretext of new science presume to change it....We are not to tolerate anyone who on his own authority wishes to modify the formulae in which the Council of Trent sets forth the mystery of the Eucharist for our belief.[8]

In the light of the words of Pope Paul, the statement of the Music Advisory Board seems to be wanting in clarity and even to be expressing false opinions. One might wonder why an advisory board in the area of music should put out a theological statement at all, and especially this paragraph:

The Eucharistic prayer is the praise and thanksgiving pronounced over the bread and wine which are to be shared in the communion meal. It is an acknowledgment of the Church's faith and discipleship transforming the gifts to be eaten into the Body which Jesus gave and the Blood which He poured out for the life of the world, so that the sharing of the meal commits the Christian to sharing in the mission of Jesus. As a statement of the universal Church's faith, it is proclaimed by the president alone. As a statement of the faith of the local assembly it is affirmed and ratified by all those present through acclamations like the great Amen.[9]

The authors of *The Place of Music in Eucharistic Celebrations* use the word *transform* to describe the effect of the words of consecration and avoid the word *transubstantiation* as commanded by Pope Paul. They employ the term "meal" twice in a short paragraph, and the term "sacrifice" is not found once in the entire document of over six pages, while in *Mysterium fidei*, Pope Paul uses it repeatedly and has occasion only once to employ the word *meal*. The term *president* is used instead of *priest*. The document clearly was intended to be an expression of theological ideas quite different from those taught by Pope Paul, including such questions as the purpose of prayer, the distinction between the hierarchical priesthood and the common universal priesthood, the nature of Christ's presence in the Holy Eucharist and His presence among us, and the very purpose of the Mass itself. In a variety of issues, the document of the Music Advisory Board offends against the clear teaching of the encyclical. What is obvious from such a comparison is that the theological convictions of the progressive liturgists and the thinking of the Universa Laus group are closely associated with doctrinal deviations that the Council Fathers voted to reject but which surfaced after the Council not only in theological writings but in such practical applications as these published for musicians.

But *The Place of Music in Eucharistic Celebrations* is not confused only in doctrinal matters. It fails in musical questions to conform to directives from the Holy See. *Musicam sacram* says: "The distinction between solemn, sung and read Mass, sanctioned by the *Instruction* of 1958, is to be retained."[10] But the Music Advisory Board says: "While it is possible to make technical distinctions in the forms of Mass... there is little distinction to be made between the solemn, sung and recited Mass."[11] *Musicam sacram* uses the long-standing terminology of "Ordinary" and "Proper" parts of the Mass; but the Music Advisory Board says that "the customary distinction between the Ordinary and Proper parts of the Mass with regard to musical settings and distribution of roles is irrelevant."[12] The Music Advisory Board says that "the musical settings of the past are usually not helpful models for composing truly contemporary pieces."[13] But *Musicam sacram* says:

> Musicians will enter on this new work with the desire to continue that tradition which has given the Church a truly abundant heritage. Let them examine the works of the past, their style and characteristics, but let them also pay careful attention to the new laws and requirements of the liturgy, so that new forms may in some way grow organically from forms that already exist.[14]

The chief error to be found in the American document, however, is concerned with the very purpose of sacred music, and this error lies at the root of most of the problems that have arisen since the issuing of the unfortunate statement. The *Constitution on the Sacred Liturgy* repeats the centuries-old position of the Church: "The purpose of sacred music is the glory of God and the sanctification of the faithful."[15] But the Music Advisory Board says:

> Music, more than any other resource, makes a celebration of the liturgy an attractive human experience. Music in worship is a function [sic] sign. It has a ministerial role. It must always serve the expression of faith. It affords a quality of joy and enthusiasm to the community's statement of faith that cannot be gained in any other way. In so doing, it imparts a sense of unity to the congregation.[16]

With the purpose of sacred music reduced to the "creating of a truly human experience," one can easily explain the secularization of wedding music, the introduction of various combos, show tunes, folk music, ballads and much of the newly composed religious pieces that lack all artistic merit. The criterion has become "We like it." The requirements of sanctity and good art have been replaced. Music is no longer *pars integrans*, as the Council Fathers called it, but it has become entertainment at worship.

The Music Advisory Board's document teaches that there are now four principal classes of texts: readings, acclamations, psalms and hymns, and prayers. This comes directly from *Voices and Instruments in Christian Worship* by Father Joseph Gelineau.[17]

Because these theories were imposed on the church musicians of the United States, the various *Instructions* of the Holy See failed to get a hearing. The liturgists refused to accept the sixth chapter of the *Constitution on the Sacred Liturgy* as well as the *Instruction, Musicam sacram*, and in their place they promoted the tenets of Universa Laus as expressed in *The Place of Music in Eucharistic Celebrations*.

One may ask how such a body as the Music Advisory Board could impose its opinions on the musicians and clergy of the United States. What was their legal foundation? The *Constitution on the Sacred Liturgy* says: "It is desirable that the competent ecclesiastical authority, mentioned in article 22, set up a liturgical commission, to be assisted by experts in liturgical sciences, sacred music, art and pastoral practice."[18] Advisory boards were set up in other areas besides music. Their capacity was seen as exclusively advisory to the Bishops' Committee on the Liturgy.

The Bishops' Committee finds its purpose and description in a document from the Holy See, *The First Instruction on the Orderly Carrying Out of the Constitution on the Sacred Liturgy*, dated September 26, 1964:

> The territorial authority may, as circumstances suggest, entrust the following to this commission:
>
> a) studies and experiments to be promoted in accordance with the norm of article 40, 1 and 2 of the *Constitution*;
>
> b) practical initiatives to be undertaken for the entire territory, by which the liturgy and the application of *The Constitution on the Liturgy* may be encouraged;
>
> c) studies and the preparation of aids which become necessary in virtue of the decrees of the plenary body of bishops;
>
> d) the office of regulating the pastoral-liturgical action in the entire nation, supervising the application of the decrees of the plenary body, and reporting concerning all these matters to the body;
>
> e) consultations to be undertaken frequently and common initiatives to be promoted with associations in the same region which are concerned with scripture, catechetics, pastoral care, music and sacred art, and with every kind of religious association of the laity.[19]

The question arises concerning the fact of how many of these functions have been entrusted to the committee by the territorial authority. But presuming that all of them have been so entrusted, it still remains a fact that in each of the cases enumerated in the *Instruction* from the Holy See, the committee is concerned only with studies and experiments, with regulating what the plenary body has already decreed, with preparation of aids and consulting learned societies and individuals, and with practical initiatives to promote the *Constitution on the Sacred Liturgy*. Committees are normally set up by a plenary body and are responsible to that body that has created them; they report their findings to that body which then, having received or not received the report, may or may not determine to take action on the subject in question. Thus the "legislative" authority in liturgy in this country as a whole remains the "territorial authority," the plenary body of bishops, subject always to the Holy See.[20]

An interesting note appeared in the Newsletter of the Bishops' Committee on the Liturgy when *The Place of Music in Eucharistic Celebrations* was issued:

> The following statement was drawn up after study by the Music Advisory Board and was submitted to the Bishops' Committee on the Liturgy. The Bishops' Committee has approved the statement, adopted it as its own, and recommends it for consideration by all.[21]

The question is obviously just what authoritative value does this document possess, and therefore, what respect and even obedience does it demand. Can it be construed as the basis for local diocesan legislation on musical matters, as has, in fact, so often been done?

The answer must be that it has no legal binding force, since it is merely the opinion of a board that is only advisory to a committee that in itself has no legislative authority but is constituted to report to the full body that empowered it, an act that doubtfully was ever done at all. In addition, when the opinions of an advisory board are found to be in contradiction to authoritative Roman *Instructions*, then they clearly must be rejected.[22] But, in fact, they were not, and *The Place of Music in Eucharistic Celebrations* became the basis for great activity in most dioceses where many musicians in good faith accepted the propaganda delivered to them by Universa Laus, acting through the Music Advisory Board.

Two national meetings were arranged in order to launch *The Place of Music in Eucharistic Celebrations*, one in Kansas City, Missouri, December 1 and 2, 1966, when the Music Advisory Board met, reorganized itself to be free of members who would likely oppose the projected statement, and then appointed a committee to write the desired document. Members of the committee were Fathers Eugene Walsh, S.S., and Robert Leodogar, M.M., and Dennis Fitzpatrick. The other major meeting was in Chicago, Illinois, November 20 to 23, 1968, jointly attended by members of diocesan music and liturgy commissions from across the nation. Under the watchful eye of Father Frederick McManus, papers were given by Reverend Joseph M. Champlin, Reverend Robert Leodogar, M.M., Reverend

Eugene Walsh, S.S., Reverend Neil McEleney, C.S.P., Bishop John J. Dougherty, Reverend Gary Tollner and Reverend William A. Bauman. Statements made and left unchallenged included these: "Without faith, there can be no sacrament; community faith is necessary; it exists in the community before it exists in the individual"; "The faith of those present accomplishes the marvelous change called transubstantiation"; "The primary sign of the Eucharist are (sic) people gathering together, not the bread and wine or words."

With only a few objections, which were quickly disposed of, the document, *The Place of Music in Eucharistic Celebrations*, was considered approved, although it had scarcely been considered by the assembly and little or no discussion was permitted or encouraged. But the true colors of those who were manipulating the reforms of music and liturgy in the United States became crystal clear in Chicago. The practical application of the principles set forth in the document was presented at the Mass celebrated by Reverend J. Paul Byron at Old Saint Mary's Church, November 21, at which the folk music of Phil Ochs and Pete Seeger was performed.[23] Present at most of the sessions and the Masses were many members of the hierarchy, members of the Bishops' Committee on the Liturgy, none of whom raised any objections to the statements made or the music performed.[24]

With the document now enjoying an "official" position, taken by some to be even legislative and authoritative and equal if not surpassing Roman legislation, the disintegration of church music across the country began in earnest. "Beat" music, so-called folk music, combos, jazz and rock groups, country western and ballads became the accepted music for parish liturgies, weddings, graduations and even ordinations. The Catholic and the secular press have recorded the aberrations.[25] With the introduction of profane and trivial compositions and performances, good music became ever more disused, as choirs were disbanded and even prohibited. Seminaries, novitiates and colleges led the way, and little official effort was expended to curtail it.[26] In some dioceses the bishops did speak up forcefully against abuses.[27] Writers in Catholic periodicals generally backed the revolution, but others expressed caution and concern.[28] As music for "special groups," originally intended for college and high school students, came to mean music for elementary pupils too, so that they could participate more fully, some liturgists promoted the writing of music by grade school children for performance at their Masses. *Living Worship*, a publication of the Liturgical Conference, assured church musicians that the piano had at least four advantages over the organ as a liturgical instrument, and that ukuleles are amazingly simple for young children to learn to play.[29] In a more learned idiom, *Worship* published an explanation of the entire reform: "The hootenanny Mass can give explicit eucharistic and Christological specification to youth's intense involvement in the movements for racial justice, for control of nuclear weapons, for the recognition of personal dignity."[30]

With the very purpose of sacred music undermined, the repertory of centuries set aside, the language of the Church even outlawed, choirs disbanded and a rash of secular compositions and ensembles put in the place of a thousand-year tradition, there is little wonder that church musicians were baffled and disheartened. The hope and development promised by the Council Fathers had not materialized in this country, chiefly because what came from Rome never reached the United States.

Monsignor Richard J. Schuler
(*Sacred Music*, Vol. 110, No.1, Spring 1983, p. 5-11)

NOTES

1. Cf. *Notitiae*, 195-196 (October-November, 1982), p. 466.

2. This writer once was asked by a priest if the Latin *Missale Romanum* that he was unfamiliar with was a translation into Latin from the English missal! It demonstrates how the Latin missal was kept from the American priests.

3. See *Sacred Music*, Vol. 102, No. 4 (Winter 1975), p. 31-35; Vol. 103, No. 3 (Fall 1976), p. 3-6.

4. See *Sacred Music*, Vol. 103, No. 4 (Winter 1976), p. 19-28; Vol. 104, No. 1 (Spring 1977), p. 21-25.

5. In 1966, Pope Paul VI warned religious communities bound to the singing of the Office that, "if this language, noble, universal and admirable for its spiritual vigor, if the Gregorian chant that comes from the depths of the human soul – if these two things be remodeled, then the choir will become like an extinguished candle which no longer illuminates or attracts the attention of the minds of men. The Church introduced the vernacular among the faithful for pastoral reasons; but she looks to you to preserve the ancient beauty, gravity and dignity of the Divine Office in both language and chant." Quoted in *The Wanderer*, Oct. 6, 1966.

6. For a partial list of dioceses in the United States with regulations against the use of Latin, see Johannes Overath, ed. *Sacred Music and Liturgy Reform after Vatican II*, Rome: 1969, p. 22-23.

7. Newsletter of Bishops' Committee on the Liturgy, Vol. 4, No. 1-2 (January-February 1968).

8. Paragraph 23, 24.

9. IV, B, 1, a.

10. Paragraph 28.

11. II, B, 1.

12. II, B, 3.

13. II, B, 3.

14. Paragraph 59.

15. Article 112.

16. III; III, B.

17. Joseph Gelineau, *Voices and Instruments in Christian Worship*. Collegeville, Minnesota: The Liturgical Press, 1964.

18. Article 44.

19. Paragraph 45.

20. Cf. *Acta Apostolicae Sedis*, June 28, 1968). No bishops' conference can delegate any of its legislative authority to any of its committees.

21. Vol. 104, No. 1-2 (January-February 1968).

22. See Richard J. Schuler, "By Whose Authority?" *The Wanderer*, April 4, 1968, p. 3.

23. The official program of the meeting prints the texts for "Oh, Had I a Golden Thread," by Pete Seeger; "When I've Gone," by Phil Ochs; and "This Little Light of Mine."

24. Members of the Bishops' Committee on the Liturgy were Most Reverend Leo C. Byrne, Coadjutor Archbishop of Saint Paul and Minneapolis; Most Reverend John L. Morkovsky; Most Reverend James W. Malone; Most Reverend Francis J. Furey; Most Reverend Aloysius J. Wycislo and Most Reverend John J. Dougherty.

25. Some of the "top ten" of the liturgical hits in the late sixties were: "Michael, Row the Boat"; "Blowing in the Wind"; "Gypsy Rover"; and "Kum-bay-a." Often these had newly composed words the literary worth of which was worse than the liturgical value of the melodies. Others were totally secular in both words and music, e.g., "Hush Little Baby"; "There is a Ship"; "Try to Remember"; "This Land is Your Land," etc.

26. For example, in a letter to this writer, dated March 31, 1966, Archbishop Hallinan of Atlanta, Georgia, said: "I am sympathetic to the adaptation of popular music in church to include the use of folk songs. I would not want the bishops' commission to take a strong stand against such folk music. Rather, I prefer the free development of it, with of course, proper care and exercise of caution at all times."

27. For example, Archbishop Cousins in Milwaukee and Bishop Gorman in Dallas both spoke out against the abuses.

28. Cf. Michael D. Cordovana, "Perspective of Change," *Musart*, September-October 1967, p. 10-11, 41; Robert F. Hayburn, "Music for Special Groups," *Musart*, September-October 1967, p. 16, 33-38.

29. William Flanders, "Music for Children's Liturgies – Practical Excerpts from a New Book," *Living Worship*, Vol. 6, No. 7, September 1970.

30. Patrick Regan, "The Change Behind the Changes," *Worship*, Vol. 40, No.1, January 1966.

PART VI

"Music in Catholic Worship"

The seventies were a decade of unrest for the whole world. In the United States, the effects of the cultural revolution that began in China and spread through Europe caused protests and strikes on college campuses that echoed down into high schools and other educational institutions generally. The protests associated with the war in Viet Nam involved nuns and priests in activity not formerly a part of the religious life. The concept of authority in the Church was challenged in every area: education, liturgy, catechetics, religious vows, the role of the laity. Much of the ferment was justified by the activists in their own minds as being an expression of the "spirit of Vatican II." The progressivists pushed far beyond the intentions of the Council Fathers in an effort to establish a church that reflected their own specifications rather than the directives that came out of the Council and the curia. Since few among the laity and even among the clergy actually had ever read the writings of the Council Fathers or the papal and curial documents that followed on the close of the Council, most of the activity that was promoted so feverishly in the seventies, supposedly to implement the Council's directives, was based on opinions rather than on facts, on newspaper accounts of interviews with the statements by *periti*. Church music was among the first areas to suffer devastation under the attacks of the reformers.

On an international scope, the Consociatio Internationalis Musicae Sacrae continued its efforts to implement the decrees of the Council in accord with the commission given to it by its founder, Pope Paul VI. It organized and sponsored the Sixth International Church Music Congress, held in Salzburg, Austria, in August of 1974.[1] Special efforts were made there in the practical order to foster new compositions. New works in a variety of languages, many from areas under Communist domination, were presented along with

Gregorian chant and music from all periods of the Church's treasury of polyphony. Before and after the Congress, several symposia were organized by the Consociatio in various areas of music that were opened up for study as a result of conciliar statements. In Rome, in 1975, ethnomusicologists from all the continents met to consider the place of native music in missionary lands as ordered by the Council.[2] In 1972, the subject of music for cathedral churches was studied in Salzburg,[3] and in 1977, at Bolzano in the South Tirol, questions confronting composers for the revised liturgy were discussed.[4] An international house for the study of hymnology, ethnomusicology and Gregorian chant was established at Maria Laach in West Germany in 1975 with the purpose of aiding musicians and bishops from all parts of the world in carrying out the music reforms of Vatican II. The Consociatio published a volume of chants common to all peoples, the *Liber Cantualis*,[5] containing a basic repertory to be sung by all Catholic congregations, and four years earlier, in 1974, Pope Paul VI sent a booklet of chants, entitled *Jubilate Deo*,[6] to all the bishops of the world as his special Easter gift to them and their people. Despite constant opposition to its work from the progressivists who wished to impose a "spirit of the Council" in place of the decrees of the Council, the work of the Consociatio, coupled with the academic activity of the Pontifical Institute of Sacred Music in Rome, advanced clearly if somewhat slowly.

During the first part of the decade, the officers of the Consociatio, appointed by papal letter, were: Jacques Chailley of France, president; Monsignor Johannes Overath of Germany and Monsignor Richard J. Schuler of the United States, vice-presidents; Canon René B. Lenaerts of Belgium, Joseph Lennards of the Netherlands, Monsignor Fiorenzo Romita of Italy, Monsignor Jean-Pierre Schmit of Luxembourg and Monsignor Ferdinand Haberl of Germany were consultors. During the second half of the decade, the *praesidium* of the Consociatio was: Monsignor Johannes Overath, president; Monsignor Richard J. Schuler and Canon René B. Lenaerts, vice-presidents; Joseph Lennards, Monsignor Jean-Pierre Schmit, Monsignor Gerard Mizgalski of Poland and Edouard Souberbielle of France, consultors.

In the United States, the Church Music Association of America continued its efforts to carry out the wishes of the Council. Meeting in Boston, Massachusetts, April 1-3, 1970, church musicians from all parts of the United States considered the challenges presented to them by the reform, but the influence of the progressivists was very apparent at the meeting, both in discussions and in practical demonstrations.[7] The previous national convention at Detroit, Michigan, April 16-19, 1968, had been a financial disaster because racial tensions in the city had kept many from attending.[8] The Boston meeting did much to help recoup the monetary losses incurred in Detroit, but a clear direction for the association in the turmoil of the liturgical and musical reforms was not forthcoming. Later meetings of the association in Saint Paul, Minnesota, in December 1973,[9] and in Pueblo, Colorado, January 31 to February 2, 1975,[10] were poorly attended and of little significance. Cost of travel and lodging and adverse economic conditions prohibited many musicians from attending national conventions at great distances from their homes. The meeting in Saint Paul marked the centenary of the establishment of the Society of Saint Caecilia of America and the founding of the journal *Caecilia*. The event was observed with Pontifical Mass at the Church of Saint Agnes, a blessing from the Holy Father and the presentation of medals from the Allgemeiner Cäcilien-Verband fur die Lander deutscher Sprache. After Pueblo, the Church Music Association of America has confined its activity to the publication of its quarterly journal, *Sacred Music*.

Officers of the association during the seventies were: 1970-72: Roger Wagner, president; Noel Goemanne, vice-president; Reverend Robert A. Skeris, general secretary; Frank D. Synskie, treasurer; Robert I. Blanchard, Reverend Ralph S. March, Theodore Marier, John McManemin, Reverend Elmer F. Pfeil, Paul Salamunovich, Reverend Richard J. Schuler and James Welch, directors. 1972-74: Roger Wagner, president; Reverend Robert A. Skeris, vice-president; Monsignor Richard J. Schuler, general secretary; Sister Miriam Joseph, C.S.J., treasurer; Mrs. Richard K. Biggs, Arthur F. Edwards, Reverend Ralph S. March, John McManemin, Reverend Elmer F. Pfeil and Paul Salamunovich, directors. 1974-76: Gerhard Track, president; Reverend Robert A. Skeris, vice-president; Monsignor Richard J. Schuler, general secretary; Mrs. Richard H. Ores, treasurer; Mrs. Richard K. Biggs, Arthur F. Edwards, Reverend Ralph S. March, John McManemin, Noel Goemanne, Mrs. Donald G. Vellek, directors. 1977-80: Monsignor Richard J. Schuler, president; Gerhard Track, vice-president; Virginia A. Schubert, general secretary; B. Allen Young, treasurer; Mrs. Richard K. Biggs, Reverend Ralph S. March, Mrs. Donald G. Vellek, William P. Mahrt and Reverend Robert A. Skeris, directors.

During the seventies, many ecclesiastical organizations ceased functioning, chiefly because of financial troubles caused by inflation in the economy, but also because a clear direction and purpose could not be maintained. Pressure from the progressivist element was too strong. Among the societies that disappeared was the National Catholic Music Educators Association, publishers of *Musart*. The NCMEA was primarily interested in classroom music teaching, but the music of the liturgy always had an important place in Catholic schools. Thus, considerable effort was directed toward Gregorian chant, formation of boys' choirs, state-wide festival Masses and the liturgical formation of students in addition to the usual work of music educators. When Catholic schools and most religious orders of Sisters experienced the turmoil of the seventies and many failed and closed, the teachers' associations also suffered. NCMEA ceased publication of its magazine in the middle of the decade.[11]

While strictly speaking it is not the successor organization to NCMEA, the National Association of Pastoral Musicians was organized after the demise of the music teachers' society. Its publication, *Pastoral Music*, began in 1976, with Reverend Virgil C. Funk as publisher. The society has the approval of the American bishops, and its journal reflects the position of the music advisors to the Bishops' Committee on the Liturgy as well as the National Liturgical Conference, the Federation of Diocesan Liturgical Commissions, and ultimately, Universa Laus. *Pastoral Music* publishes current developments in liturgical innovations and musical fads. References to folk music, combos, dancing, banners and theological trends dominate its pages, and yet a decade after its beginning, it is already becoming *passé*, tied to the ideas of the sixties and seventies. The true liturgical reforms of the Council, as announced by the Holy See, are not clearly set forth in the pages of *Pastoral Music*, although they are slowly beginning to appear on the American scene despite the fads and trendy positions proposed by the Association of Pastoral Musicians. Its conventions and workshops are scheduled in a wide variety of places across the country. They have attracted large numbers of church musicians who truly seek help in bringing to their parishes the reforms sought by the Church, but the number who have found answers to their problems is beginning to dwindle. Basic in the stance of the National Association of Pastoral Musicians is a confusion over the nature of the "sacred."[12] Until the requirements as given by the Church in its *Instructions* on music in the liturgy are accepted, viz., holiness and goodness of form, nothing positive toward implementing the wishes of the Council will be achieved by the activities of this group. Liturgical music must be sacred and it must be art. So many of the suggested innovations are lacking in one or both of these requirements.

The seventies proved to be the decade of the *piccolomini*, the little men. Church music became the domain of the "do-it-yourself" composer and performer. In the name of *actuosa participatio*, guitar players, various combos, folk singers and even grade school children undertook to write and perform music for church, providing both texts and notes. That such ineptitude and ignorance, albeit sincere, could have taken hold of a serious and sacred sector of life, the worship of God, can only be explained by reference to the direction given from the central authority in the country. The phenomenon was witnessed in all parts of the country; it came from a common source. That source was the Music Advisory Board of the Bishops' Committee on the Liturgy. The group acted chiefly through the documents issued in its name: *The Place of Music in Eucharistic Celebrations*;[13] and "Music in Catholic Worship," which was released in 1972.

On September 5, 1970, the Sacred Congregation for Divine Worship published its *Third Instruction on the Correct Implementation of the Constitution on the Sacred Liturgy* of the Second Vatican Council.[14] Entitled *Liturgicae instaurationes*, it put an end to experimentation in liturgical matters and called for the careful fulfillment of the *Instructions* given by the Council and the curial documents that followed. The decrees contained in *Musicam sacram* of 1967 are repeated, and abuses are ordered to be eliminated. Only a passing reference to this significant document from Rome occurs in "Music in Catholic Worship." Just as with *Musicam sacram*, the Roman *Instruction* was ignored in the United States, and the abuses continued to grow. There is little wonder that the laity objected to many innovations made in the name of the Council and the reform, because their very right to have the liturgical reform carried out properly and orderly was being violated. The *Instruction* of 1972 clearly stated that "the priest should keep in mind that, by imposing his own personal restoration of sacred rites, he is offending the rights of the faithful and is introducing individualism and idiosyncrasy into celebrations which belong to the whole Church."[15] The true nature of the liturgical reform was once again clarified:

> The effectiveness of liturgical actions does not consist
> in the continual search for newer rites or simpler forms,
> but in an ever deeper insight into the word of God and
> the mystery which is celebrated. The priest will assure
> the presence of God and His mystery in the celebration
> by following the rites of the Church rather than his own
> preferences.[16]

The *Third Instruction* repeats the statement of *Musicam sacram* which says that "the Church does not exclude any kind of sacred music from the liturgy."[17] It says further that "not every type of music, song or instrument is equally capable of stimulating prayer or expressing the mystery of Christ." True sacred music must have the qualities of holiness and good form, as the Church has been repeating at least since the days of Pope Pius X. Interestingly, "Music in Catholic Worship" omits the word *sacred* in its treatment of this subject, even when it quotes *Musicam sacram* in the *Newsletter* of the Bishops' Committee: "In modern times the Church has consistently recognized and freely admitted the use of various styles of music as an aid to liturgical worship."[18] The fact is, that the word *sacred* and the very notion of sacredness is usually absent in the American documents, despite frequent use in the Roman ones. The issue of the "sacred" continues to be a basic difficulty between the American and Roman statements. If one eliminates the quality of holiness, then "many styles of contemporary composition"[19] can be employed, and if the quality of good form is overlooked, then "music in folk idiom (can) find acceptance in Eucharistic celebrations."[20] But these actions go contrary to the clear Roman *Instructions*.

As was the case with *The Place of Music in Eucharistic Celebrations*, the most unfortunate part of "Music in Catholic Worship" is its theology. Why a document on music needs such theological reflections is not clear, unless a new theology is being taught, something until now unknown to the Catholic musician. In the chapter entitled "The Theology of Celebration," we read such nebulous statements as these:[21]

> We are Christians because through the Christian community we have met Jesus Christ, heard his word in invitation, and responded to him in faith. We gather at Mass that we may hear and express our faith again in this assembly and, by expressing it, renew and deepen it.
>
> We come together to deepen our awareness of, and commitment to, the action of his Spirit in the whole of our lives at every moment. We come together to acknowledge the love of God poured out among us in the work of the Spirit, to stand in awe and praise.[22]

Catholic truth is not based on feelings. The divine life in a baptized person redeemed by the sacrifice of Christ is a deeper reality than that expressed in "The Theology of Celebration." The purpose of the Mass for the Catholic is inadequately expressed in the words quoted above. Such watered-down statements cannot be the basis for liturgy or for music that forms an integral part of liturgy. The taint of a false ecumenism with its roots in Modernism can be detected in this statement on celebration. It is only a partial truth and not a good or adequately complete expression of Catholic faith. Where is there in it any reference to transubstantiation or the consecration or the real presence of Jesus, all essential to a Catholic understanding of the Mass? Truly, the Mass is more than a mere prayer, more than even the greatest prayer.

"Music in Catholic Worship" is the work of liturgists, not of church musicians. It was drawn up by a committee of the Federation of Diocesan Liturgical Commissions. In the seventies, a new class of "expert" emerged.[23] Despite limited theological study, historical knowledge and artistic achievement, the liturgist acquired command of parish worship, including virtual control of the clergy, musicians and the laity in their separate roles. Selection of music, scheduling of cantors and lectors, decisions on vestments, decorations, ceremonial movement and even the hours of choir practice came under the jurisdiction of a new type of bureaucrat. Trained at Notre Dame University and at Catholic University in Washington, the first liturgists were able to find employment and command significant salaries, and thus many other schools and colleges added courses to train liturgists. With "creativity" as a basic principle of action, the liturgist is constantly seeking the innovative despite the warning of the Sacred Congregation of Divine Worship which insists that "the effectiveness of liturgical action does not consist in the continual search for newer rites or simpler forms."[24]

Most of the difficulties between liturgists and church musicians arise precisely because of this problem. Musicians need time to develop repertory, and once repertory is built, opportunity to use it frequently is necessary. The very construction of the Roman liturgical books assures this repetition with the recurring cycles of the liturgical texts and the Gregorian melodies. Thus the musician asks only for the right to carry out the liturgy according to the directions of the Roman books. Indeed, the third *Instruction* of 1970 says: "One should not add any rite which is not contained in the liturgical books."[25]

Thus, by the end of the decade, fifteen years after the promulgation of the *Constitution on the Sacred Liturgy*, the state of church music in the United States had so deteriorated that serious observers began to question what had gone wrong with the reform. The Consociatio Internationalis Musicae Sacrae conducted a survey of musicians in all parts of the world seeking to ascertain if current practices in liturgical music actually corresponded to the requirements of the conciliar decrees and the post-conciliar *Instructions*.[26] It asked if there was greater *actuosa participatio* now than before, if Latin and Gregorian chant were truly being fostered as the Council had directed, if church music was being taught in seminaries and novitiates, if congregational singing was improving, if the organ was being given its legitimate role in liturgical services. For each question, the proper quotation from the official documents was given. The survey proved that far from a new springtime for church music, the hoped-for reform had come to ruin, and even the achievements of the past seventy-five years since the *motu proprio* of Pope Pius X had been for the most part lost. A new beginning would have to be made, based on a renewed understanding of the "sacred" and a re-established system of education in liturgical music at all levels from grade schools through seminaries and novitiates. By the beginning of the eighties, it was becoming clear that the next generation would have to correct what had been wrought in the sixties and seventies if it wished to implement the directives of the Second Vatican Council and continue the reform originally begun by Saint Pius X.

Monsignor Richard J. Schuler

(*Sacred Music*, Vol. 110, no.2, Summer 1983, p. 11-16)

NOTES

1. Johannes Overath, ed., *Conservare et Promovere: VI Internationaler Kongress fur Kirchenmusik, Salzburg, 26. August bis 2. September 1974.* Rome: Consociatio Internationalis Musicae Sacrae, 1975. American participation in the Congress included the presence of two choirs, the Dallas Catholic Choir, directed by Father Ralph S. March, and the Twin Cities Catholic Chorale, directed by Monsignor Richard J. Schuler; new compositions commissioned for the occasion by American composers, Noel Goemanne and Paul Manz; and lectures presented by William Peter Mahrt and Monsignor Schuler.

2. Josef Kuchertz and Johannes Overath, eds. *Musica Indigena: Musikethnologisches Symposium, Rom, vom 14. bis 22. November 1975.* Rome: Consociatio Internationalis Musicae Sacrae, 1976. See also Richard J. Schuler, "Native Music for the Missions," *Sacred Music*, Vol. 102, No. 4 (Winter 1975), p. 27-30.

3. Johannes Overath, ed. *Magna Gloria Domini, Die liturgische Musik in den Kathedralen, Abteikirchen und Ecclesiae maiores nach dem Vaticanum II: Symposion der Consociatio Internationalis Musicae Sacrae, vom 4. bis 8. April 1972 in Salzburg.* Rome: Consociatio Internationalis Musicae Sacrae, 1972.

4. Johannes Overath, ed. *Confitemini Domino: Internationales Komponisten-Symposion, Bolzano dal 13 al 17 Aprile 1977.* Maria Laach: Haus der Kirchenmusik, 1977.

5. *Liber Cantualis.* Sablé-sur-Sarthe (France): Abbaye Saint-Pierre de Solesmes, 1978.

6. *Jubilate Deo.*

7. See *Sacred Music*, Vol. 96, No. 1 (Spring 1970), p. 42-43, for Father Ralph S. March's comments on the convention.

8. Cf. Theodore Marier, "National Convention in Detroit," *Sacred Music*, Vol. 95, No. 1 (Spring 1968), p. 3-4.

9. See *Sacred Music*, Vol. 101, No. 1 (Spring 1974), p. 41-42.

10. See *Sacred Music*, Vol. 102, No. 1 (Spring 1975), p. 35-36.

11. Published from 1948 to 1976.

12. *Pastoral Music*, Vol. 7, No. 4 (April-May 1983), contains several articles on the question of sacred and secular music.

13. *Newsletter* of Bishops' Committee on the Liturgy. Vol. 4, No. 1-2 (January-February 1968). See Part V of "Chronicle of the Reform" for a treatment of this document, *Sacred Music,* Vol. 110, No. 1 (Spring 1983), p. 5-11.

14. See *Documents on the Liturgy, 1963-1979: Conciliar, Papal and Curial Texts.* Collegeville: The Liturgical Press, 1982. p. 159-167.

15. *Ibid.,* para. 1.

16. *Ibid.*

17. *Musicam sacram,* No. 9.

18. *Ibid.,* No. 4.

19. "Music in Catholic Worship," Revised edition. Bishops' Committee on the Liturgy, 1983, No. 28.

20. *Ibid.*

21. Compare these statements with *Liturgicae instaurationes,* the *Third Instruction,* No. 1, which says: "Liturgical reform is not at all synonymous with so-called desacralization and is not intended as an occasion for what is called secularization. Thus the liturgy must keep a dignified and sacred character."

22. "Music in Catholic Worship," No. 1, 2.

23. Cf. Editorial statement, "The Liturgist," *Sacred Music,* Vol. 108, No. 3 (Fall 1981), p. 19-21.

24. *Liturgicae instaurationes,* No. 1.

25. *Ibid.*

26. The questions made reference to particular articles of the *Constitution on the Sacred Liturgy,* the *Instruction, Musicam sacram* of 1967, and the *Institutio generalis* of the *Ordo Missae.* cf. *Sacred Music,* Vol. 104, No. 4, p. 5-12.

PART VII

Documents on the Liturgy

By the end of the seventies, the condition of church music in the United States had so far deteriorated that the very purposes of the reform set in motion by Pope Pius X eighty years before had all but disappeared. Just what the Church intended as reform, and how it was to be accomplished was so confused in the minds of church musicians that aberrations worse than the abuses decried by Pius X were even being promoted as reforms.

To catalog the abuses would take volumes. When the nadir was thought to have been reached, the next day produced even greater and more unfortunate disorders. The problems were based in a disregard for the two elements required of church music, qualities clearly called for by Pius X and by every document issued since, including the *Constitution on the Sacred Liturgy* from the Second Vatican Council: holiness and goodness of form. Church music must be sacred and it must be true art. In nearly everything that in recent years was promoted by publishers, performing groups, musical congresses and conventions, one or both of these essential qualities was lacking. With the basic requirements wanting, the incidental and peripheral innovations had no foundation, and utter confusion resulted. Educated musicians and many Catholics with a *sensus ecclesiae* asked openly what had happened. Could it be that what we have experienced in the past twenty years is what the Church, under the guidance of the Holy Spirit, in a general council, intended the worship of God to become?

The answer was hard to arrive at, because the vast number of documents, papal, conciliar and curial, that had come forth since the opening of the Second Vatican Council lay beyond the grasp of most musicians and clergy. Even those who had attempted to become acquainted with every decree were not sure that they had really seen them all. No orderly compilation of the documents of the reform had as yet appeared. Monsignor Robert F. Hayburn had collected the historical documents on church music, but his work was concluded with the Second Vatican Council.[1] Need for an orderly collection, that showed the intentions of the law givers, the direction of the reform, and the purpose behind the art of music as a part of liturgy was finally met by the publication of a monumental work, *Documents on the Liturgy, 1963-1979, Conciliar, Papal and Curial Texts.*[2]

In studying this volume the first idea that strikes the reader is the order and plan behind the ongoing decrees from the Holy See and the conciliar bodies. The goal of reform was clear and the means of attaining the goal were likewise fully laid out. The purpose of sacred music is given: the glory of God and the edification of the faithful, not the creation of a truly human situation, as the Bishops' Advisory Board on Music stated.[3] Music for use in church must be sacred, a requirement that is called for again and again in the Roman documents, but hardly ever in statements from Americans. Music for the liturgy must be true art, a judgment that belongs to well-trained professional church musicians, despite the abundance of well-meaning but uneducated amateurs in composition, performance and criticism of church music in this country. In reality, what the documents of the Council, the Pope and his curia spelled out in the past twenty years does not differ significantly from the original directives given by Pope Pius X. In a way they are a kind of capstone placed on the top of a structure that has long been building. Now the view of the whole is apparent and those who have strayed from the plan can return to the clearly outlined goal.

Not all the reform has been contained in decrees and documents. More important, from a practical standpoint, has been the publication of new liturgical books. In these newly revised and edited volumes what has been ordered for liturgical use in the universal Church is definitely set down. While all the liturgical books issued since the Council are important, at least remotely, to the church musician, those that are specifically musical are of the utmost concern. Those that have been published and are available for use in the Latin liturgy are:

> *Graduale Romanum* (1974). Contains the Proper of the
> time, Common of the saints, Proper of the saints, ritual
> Masses, Masses for various occasions, Votive Masses, the

Liturgy of the Dead and the Ordinary of the Mass.

Graduale simplex (1975). Intended for use in small churches, it contains simplified settings for the texts of the Mass.

Jubilate Deo (reprinted 1974). A collection of chants for Mass and other occasions.

Lectionarium (1970-72). In three volumes, the readings in Latin for the whole church year in all cycles, together with the responsorial psalm and verse before the Gospel (without musical settings).

Liturgia Horarum (1980). In four volumes, the Divine Office (without musical settings).

Missale Romanum (revised edition, 1975). Originally published in 1969, this is the *Novus Ordo Missae* of Pope Paul VI, containing what is needed by the priest at the altar and the chair. Some musical indications are given.

Missale Romanum cum lectionibus ad usum fidelium (1977). In four volumes, all the prayers and readings for the whole year for use as a hand missal for the faithful. Musical settings include some chants for the Mass.

Ordo Missae in Cantu. The priest's chants at the chair and the altar, including the opening prayers, various intonations, all the prefaces, the four Eucharistic prayers, concluding chants. Notation is provided for all the texts.

Pontificale Romanum and *Rituale Romanum*. Still in preparation, containing rites performed by bishops and by priests. There will be musical notation.

From these books that have appeared in an *editio typica* from the Libreria Editrice Vaticana, the official publishing house of the Holy See, all the various vernacular translations have been made. But the Latin originals have been printed for use not simply as sources of translations.[4] When the Council ordered that the Gregorian chant books be revised and extended, it was the intention of the Fathers that the chant should be sung within the Latin liturgy. They were not merely promoting musicological research; they were directing the faithful to the means of Catholic worship in song. Other books are in progress, including the musical settings of Vespers and an updated *Liber Usualis*, containing the most commonly used chants for Mass and Vespers. The revision is the work of the monks of Solesmes, and their publications in the past decade include not only the official chant books, but they have also issued research volumes indicating their musicological methods.[5]

With the publication of the official books and decrees emanating from Rome and from the Abbey of Solesmes, the long process of implementing the wishes of the Council Fathers for a liturgical reform takes shape and gains momentum throughout the world. Unfortunately in the United States it has scarcely begun, chiefly because an anti-Latin propaganda was so effective among both clergy and laity that the use of Latin is still thought to be forbidden. The official liturgical books in Latin have hardly been seen in this country even in the seminaries, contrary to explicit legislation ordering candidates for the priesthood to be trained in Gregorian chant and Latin, and other rules commanding that the liturgy celebrated in seminaries be done in Latin as the usual procedure. As long as a disobedience to these commands persists in the seminaries, the liturgical reforms of the Second Vatican Council will not be accomplished in the United States. Without the solid foundation of the Latin liturgy, the aberrations found in so many vernacular celebrations will continue and increase.

From June 19 to 22, 1983, an international Gregorian chant symposium was held in Washington, D.C., sponsored jointly by the Catholic University of America, the Dom Mocquereau Foundation, the Pontifical Institute of Sacred Music in Rome and the Consociatio Internationalis Musicae Sacrae. Over five hundred participants came from all over the world to study, sing and learn about Gregorian chant.[6] The significance of this gathering lies in the demonstration that Gregorian chant is alive and prospering in some parts of the world in accord with the Church's wishes, and secondly, that in the United States, for the most part, the wishes of the Church have been ignored.

In contrast with the chant symposium, the several meetings of the Association of Pastoral Musicians show how far astray the reform has gone in the United States. In Saint Louis, Missouri, after the closing Mass of the convention in the cathedral, the archbishop found it necessary to apologize to the people for the liturgy carried on by the delegates.[7] *Pastoral Music, Aim, Worship,* and *Modern Liturgy* continue to record the theorizing and the practical applications of the theories that propose to be the implementation of the Church's reform of the liturgy. But a younger generation is arising of priests and people who see the discrepancy between what is being promoted in this country and what the official directives have indicated. They see that what is still being promoted by various publishers, performing groups and national organizations of liturgists and musicians does not correspond to the reality of the present. Rather these groups are *passé,* tied to the ideas of the sixties when experimentation was widespread. Now that the experiments, for the most part, have been shown to be unfortunate and useless, they continue to hold to them while the Church prepares to implement its well-planned reform according to its documents. Only when we are freed of the errors and unfounded innovations of the present liturgical establishment will progress be made in the United States and the reform again be allowed to continue.

Certain distinctions must be learned in this country about music for worship. They are clearly indicated in the documents.[8] First, the difference between music intended as *liturgical* music and that intended as *religious* music must be established. When composing for the very words of the Mass or the Hours, one is creating music which is itself *pars integrans,* an integral part of the liturgy itself. Whether the texts are Latin or the vernacular, the music must always be in a sacred style and truly and seriously artistic, worthy of the exalted purpose for which it is intended. It can, indeed, be simple and within the scope of lesser performers, but it must always be holy and of good form. The Council itself calls for just that, both in Latin and in the vernacular tongues. The treasures of the past will supply the bulk of such repertory for many years to come, but new composition must surely be encouraged and used.

Secondly, *religious* music, as distinguished from *liturgical* music, truly has a place both within the liturgy and in para-liturgical and extra-liturgical services, as well as in gatherings apart from formal worship. Through the centuries the Church has encouraged such pious activity. The Medieval world was filled with compositions in both Latin and the vernacular that were religious and prayerful. Some, indeed, found their way into the liturgy as hymns and sequences. Others remained always as nonliturgical compositions.

We can further distinguish within this *religious* music pieces that might well be used at Masses in which the liturgical texts themselves are not sung.[9] Hymns constitute the largest body of such music. They must, of course, have sacred texts and they must be composed according to the proper rules of hymn-writing. Since by their very nature they fall within the capabilities of the entire congregation, they are most useful for the promotion of *actuosa participatio populi*. A great body of such music exists, especially from the 16th century, but 19th century hymns and some from our own time may likewise be suitably employed.

Other *religious* music, especially what is known today as folk songs, or pieces in ballad style, music reminiscent of country or western songs but set to texts of a religious nature, has no place in services within the church, either liturgical or non-liturgical. The texts are not taken from the Sacred Scriptures or from liturgical books as the *Constitution on the Sacred Liturgy* orders.[10] The music is not in a serious artistic style. Rather these pieces, good in themselves, are best used in gatherings outside the church, meetings of youth groups, excellent for singing as part of entertainment.

There are also those great religious works, such as oratorios and cantatas, written on texts from the Bible or on sacred poems, set with melodies of great beauty and harmony of great value, some with orchestration and both choral and solo sections. Again, these are not intended for liturgical use, but rather for occasions when performances of this genre of religious music can bring the minds and hearts of the audiences to the contemplation of holy things.

In a word, as there exist both secular and sacred compositions, so within the category of sacred one must further distinguish between liturgical and religious works. And often one must further refine the distinction "religious" by determining what is suitable for use within the house of God and what belongs in activity that is good and worthwhile in itself, but not directly a part of God's worship. It is in the confusion of these forms and styles that many of today's problems in church music in the United States lie. Most contemporary guitar ensembles, campus ministry combos, folksingers and religious ballad singers, often very skilled and professional, are not aware of the distinction in forms that must determine the use of all religious music. Frequently, criticism is misunderstood when objection is made to the kind of religious music employed in some liturgical services. Ignorance of what the Church wishes for the liturgy and what the Church approves for non-liturgical services, and what it admits and even blesses for activities outside the house of God is widespread.

With composition for liturgical texts at a low ebb, many choirs are resorting to Protestant anthems. Unfortunately, the texts are not from the Catholic liturgy, and in singing general religious anthems, the richness of the ever-changing liturgical texts of the Roman rite is lost. One Sunday becomes as every other, and feast and ferial, solemnity and memorial, all become the same. The riches of the Roman rite are ignored. The same can happen when hymns replace the texts of the day, even though the hymns themselves may often be varied. The poverty of liturgical celebration experienced in the eighties is caused chiefly by the abandoning of the liturgical texts of the *Missale* or the *Graduale* in favor of general anthems or hymns.[11] The true reform intended by the Church lies in the full use of all the liturgical books, the implementation of the directives contained in the post-conciliar documents, and above all, a clear understanding of what divine worship is, particularly its essential characteristics of holiness and goodness of form. Music as an integral part of divine worship must share in and clearly exemplify those same qualities.

In conclusion, having traced the liturgical reform from its inception in the work of the second half of the 19th century, through the pontificates of several popes, the high point of the Council and the decline that followed, what can one expect will be the course of that reform in the eighties and nineties of this century? One cannot know the future and frequently guesses about it are totally wrong. But by observing present trends one may arrive at probable results.

First, a new expression of Catholic truth in a new theological language is coming from the Holy Father, Pope John Paul II. Signs of a new flowering, the result of the Council, are beginning to be apparent, even though many theologians continue to hold to the errors of Modernism that surfaced just after the Council. But they are living in the past, shackled to the sixties. As a new wind is blowing in theological expression, so in liturgy and church music. So, also, in the religious life, in catechetics and canon law. The work of implementing the decrees of the Council, freed of the dross of those who wished to have their own way, is at last taking hold.

In church music, the renewal can be seen especially in eastern Europe, in Poland, Croatia and in Germany. In the United States, such activity has not yet begun, chiefly because the musical establishment is in the hands of those who are living in the past, holding to ideas that have long since been discarded abroad. The errors foisted on the church musicians of this country twenty years ago are still being peddled by official and semi-official organizations and periodicals.

What must be taken as the basis for putting the reform back on the track in this country? Simply, a full and impartial acceptance of all directives, conciliar, papal and curial.[12] That means the use of Latin as well as the vernacular, the fostering of choirs as well as congregational singing, the acceptance of the distinction between sung and spoken liturgy, the creation of new serious music as well as the use of the great works of the past. Above all, it means that the distinction between sacred and profane must be held to, along with the admission that a professional judgment must be made on the artistic merit of musical composition. In a word, the reform must be put in the hands of educated, professional musicians who are dedicated to carrying out the wishes of the Church as expressed in the documents. The same malaise that afflicted this country when the reforms of Pope Pius X were promulgated still persists. It is still a question of education, an understanding of what the Church wants and a willingness and an expertise to carry it forward.

Monsignor Richard J. Schuler

(*Sacred Music*, Vol. 110, no.3, Fall 1983, p. 7-11)

NOTES

1. *Papal Legislation on Sacred Music, 95 A.D. to 1977 A.D.* Collegeville, Minnesota: The Liturgical Press, 1979.

2. *Documents on the Liturgy, 1963-1979, Conciliar, Papal and Curial Texts*, Collegeville, Minnesota: The Liturgical Press, 1983.

3. *The Place of Music in Eucharistic Celebrations*, III; III, B. Published in *Newsletter* of the Bishops' Committee on the Liturgy, Vol. 4, No. 1-2 (January-February 1968).

4. Father Frederick R. McManus, while head of the secretariat of the American Bishops' Committee on the Liturgy, stated that "it may be that in some areas retention (of Latin) will simply mean employing the Latin texts as the basis for translations into the vernacular, at least in the case of those parts of the Roman rite which are themselves original, such as the collects." *Worship*, Vol. 38, No. 6, p. 351.

5. Cf. *Graduale Triplex*; Eugène Cardine, *Neume; Première Armée de Chant Grégorien; Sémiologie Grégorienne; Graduel Neumé; Offertoires Neumés.*

6. For accounts of the meeting, see Paul LeVoir, "The International Gregorian Chant Symposium" in *Sacred Music*, Vol. 110, No. 2 (Summer 1983), p. 17-21; Christopher M. Schaefer, "International Symposium on Gregorian Chant" in *The American Organist*, Vol. 17, No. 10 (October 1983), p. 40-42; Msgr. Francis Schmitt, "International Symposium on Gregorian Chant" in *The American Organist*, (Vol. 17, No. 10 (October 1983), p. 42-43.

7. *St. Louis Review*, April 29, 1983, p. 4.

8. Cf. The *Constitution on the Sacred Liturgy; Musicam sacram, Instruction on Music in the Liturgy*, March 5, 1967, Para. 4a, b.

9. *Musicam sacram*, Para. 32.

10. Para. 121. Pope Paul VI spoke to a thousand religious women participating in a convention of the Italian Society of St. Cecilia, April 15, 1971, about a true sense of what is sacred and therefore fitting for the liturgy. For a commentary on his words, see Richard J. Schuler, "Pope Paul on Sacred Music" in *Sacred Music*, Vol. 98, No. 2 (Summer 1971), p. 3-5.

11. "What must be sung is the Mass, its Ordinary and Proper, not 'something,' no matter how consistent, that is imposed on the Mass. Because the liturgical service is one, it has only one countenance, one motif, one voice, the voice of the Church. To continue to replace the texts of the Mass being celebrated with motets that are reverent and devout, yet out of keeping with the Mass of the day...amounts to continuing an unacceptable ambiguity; it is to cheat the people. Liturgical song involves not mere melody, but words, text, thought, and the sentiments that the poetry and music contain. Thus texts must be those of the Mass, not others, and singing means singing the Mass not just singing during Mass." *Notitiae*, Vol. 5 (1969), p. 406.

12. These are all readily available in *Documents on the Liturgy, 1963-1979: Conciliar, Papal and Curial Texts*. Collegeville, Minnesota: The Liturgical Press, 1983.

"It's in the Book" –
Monsignor Schuler and Pride of Place in the Liturgy

"Thank God for the new Mass."

These words of Monsignor Richard J. Schuler, spoken with conviction, formed the basis of the development of the liturgy at the Church of Saint Agnes in Saint Paul, Minnesota, in the years following the Second Vatican Council.

Before the end of the Council in 1965, it was not considered appropriate to include "operatic" choral-orchestral music in the liturgy. Monsignor Schuler observed that it was looked upon as "naughty." However, the Council documents on the liturgy and music actually called for the use of the vast treasury of sacred music and thus opened the door to including the works of the great masters of the Classical and Romantic eras in the liturgy. Monsignor recognized the opportunity and characteristically made the most of it. The result was the Latin liturgy at the Church of Saint Agnes.

The Twin Cities Catholic Chorale, with its impressive repertory of Classical and Romantic Masses and motets fit into the Council's desires for the liturgy and thus played an important role in the liturgy at Saint Agnes in the years after the publication of the new Roman *Missal*. All of these components are present to this day, including the use of the Latin language, Gregorian chant, and the pipe organ in the principal Sunday Mass. Monsignor Schuler implemented it all, *following the Council's requests* to use the Latin language, preserve and foster sacred polyphony with great care, hold the pipe organ in high esteem, and give Gregorian chant pride of place in the sacred liturgy.

Gregorian chant was exceptionally prominent in the liturgical life of Saint Agnes while Monsignor was pastor, again in accord with Council directives. Not only did the *Schola* sing the Gregorian Propers every Sunday at the principal Mass, it provided the Propers and the Ordinary during Advent and Lent as well as during the summer months when the Twin Cities Catholic Chorale was between seasons. In addition, the 8:00 a.m. Latin Mass on Saturdays was all Gregorian chant (Propers, Ordinary, and much in between), as were the Office of Readings on Christmas Eve, the entire office of Tenebrae in the traditional form during Holy Week, and solemn Vespers every Sunday afternoon. Once again, all of these practices are still in place.

Monsignor Schuler's writings on the sacred liturgy published here are among his most important. They cover succinctly and accurately a period of great change in the life of the Church and offer a perspective that is unique and deeply informed and in accord with the Council's desires. His series on the reform of the liturgy (Section One of this volume) along with his landmark review of Archbishop Annibale Bugnini's *The Reform of the Liturgy (1948–1975)* (in Section Two) are indispensable for a thorough understanding of the impact of liturgical reforms on the Church and on the faithful. His other writings explore the liturgy of the Second Vatican Council and how it can be celebrated solemnly, reverently, and in Latin.

The liturgy was always at the center of everything Monsignor developed at Saint Agnes, even though he is best remembered for his contributions to the promotion of sacred music in the liturgy. For him, sacred music was not just an add-on, it was an integral part of the liturgy. It *was* liturgy. As Pope Benedict XVI stated in his address to *Scholae Cantorum* pilgrims (November 11, 2012), the music they provide for the liturgy "is not an accessory or only an external ornament of the liturgy, but it is liturgy itself."

Many misunderstood or disagreed with Monsignor's liturgical practices and ideas, missing the point that these practices and ideas were absolutely in conformity with the mind of the Church and were always based solidly on current, official liturgical sources. So whenever anyone challenged him on something specific — such as how he could "get away with" having a Latin Mass, for example, or how he could justify celebrating Mass *ad orientem* — he would often simply say, "It's in the book."

Paul W. LeVoir
Saint Paul, Minnesota

Section Two

COMMENTS ON
THE SECOND VATICAN COUNCIL

"There are three basic problems that have surfaced on the subject of sacred music since the close of the Council: 1) the meaning of active participation; 2) the use of the vernacular; and 3) the qualities of 'sacred' and 'artistic' as applied to music for the liturgy."

Monsignor Richard J. Schuler
"Conciliar Constitution: *Sacrosanctum concilium,*"
Sacred Music, Vol. 119, No. 4, Winter 1992

Some Comments on the New *Instruction*

The long-awaited *Instruction* for implementing the sixth chapter of the *Constitution on the Sacred Liturgy* has finally appeared [*Musicam sacram*, the *Instruction on Sacred Music in the Liturgy*, March 5, 1967]. Its formulation, over a period of nearly two years and through a series of many redactions, seemed at times would never be accomplished, but in its published version it constitutes a very adequate instrument for putting into effect what the Fathers of the Second Vatican Council intended when they wrote the chapter on sacred music. The very purpose of this *Instruction* is to specify what is general in the *Constitution*, to give detail to the more sweeping norms laid down in it, and to suggest ways and means for carrying out the restoration of church music in the post-conciliar period. Despite the objections of those who claim that true *aggiornamento* is not accomplished by carrying out "curial directives," the fact remains that it is the Holy See, through documents of this kind, that will implement the reforms called for by the Council, leaving the details to the territorial hierarchies to adapt to each country. That the renewal will be accomplished by this method is repeated in this *Instruction*.

The document is long, perhaps too long and too wordy. Since it is written for the entire world, it has resulted in a tendency to be too general and at times anomalous. Perhaps this can be explained as the result of compromise between those who fought so hard over this document. However, it does succeed in reinforcing the directives of the *Constitution*. It reaffirms the call for active participation in the liturgy by all through singing; it reaffirms the role of the choir; it calls for the continuing use of the Latin music of the past as well as new music to be composed to Latin texts; and it repeats the role of the vernacular in the liturgy, showing composers what they should do in composing for the liturgy.

The *Instruction* has a preface and nine chapters. The first chapter is concerned with general norms regulating music in the liturgy. The second chapter takes up the all-important area of personnel, which includes treatment of the various singing roles in the liturgical action. Then follow chapters on the Mass, the Divine Office, and music for various other rites and ceremonies. The sixth chapter is dedicated to the problem of preservation of the Latin language and the proper use of the vernacular tongues, together with a similar problem closely connected with the question of languages, viz., the continued use of the heritage of sacred music and the fostering at the same time of new music in the vernacular with a wider role for congregational singing. The final three chapters are given over to directions for composers (Chapter VII), the use of musical instruments (Chapter VIII), and the position of the music commission at various levels (Chapter IX).

Detailed commentaries on each section of the *Instruction* will undoubtedly be forthcoming. For the moment, it may be interesting to point out some of the highlights that will probably cause the most interest and perhaps effect the greatest good. Among the points that should not be overlooked is the statement in the preface that this *Instruction* "does not gather together all the legislation on sacred music." It is rather a continuation of a reform in church music begun by St. Pius X and advanced little by little through the pontificates of the succeeding popes. In particular, it is the "continuation and complement of the preceding *Instruction* of the Sacred Congregation of Rites, prepared by the Consilium, and published on September 26, 1964." Rather than looking for revolutionary ideas in this document or expecting that it will overthrow all previous legislation, one can expect to see in it another step in a gradual development of liturgical renewal that St. Pius began with his *motu proprio* of 1903.

Of great interest in the preface is the definition of sacred music as "that music which, being created for the celebration of divine worship, is endowed with sanctity and excellence of form." This is specified as "Gregorian chant, sacred polyphony in its various forms both ancient and modern, sacred music for the organ and other approved instruments, and sacred music of the people, be it liturgical or religious." While the discussion continues over what is sacred and what is secular, with some even denying that there is such a distinction, this definition comes as an important strengthening of the traditional position. It says clearly that there *is* a sacred music and even makes specific what it is. Much, of course, will be made of the phrase "sacred music of the people" (*cantus popularis sacer*) by those who will attempt to find in these words a justification for the so-called "folk music" being encouraged by some liturgists today. What is seriously needed is a commentary on this paragraph with a clear definition of the vocabulary in use: *cantus popularis*, folk music, popular music, music of the people, music for the people, etc.

A constant note sounded in Chapter I and frequently repeated throughout the document is the need for a variety of forms of celebration of Mass and of the music to accompany these various types of celebration. The reason for such variety is always pastoral concern for the capabilities and the nature of the worshipping community. The resources available, the solemnity of the day, the nature of the congregation and the degree of preparation will determine what the musical program will be. The need of fostering the active participation of the congregation is constantly repeated.

Chapter II elaborates on this active participation (*actuosa participatio*) which must above all be internal so that the "faithful join their minds to what they pronounce or hear." This internal participation should be shown externally by gestures, acclamations, responses and singing. An important sentence is added that through participation "by listening to the ministers and to the choir, the faithful may raise their minds to God." The old problem of what belongs to the choir and what to the congregation is resolved by application of the principles of variety in the ways of celebration and the musical capabilities of the participants. Thus, the choir is not to assume the role of singing all to the exclusion of the congregation, nor is the congregation to be expected to undertake the total service. According to its abilities, the congregation may take part in the singing of the Ordinary as well as sections of the Proper. However, if it is not capable of this, the choir may sing all these parts, provided that the congregation is not excluded from singing what it is able to do in the service, which will vary according to its training and nature. In a word, the answer to the problem is that the individual situation must be considered and the pastoral concern for the condition of the flock taken into the decision. Ultimately, we must come to the question of the possibilities and the limitations of our congregations in singing, and having made an intelligent survey of their abilities, use them as they are, neither demanding more than they are capable of nor underestimating their potential.

Many words of high commendation for choirs will give great consolation and encouragement to those who have suffered because of false opinions that trained musical groups are outmoded, unnecessary or even a hindrance to a renewed liturgy. In fact, if one could say that any one group is given preferential treatment in this document, it is the choir. An interesting note calls for the "provision for at least one or two properly trained singers, where the possibility of even a small choir" is lacking. Here we have come around the entire circle. Time was when the "soloist" was looked upon with displeasure in many places; now he is not only permitted but positively encouraged. Now he is called cantor. His presence is desirable even in those churches that have a choir especially for those celebrations in which the choir cannot take part but which may fittingly be performed with some solemnity and therefore with singing. A directive that surely should be taken to heart in this country is the one that calls for choirs in all churches, even small churches, where a small choir would be quite in order.

Chapter III on the Mass urges the frequent use of the sung Mass (*Missa in cantu*), even several times a day. The distinction between solemn, sung and read Masses as indicated in the *Instruction* of 1958 continues, but the amount of music that is required for the celebration of a sung Mass may now be varied according to the solemnity of the day, the capabilities of the congregation and the musical resources available. The degree of musical participation by ministers, choir and congregation form a rather complicated gradation, which could be summarized in the phrase "first things first." The most basic form is that which provides for the singing of the celebrant and the congregation; to this can be added further musical portions of both the Ordinary and the Proper as the congregation and the choir can provide. However, more elaborate settings or less important chants should not be introduced without the basic degrees of participation by the ministers and the congregation.

Article 34 in this chapter contains a point that was long disputed in the preparation of this document, viz., whether the choir could perform all the parts of the Ordinary in polyphonic settings without the participation of the congregation in singing those parts. There were those who insisted that the *Credo* and the *Sanctus,* for example, must always be sung by the congregation. On the other hand, it was pointed out that this would thereby exclude the singing of the *Sanctus* or the *Credo* in all polyphonic music of earlier periods. But the Council had ordered the fostering of the treasury of sacred music, not just a part of it, e.g., all but the settings of the *Credo* and the *Sanctus*. The dispute over this question is concluded by the *Instruction* which says that the choir may sing such compositions according to the "customary norms" (which means according to the performance practice that the composer wrote for), as long as the people are not completely excluded "from taking part in the singing." This means, then, that during the service other parts should be done by the congregation, which may be parts of the Proper, or acclamations, or most certainly the various responses, hymns, etc. This is a typical Roman solution: use the music that is worthwhile according to its intended manner of performance and the resources available, but at the same time it is strongly recommended that both *Credo* and *Sanctus* be sung by the entire congregation when such is possible. Again the principles of variety, musical capabilities and pastoral concern dictate the solution. Other points in this important chapter should surely be commented on in a longer article.

Chapter IV is concerned with the singing of the Divine Office. Unfortunately, the decline in the public celebration of the Office has seemed to coincide with the progress of the liturgical movement and the gradual disintegration of choirs. It would be interesting to survey the number of parishes that had Sunday Vespers in 1903 as compared to 1925, 1945 and 1967, and then try to determine the reasons for the decline. Today, even seminaries do not observe the direction calling for the singing of Vespers set forth in the *Instruction for Seminaries* (Christmas, 1965). Nevertheless, the *Instruction on Sacred Music* speaks of singing the Office and requires again that "the Latin language is to be retained for clerics in celebration of the Divine Office in choir."

Chapter V deals with music for celebration of the sacraments, sacramentals, Bible services and other popular devotions. In all these, music has its role which should become a more important one. A caution is sounded against introducing anything that is "merely secular or that is hardly compatible with divine worship," and a plea is made that the sacred rites of Holy Week be given "due solemnity, since these lead the faithful to the center of the liturgical year and of the liturgy itself."

One of the most controversial subjects is treated in Chapter VI which deals with the languages to be used in sung liturgical celebrations and the necessity of preserving the heritage of sacred music. Pertinent passages from the *Constitution* are repeated: "Latin is to be preserved in the Latin rites"; "the faithful should know how to say or sing in Latin those parts of the Ordinary of the Mass which pertain to them"; "the use of the vernacular may often be of great advantage to the people"; "it is for the competent territorial authority to decide whether and to what extent one should use the vernacular." Seminaries are again reminded of the *Instruction* concerning the liturgical formation of students, which calls for the celebration of the liturgy in seminaries in the Latin language. New musical settings should be composed for Latin texts. The question of mixing Latin and the vernacular in the same service is solved by allowing such a practice.

The need of training and study in music is again emphasized (one wonders if there has ever been anything asked for by the Holy See so frequently or any request that has so regularly fallen on deaf ears). Gregorian chant as a necessary study is ordered and its practice and use commanded. But this also continues to fall on deaf ears. Undoubtedly, the prescriptions of this chapter will be explained away by those who do not want to accept them. However, the language is clear and simple to those who will accept words at their usual meaning, and it is the Holy See that has spoken.

Chapter VII gives directions both for composers and for those responsible for preparing the vernacular texts. Permission is granted, subject to the approval of the territorial hierarchy, for using the music of previous eras even though the texts differ somewhat from the present approved versions. This has been a point long advocated by English musicians who wish to make use of the great music composed originally for the Anglican service in the English language during the Elizabethan period and later. It may be that our bishops will take advantage of this very welcome concession. The chapter adds a caution on the use of unbecoming music even for experiment, insisting that the dignity of the liturgy and the devotion of the faithful be respected.

Chapter VIII was the section of the document that particularly interested the secular press and even much of the Catholic press. The *Associated Press* news release from Rome on the publication of the *Instruction* was concerned only to point out that "Pope Paul VI changed the rules for Roman Catholic church music today, opening the way to use of beat rhythms and jazz for sacred services." Arguing that since there were no specific prohibitions against the use of certain instruments or certain types of secular music, these were consequently permitted, the press overlooked completely the earlier declaration of the Congregation of Rites on January 4th concerning this very matter. Actually, the chapter on instruments does little more than repeat the words of the *Constitution*, and since it is intended for the entire Church, lists of instruments are not given either with approval or disapproval with the exception of the pipe organ which is again extolled as the "traditional instrument that adds a wonderful splendor to the Church's ceremonies." The territorial hierarchies are left with the obligation of deciding which instruments are "by common opinion and use suitable for secular music only and thus to be prohibited from every liturgical celebration and from popular devotions."

The final section, Chapter IX, treats of the commissions on sacred music. Little that is new is to be found here. The document bears the signatures of Cardinal Larraona of the Sacred Congregation of Rites under whose authority the *Instruction* was issued, Cardinal Lercaro of the Consilium for the Implementation of the *Constitution on the Sacred Liturgy* by whom the *Instruction* was prepared, and Archbishop Ferdinando Antonelli, secretary of the Sacred Congregation of Rites. The document went into effect on Pentecost Sunday, May 14, 1967.

Publication of the *Instruction* followed designedly the convocation of the first general meeting of the Consociatio Internationalis Musicae Sacrae at Chicago in August, 1966. The work of the papal church music society in bringing the document to its present state is clear. The ideas expressed at the meeting of the Consociatio and presented to the Holy See are evident in the *Instruction*. It is the declared purpose of the Consociatio that it be a means of informing the Holy See on questions of church music. For the most part the points brought out by the papers and discussions at Chicago are reflected in the *Instruction*, and this may explain its less than enthusiastic reception in some circles.

It is interesting, also, in the light of the *Instruction* to study the program for the Masses at the Fifth International Church Music Congress in Milwaukee following the meetings of the Consociatio in Chicago. In each instance what was sung and played at the pontifical Masses was in accord with the *Instruction* which was published seven months later. The criticism that was voiced against using the *Credo* and the *Sanctus* of the *Messe in E Moll* of Anton Bruckner continues to be without foundation since the *Instruction* clearly states that the "Ordinary of the Mass sung to musical settings written for several voices may be performed by the choir according to the customary norms" (art. 34).

Lastly, a word should be written about the work of the Consociatio and its presidents, Monsignor Iginio Anglès and Monsignor Johannes Overath, who worked so heroically on this *Instruction* which preserves the great tradition of using the musical art in the liturgy of the Roman Church. The past has been glorious; it is our burden to create an even more glorious future according to the directions laid out for us in this *Instruction.*

Reverend Richard J. Schuler
(*Sacred Music*, Vol. 94, no.2, Summer 1967, p. 27-32)

Church Music After Vatican II

(This essay first appeared in *Church Music*, a semi-annual publication of Concordia Publishing House. It was part of a series of articles expressing many viewpoints on the status of church music in various denominations. It is reprinted here with permission of the editors from the 76-2 issue.)

In 1963, for the first time in Christian history, an ecumenical council of the Church turned its attention in a positive and extensive way to the subject of sacred music. It is true that the Council of Trent (1545-63) issued some decrees about music, but mostly in a restrictive sense. The Second Vatican Council called rather for a liberation and a purification of music in the service of the Church. It placed the final stone in a process of restoration begun a century earlier through the efforts of the monks of Solesmes Abbey, the Caecilian movement in the German-speaking lands, and the efforts of Pope Pius X through his *motu proprio* of 1903.

In fact, the Vatican Council decreed little that was new, but it put the approbation of the highest ecclesiastical authority on the basic principles underlying the use of music in the worship of God through liturgy. Chapter VI of the *Constitution on the Sacred Liturgy* clearly established that the musical tradition of the Church is a "treasure of inestimable value, greater even than that of any other art." This sacred music is a "necessary or integral part of the solemn liturgy." Its purpose remains the same through the ages – "the glory of God and the sanctification of the faithful." In addition, it can "add delight to prayer, foster unity of minds, and confer greater solemnity upon the sacred rites." And, significantly, the point is added that the "Church approves of all forms of true art having the needed qualities and admits them into divine worship." Truly, these words leave little doubt of the role of sacred music in worship.

A great freedom, so necessary for the cultivation of any art, marked the paragraphs on sacred music in the Council's document. There is scarcely a restrictive phrase. While former interpretations of papal documents had led to narrowing the limits of styles admitted to the church, now all styles from every age possessing the true qualities required of music for worship can be used. The classical Viennese Masses, frowned on in the pre-Vatican days by a puritanical and mistaken view of sacred music, now surely may be used in worship again. Instruments have their proper place; indigenous music, especially in mission lands, is to be encouraged; choirs should be fostered; the congregation is asked to sing; the vernacular languages are admitted to solemn liturgical rites. At the same time, Gregorian chant retains its pride of place; the pipe organ is recognized with great esteem for the wonderful splendor it adds to the ceremonies; the entire literature of the Latin rite, polyphonic as well as unison, should be the basis for further composition in both the vernacular languages and in Latin, for expert musical organizations as well as smaller amateur groups. Truly, these words were the herald of a new springtime in church music, and musicians around the world hailed them as such. New compositions, new singing groups, the revival of old music, and new life for existing choirs was to be expected. The congregation was to be brought into its rightful role. Instruments and voices would rise to God's praise. Hopes were great in 1963.

By 1973, all that had been accomplished in the musical renewal begun a century before lay in shambles. What had been envisioned by the Council Fathers had not only failed to come to pass, but rather, even what existed when they published their beautiful and encouraging decrees had now ceased to be in most places. Why? There are several basic problems involved.

First, the Council Fathers reiterated the repeated call for *actuosa participatio populi*, the active participation of the people in the liturgical action which Pope Pius X and other popes so often asked for. Unfortunately, this rather deep theological concept, based in the effects of the Sacrament of Baptism, was misunderstood by some to mean that everyone in the congregation had to be actively engaged in singing or in other ritual acts. Even though the Council documents clearly distinguish between interior and exterior participation, many insisted that true "active" participation had to do away with the singing of choirs, because "listening" to the singing of a choir was not truly "active" participation. Everyone must himself sing. In reality, the term *actuosa participatio* refers to the action of the interior spirit of one who is baptized when he is present at the sacred liturgy; thus, a person who is blind or deaf or even mute could indeed be participating actively in the liturgy even though unable to sing or even listen, while an unbaptized person, even though singing and doing many other things, in reality would not be capable of true *actuosa participatio*, because he lacked the baptismal character which is essential.[1] Musically speaking, the misunderstanding of this key concept in the *Constitution on the Sacred Liturgy* wrought untold damage. Choirs were disbanded in favor of the singing of the congregation; everyone was expected to sing and often to sing nearly all the time; the need for listening and the need for art music well performed was denied; external activity became the gauge for a successful liturgical function; the quality of the music was secondary to the fact of singing – it mattered not what one sang, as long as he sang.[2] Obviously, the blow to serious church music in the disbanding of choirs and in the abandoning of discretion in selection of music was catastrophic.

Secondly, a confusion between the sacred and the secular, even a denial of the existence of the sacred, hurt church music which had long been considered a body of music set aside by connotation and text as specially dedicated to God. When music not intended by its composer as church music, compositions connoting worldly actions, texts not taken from the Scriptures or liturgical sources, or forms meant for dancing or concert were introduced into worship, then the whole nature and purpose of sacred music was changed. Music in the service of the Church became entertainment music, directed at man rather than toward God. Texts and styles taken from the theater, concert hall, the musical comedy and even Tin Pan Alley made their entrance into worship. The "hootenanny" Mass (later dignified by the term "contemporary" Mass) introduced secular music, often poor in itself and even more poorly performed. Warnings came from Rome and various bishops; documents from the highest authorities confirmed the distinction between sacred and secular;[3] Pope Paul himself reiterated the traditional position at a convention of Italian musicians.[4] He said that secular words, love songs, folk ballads, musical comedy, or operatic arias are not sacred and do not belong in God's house, interesting and salutary as they may be in their proper place. They are not meant to cross the threshold of God's temple.[5] And yet they have, a situation that has lowered the standards required in music intended for worship.

Thirdly, the promotion of the vernacular languages resulted in the abandoning of Latin, quite contrary to the directions of the Vatican Council which clearly allowed the use of the vernacular as a privilege, but commanded the use of Latin as the language of the Roman Church.[6] In some areas, Latin was even prohibited, despite the conciliar decrees ordering its use. With the abandoning of Latin came the demise of the Gregorian chant, the polyphonic music of the Medieval and Renaissance periods, and most of the compositions of the past 200 years, which simply could not be translated into the vernacular tongues, a fact proved after many artistically disastrous attempts. In setting aside the repertory of 1,500 years, the role of art music in the Church became almost nonexistent, and while some starry-eyed enthusiasts for the vernacular hailed the opportunity for the creation of a new repertory of church music in the mother tongues, little was actually forthcoming. Every age must stand squarely on the shoulders of those who have gone before; creation *ex nihilo* is a prerogative of God alone. Musical styles develop with their roots in the past; eliminate the past and one finds that the wellsprings of musical inspiration and composition dry up too. The introduction of the vernacular should have been an opportunity for the expansion of composition for worship and also for the performance by Catholic choirs and congregations of the vast body of music created in the past 400 years since the Protestant reforms. The introduction of the vernacular was intended as an expansion of the horizon, not a restriction of the glorious Latin heritage of 15 centuries. But no other factor did more to discourage choirs than this erroneous ban on singing in Latin. Without a body of music to select from, choirs that were not deliberately disbanded by a misunderstanding of *actuosa participatio populi* disintegrated for lack of musical fare.

Finally, the question of the musical education of the clergy looms large in the post-Vatican church music scene. This is not a new problem, but its magnitude is emphasized by the role of the clergy in introducing the reforms of the Council. When ignorance and misunderstanding of what the Council ordered in musical matters are found among those responsible for implementing them, then disaster is the result. Musical training in seminaries in the United States was improving somewhat in the decade just preceding the Council, as better trained teachers were employed and serious music courses were added to the curriculum. But with the infection of so many seminaries with the errors mentioned above, the present status of liturgical music in most seminaries in this country is lamentable. The truth is that there will be no flowering of the hopes embodied in Vatican II until students for the priesthood learn what truly is meant by *actuosa participatio*, by the distinction between sacred and secular, and by the commands of the Church that Latin is to be used and fostered. Without true understanding of these facts, little can be accomplished in any musical education for clerics.[7]

Is there, then, any hope for a new springtime? I would say a resounding yes. It lies, as always, with the youth. Little by little, a new generation is learning about the treasure that has been abandoned – Gregorian chant, the polyphonic Masses and motets, the orchestral Masses of Mozart, Haydn, Beethoven, and Schubert, the great liturgical works of the romantic 19th century. This is their heritage and they want it. Some day a finger will be pointed at those who have deprived them of it. It is interesting to note the age of the worshipers in a congregation in Paris or in Amsterdam who have come to hear a Mass sung in Gregorian chant, or the people coming out of the Augustinerkirche in Vienna after a classical 18th-century Mass, or at Westminster Cathedral in London, where they have heard an *a cappella* 16th-century composition. They are predominantly young people. Only when this heritage of centuries is restored, used, fostered and loved will a new music be added to that continuing tradition of musical worship and the decrees of Vatican II be implemented in fact.

Monsignor Richard J. Schuler

(*Sacred Music*, Vol. 103, no.4, Winter 1976, p. 15-18)

NOTES

1. See Colman E. O'Neill, "The Theological Meaning of *Actuosa Participatio* in the Liturgy," *Sacred Music and Liturgy Reform after Vatican II*. Rome: Consociatio Internationalis Musicae Sacrae, 1969, p. 89-108.

2. Many of these ideas were expressed by Joseph Gelineau in *Voices and Instruments in Christian Worship*. Collegeville, Minn.: The Liturgical Press, 1964. See a review of the work in *Response*, VII, 2 (1965), 104-107.

3. An *Instruction* from the Sacred Congregation of Rites, March 5, 1967, begins with the very words "Sacred music." Article 4 of that document specifies very clearly just what is understood as sacred music.

4. To the Italian Society of Saint Cecilia, April 15, 1971.

5. See Richard J. Schuler, "Pope Paul on Sacred Music," *Sacred Music*, Vol. 98, No. 2 (Summer 1971), p. 3-5.

6. See Richard J. Schuler, "How Can You Have a Latin Mass?" *Sacred Music*, Vol. 103, No. 1 (Spring 1976), p. 26-31.

7. See Richard J. Schuler, "Preparation of the Diocesan Clergy in Church Music," *Sacred Music*, Vol. 101, No. 3 (Fall 1974), p. 3-8.

1967 *Instruction* – Ten Years Later

Ten years ago, the Holy See, through the Sacred Congregation of Rites and the Consilium for the Implementation of the *Constitution on the Sacred Liturgy*, issued the *Instruction on Sacred Music in the Liturgy* that began with the words, *Musicam sacram*. As in other matters treated by the Council, *Instructions* were prepared by bodies set up to implement the decrees of the Council Fathers and bring into practical and specific detail what had been ordered by them in a more general way. Now, ten years later, it is interesting to review the 1967 document on sacred music and assess what effect it has had on liturgical music, especially in the United States.

First, it is apparent that a constant secularization process, leading almost to a denial of the sacral even in worship, has unfortunately been the pattern of the past ten years, despite the very opening words of the *Instruction* – *Musicam sacram*. With the demise of the sacred, we find the strange phenomenon of ecclesiastical institutions and structures searching for their meaning and mission, an occupation not needed when the quest for holiness was recognized as the work of the Church. Herein lies the basic malaise in worship, and indeed, in the whole life and activity of the Church. Until the debate between the sacred and the secular is resolved, music and liturgy will continue to flounder.

A corollary of the secularization process appears quickly as some begin even to question the very purpose of church music, although the *Constitution on the Sacred Liturgy* makes it quite clear and the 1967 *Instruction* repeats what the Council Fathers and the Church for centuries has been saying: "the true purpose of sacred music is the glory of God and the sanctification of the faithful."[1] Yet, hardly a year after the *Instruction* was published, the Music Advisory Board to the American bishops' conference declared in a published statement that the purpose of church music is "to create a truly human experience."[2] Secularization and its progenitor, secular humanism, have disposed of the sacred and of sacred music.

The 1967 *Instruction* makes it quite clear what is meant by sacred music. It even lists what is to be so considered: "Gregorian chant, sacred polyphony in its various forms both ancient and modern, sacred music for the organ and other approved instruments, and music of the people, be it liturgical or religious."[3] There is no reference here to the flood of profane compositions that has been admitted to our churches. At the same time, one looks in vain so often in so many churches to find that truly sacred music which the *Instruction* says should be "endowed with sanctity and excellence of form."[4]

The *Instruction* orders that there be choirs, especially in cathedrals and other major churches, in seminaries and religious houses of studies, and they should be carefully fostered. Similar choirs, although small ones, should be organized in small churches. On diocesan, national and international levels, associations for sacred music should be formed. Today, ten years later, choirs and associations for sacred music seem to have dwindled and in some places even to have disappeared altogether.

The *Instruction* repeats the words of the *Constitution* and again insists on the use of Gregorian chant, which should be given "pride of place." It must be taught in seminaries and sung in parish churches, both in Masses celebrated in Latin and in the vernacular, since nothing prohibits that in the same celebration different parts be sung in different languages. How many seminaries today teach Gregorian chant?[5] When did you last sing a chant in your parish church? What has happened to the Holy Father's direct request that his gift booklet, *Jubilate Deo*, sent to all the bishops of the world, be widely and frequently used?

The *Instruction* orders that the distinction between solemn, sung and read Masses, sanctioned by the *Instruction* of 1958, is to be retained.[6] But many dioceses have followed the lead given by the American Bishops' Committee on the Liturgy and have ordered such a distinction abolished. A real disintegration of the *Missa cantata Romana* in its thousand-year-old form has taken place since 1967, despite all efforts through various *Instructions* issued to preserve it. There seems to be little doubt at all that what one witnesses in most parish churches today was not in the wildest imagination of most of the Council Fathers when they approved the *Constitution on the Sacred Liturgy*.

It seems almost incredible that only ten years ago, the Church was ordering that "in accordance with the norm of the *Constitution on the*

Sacred Liturgy and the centuries-old tradition of the Latin rite, the Latin language is to be retained for clerics in celebrating the Divine Office in choir."[7] Indeed, how many even sing the Office at all, let alone in the Latin language? And yet the *Instruction* says that the faithful are to be invited to celebrate in common on Sundays and feast days certain parts of the Divine Office, especially Vespers. Where today can one assist at Vespers in a parish church?[8]

Of course, the question of Latin remains the most sorely misunderstood point in the *Constitution* and in the *Instruction*. The documents from Rome have continued to insist on Latin, but many American dioceses have rules prohibiting the celebration of the liturgy in Latin.[9] The confusion deliberately fostered between the Mass in Latin and the Mass celebrated in the old rite continues to come up in the press and even among the clergy. Today the possibility of participating in a Mass celebrated in Latin is most remote. And yet, the 1967 *Instruction* very clearly states what the *Constitution* had decreed: "particular laws remaining in force, the use of the Latin language is to be preserved in the Latin rites." "Pastors of souls should take care that besides the vernacular the faithful also know how to say or sing, in Latin also, those parts of the Ordinary of the Mass which pertain to them."[10] The great fear, almost hatred, of Latin, seemingly engendered intentionally, especially in seminaries, stands directly contrary to the *Instruction* and other orders of the Holy See. The *Instruction* says that in seminaries "the study and practice of Gregorian chant is to be promoted, because with its special characteristics it is a basis of great importance for the cultivation of sacred music."[11]

Looking back over ten years, one can ask many questions about the implementation of the 1967 *Instruction* and the *Constitution* on which it was based. In asking them, one can well assess the state of church music today and contrast it with the decrees of the Council and the Holy See. Have the last ten years brought about the renewal envisioned by the Council Fathers and specified in the 1967 *Instruction*?

A few years ago, the Consociatio Internationalis Musicae Sacrae drew up a questionnaire that was circulated widely around the world. The series of questions is still valid today, perhaps even more so because a great perspective exists now. The questions are presented here, preceded by the proper statement from the Council and the 1967 *Instruction*. When honestly answered, the picture drawn does not usually portray a renewal nor does it match very closely the blueprint set up by either the Council Fathers or the writers of the *Instruction*.

1. *Actuosa participatio*

The *Constitution on the Sacred Liturgy* speaks of *actuosa participatio* frequently (Articles 11, 14, 19, 21, 27, 30, 41, 48, 50, 113, 114, 121, 124). It has been defined in a precise and complete manner in the *Instruction on Sacred Music* (Article 15): "The faithful fulfill their liturgical role by full, conscious and active participation which is demanded by the nature of the liturgy itself and which is, by reason of baptism, the right and duty of the Christian people."

This participation must first of all be interior in the sense that by means of it, the faithful unite their souls to what they pronounce or hear and by so doing cooperate with God's grace.

This participation must also be exterior, i.e., the interior participation is expressed by gestures and bodily attitudes, acclamations, responses and songs. The faithful must be taught to unite themselves interiorly with the singing of the ministers and the choir in order to elevate their souls to God by listening to them.

Questions:

a) Do you think that interior participation by the faithful has improved since the Council?
b) Do you think that exterior participation by the faithful has improved since the Council?
c) Have the faithful been taught sufficiently well to unite themselves interiorly with the ministers and the choir?

2. Liturgical language

Article 36, 1, of the *Constitution on the Sacred Liturgy* says: "Particular law remaining in force, the use of the Latin language is to be preserved in the Latin rites."

Article 36, 2, of the same *Constitution* says: "Since the use of the mother tongue...frequently may be of great advantage to the people, the limits of its employment may be extended. This will apply in the first place to the readings and directives, and to some of the prayers and chants, according to the regulations on this matter to be laid down separately in subsequent chapters." Those chapters are:

Article 54, 1: "In Masses which are celebrated with the people a suitable place may be allotted to their mother tongue. This is to apply in the first place to the readings and the 'common prayer,' but also, as local conditions may warrant, to those parts which pertain to the people, according to the norm laid down in Article 36 of this *Constitution*."

Article 54, 2: "Steps should be taken so that the faithful may also be able to say or to sing together in Latin those parts of the Ordinary of the Mass which pertain to them." But if in some place a more extensive use of the vernacular in the Mass seems expedient, one should consult the directives of Article 40. (Article 40, which will be examined later, limits jurisdiction in these matters without treating the basic question itself. It says that the more extensive use of the vernacular is intended especially for mission countries.)

Article 101, 1: "In accordance with the centuries-old tradition of the Latin rite, the Latin language is to be retained by clerics in the Divine Office. But in individual cases, the Ordinary has the power of granting the use of a vernacular translation to those clerics for whom the use of Latin constitutes a grave obstacle to their praying the Office properly."

These prescriptions are reiterated and confirmed in the *Instruction on Sacred Music*, Articles 47-49, which suggest among other things that the Ordinaries of places, where the vernacular is used in the celebration of Mass, should see to it that in one or several Masses, Latin be used in certain churches where there is a large enough number of faithful who speak diverse languages. They are to be the judges of the advisability of such action.

Questions:

   a) Are the rules concerning the use of Latin observed?
   b) Are the rules prescribed in Article 36, 2, observed?
   c) Are the directives prescribed in Article 101, 1, observed?
   d) Are the directives prescribed in Article 47-49 of the *Instruction on Sacred Music* observed?

3. The role of the hierarchy

Articles 22, 40 and 44 of the *Constitution on the Sacred Liturgy* define the rights and powers of the Holy See and the bishops.

Article 22, 3, stipulates expressly that no one, even if he be a priest, has the right to add, suppress or change anything whatsoever in the liturgy.

Article 40 (which is referred to above on the question of the use of the vernacular) uses a criterion that "in some places and circumstances an even more radical adaptation of the liturgy is needed." The power of decision is returned to the "competent ecclesiastical authority," specifying that adaptations which are judged useful or necessary should be proposed to the Holy See in order to be introduced with its consent (Article 40, 1, 2).

Article 40, 3, orders that men who are experts in these matters be employed to formulate them and it further says specifically that this article is directed to mission countries. The *Instruction* of 1970 repeats these ideas and closes the period of experimentation.

Questions:

a) Is experimentation, which is not in accord with prescribed norms, still going on at the present time?

b) What is the attitude of the competent authority concerning this kind of experimentation? Does it prohibit it? Is it neutral? Does it encourage it?

4. Commission of experts

Summary of Articles 44, 45 and 46 of the *Constitution on the Sacred Liturgy*: Episcopal conferences must establish a liturgical commission which should be assisted by experts in liturgical studies, sacred music and pastoral theology. A liturgical and pastoral institute, composed of experts and, on occasion, of lay people, may be founded to help the commission.

Such a liturgical commission must be established in each diocese under the authority of the bishop. A commission for sacred music and religious art should also be established in each diocese. These three commissions must work together and unite their efforts.

Questions:

a) Has the national commission asked for the assistance of expert musicians?

b) If so, does the commission listen to their opinion?

c) Are expert musicians represented on diocesan liturgical commissions?

d) If so, are their opinions listened to?

e) Do commissions on sacred music exist in individual dioceses?

5. Divine Office

In Article 100 of the *Constitution on the Sacred Liturgy*, it is stipulated that the canonical Hours, especially Vespers for Sundays and important feasts, be celebrated in common in the churches.

Questions:
- a) Did this practice exist before the Council?
- b) Has it been introduced, if it did not exist?
- c) Has it disappeared, if it previously existed?

6. The choir

Article 114 of the *Constitution on the Sacred Liturgy* says: "Choirs must be diligently promoted, especially in cathedral churches; but bishops and other pastors of souls must be at pains to ensure that, whenever the sacred action is to be celebrated with song, the whole body of the faithful may be able to contribute that active participation which is rightly theirs, as laid down in Articles 28 and 30." (N.B. Article 28 specifies that the choir must fulfill its function and not assume other roles. Article 30 says that "the people should be encouraged to take part by means of acclamations, responses, psalmody, antiphons and songs" and at the proper times should be allowed to observe a reverent silence.

This recommendation is developed and made more specific in the *Instruction on Sacred Music*, Articles 19-23, 33, 34.

Article 19: "Because of the liturgical ministry it performs, the choir or the *capella musica*, or *schola cantorum*, deserves particular mention. Its office has been given even greater importance and weight by reason of the norms of the Council concerning the liturgical renewal. Its duty is, in effect, to ensure the proper performance of the parts which belong to it, according to the different kinds of music, and to encourage the active participation of the faithful in the singing."

Article 16, c, says explicitly that one may give certain parts assigned to the people to the choir alone, provided that the people are not excluded from other parts that belong to them.

Article 33 states that the Proper parts of the Mass may be sung either "while all are seated and listen to it" or as much as possible with the participation of the people.

Article 34 provides that the Ordinary parts of the Mass can be sung in part music by the choir "provided that the people are not completely excluded from participation in the singing." It also suggests several forms of alternation between the choir and the people with special rules for the *Credo, Sanctus* and *Agnus Dei*.

Questions:

- a) Since the Council, has the number of choirs increased?
- b) Do they actually carry out the two-fold role assigned to them of singing alone and helping the congregation?

7. Musical education

Article 115 of the *Constitution on the Sacred Liturgy*: "Great importance is to be attached to the teaching and practice of music in seminaries, in the novitiates and houses of study of religious of both sexes, and also in other Catholic institutions and schools. To impart this instruction, teachers are to be carefully trained. It is desirable also to found higher institutes of sacred music whenever this can be done."

Questions:

- a) Is there a regular and well-established program of musical education in the seminaries? In novitiates and houses of study?
- b) Is this musical education given by qualified professors?
- c) Are the results satisfactory?
- d) Do clerics and future priests have an opportunity to put their theoretical instruction to practical use and specifically do they meet regularly as a choir under a qualified director?
- e) Do they study the solfeggio, organ, harmony, history of sacred music, etc.?
- f) Is there a properly accredited school for the training of choirmasters and organists in your area?
- g) Are there one or several schools for higher studies in sacred music?
- h) Is sacred music taught in a satisfactory manner in Catholic schools at every level?

8. Gregorian chant

Article 114 of the *Constitution on the Sacred Liturgy*: "The treasure of sacred music is to be preserved and fostered with great care."

Article 116: "The Church acknowledges Gregorian chant as especially suited to the Roman liturgy; therefore, all things being equal, it should be given pride of place in liturgical services."

Article 117: "It is desirable also that an edition be prepared containing simpler melodies, for use in small churches."

Questions:
   a) Have these texts been brought to the attention of the faithful
      without being changed?
   b) Is the entire Proper of the Mass sung in Gregorian chant?
   c) In the teaching given to the clergy, has Gregorian chant been
      presented as "the chant proper to the Church, having pride of
      place, all things being equal?"
   d) If not, is at least a part of it sung in Gregorian chant?
   e) Is the entire Ordinary of the Mass sung in Gregorian chant?
   f) If not, is at least a part of it sung in Gregorian chant?
   g) If Gregorian chant has been abandoned, do you think that
      this has resulted in the fostering of the meditation and interior
      participation of the faithful?
   h) If Gregorian chant has been abandoned, do you think that this
      has resulted in the fostering of exterior participation?
   i) Are the simplified editions of Gregorian chant recommended
      and made available in your area?

9. Polyphony and other types of music

Article 116 of the *Constitution on the Sacred Liturgy* says: "Other
kinds of sacred music, especially polyphony, are by no means excluded
from liturgical celebrations, so long as they accord with the spirit of
the liturgical action as laid down in Article 30."

Questions:
   a) Is the opportunity to sing polyphony in Latin given?
   b) Is an opportunity to sing polyphony in the vernacular given?
   c) How is the style and musical quality of new compositions?
   d) Must new compositions be approved by the competent
      authority?
   e) Does this competent authority seek out qualified opinions for
      judging?

10. Congregational singing

This is one of the most important ideas in the conciliar texts.
Article 113 of the *Constitution on the Sacred Liturgy* says: "Liturgical
worship is given a more noble form when the divine offices are
celebrated solemnly in song, with the assistance of sacred ministers
and the active participation of the people."

The extent of this participation is given in the *Instruction on Sacred*

Music. This *Instruction* distinguishes between the solemn, sung and read Mass (Article 28), and establishes three degrees of participation by the people (Articles 29-31). This participation is adapted to the ability of the congregation, and may be limited to the minimum of the first degree.

Articles 33 and 34 of the *Instruction* determine the distribution of the parts of the Proper and the Ordinary of the Mass among the congregation, the ministers and the choir.

Article 118 of the *Constitution on the Sacred Liturgy* says: "Religious singing by the people is to be skillfully fostered."

Questions:

a) Since the Council, do the people sing more?

b) If so, do you judge that this greater participation could also have been achieved while preserving the Latin language and Gregorian chant?

c) Where does this participation occur? In acclamations and responses? In the Ordinary parts of the Mass? In the Proper parts of the Mass? In nonliturgical singing?

d) What language is used in this participation? Latin only? Vernacular only? Latin and the vernacular?

e) Are the distinctions of the kinds of Masses, established by the *Instruction*, respected?

f) Is it widely held that these distinctions are outdated by the new *Ordo Missae*?

g) Does the competent authority hold this opinion?

h) Is there a strong tradition of worthwhile congregational hymns in your area?

i) If so, is this repertory still fostered or have new hymns been substituted?

j) Are conditions and opportunities for preparation of the congregational singing conducive to its success?

11. The organ

Article 120 of the *Constitution on the Sacred Liturgy* says: "In the Latin church, the pipe organ is to be held in high esteem, for it is the traditional musical instrument which adds a wonderful splendor to the Church's ceremonies and powerfully lifts up man's mind to God and to higher things."

Article 65 of the *Instruction on Sacred Music* says: "In sung or said Masses, the organ...can be used to accompany the singing of the choir and the people; it can also be played solo at the beginning before the priest reaches the altar, at the offertory, at the communion, and at the end of the Mass." (Exception is made for Advent, Lent, the last three days of Holy Week, and in the funeral ceremonies and the Mass for the Dead.)

The use of the organ as a solo instrument is also implicitly encouraged by the admonition of the *Constitution on the Sacred Liturgy* (Article 30) and the *Instruction on Sacred Music* (Article 17) to preserve a "reverent silence," because it is not forbidden to use an organ piece during these periods of "reverent silence."

Questions:

a) Can the organist exercise his office according to the above norms?

b) Can he play a sufficiently long time to justify his presence?

12. Other instruments

Article 120 of the *Constitution on the Sacred Liturgy* says: "Other instruments may be admitted for use in divine worship with the knowledge and consent of the competent territorial authority. This may be done, however, only on condition that the instruments are suitable, or can be made suitable, for sacred use, accord with the dignity of the temple, and truly contribute to the edification of the faithful."

Article 63 of the *Instruction on Sacred Music* says: "In admitting and using musical instruments, the culture and traditions of individual peoples must be taken into account. However, these instruments which are, by common opinion and use, suitable for secular music only, are to be altogether prohibited from every liturgical celebration and from popular devotions. Any musical instrument admitted into divine worship should be used in such a way that it meets the needs of the liturgical celebration, and promotes the beauty of worship and the edification of the faithful."

These regulations are made more specific in the *Instruction* of 1970 (Article 3, c): "The bishops' conferences should indicate selections of songs to be used at Masses for special groups, e.g., young people or children; the words, melody and rhythm of these songs, and the instruments used for accompaniment, should correspond to the sacred character of the celebration and the place of worship. The Church does not exclude any kind of sacred music from the liturgy. However, not every type of music, song or instrument is equally capable of stimulating prayer or expressing the mystery of Christ....Attention should be given to the choice of musical instruments: these should be few in number, suited to the place and the community, should favor prayer and not be too loud."

Questions:

    a) Are these regulations known, promulgated and invoked to support the decisions of religious authority?

    b) Are there difficulties in deciding which instruments the *Instruction on Sacred Music* excludes from use in the liturgy?

    c) Is it commonly understood that it is specifically excluding jazz instruments (drums, guitar, electric guitar, saxophone, jazz clarinet, etc.)?

    d) Are such instruments permitted in your church?

    e) What is the opinion of the young people about these instruments: Divided opinion? Great interest? Indifference? Rejection?

    f) What is the opinion of the adults?

    g) What is the attitude of the religious authorities: Encouragement? Tolerance? Rejection?

    h) Is recorded music used in the liturgy? What is the attitude of the religious authorities?

13. The new *Ordo Missae*

The new *Ordo* in no fundamental way modifies the principles stated above. The *Institutio generalis* permits a choice of either the vernacular or the Latin and even provides for the use of the *Graduale Romanum* in order to promote participation in Gregorian chant (Articles 26, 36, 37, 56, 100, 147, 168, 324). It excludes neither the organ nor polyphony.

Questions:

    a) Is it generally known that the use of the *Graduale Romanum* is still permitted according to the new *Ordo*?

    b) Is it known that polyphony is also permitted? Is it still sung?

    c) Are the rules about the use of the organ known? Can the organist still exercise his role in a satisfactory manner?

    d) Have the competent authorities given instruction in these matters?

e) Since the appearance of the new *Ordo*, has the active participation of the people increased? Decreased? Remained the same?

f) From a pastoral viewpoint, does it seem that the musical quality of liturgical services has improved? Deteriorated? Remained the same?

g) From an artistic viewpoint, does it seem that the musical quality of liturgical services has improved? Deteriorated? Remained the same?

14. Miscellaneous Questions:

a) Are the exact texts of the various decrees known and available?

b) Have deceptive slogans, such as "the Council wants to suppress Gregorian chant," etc. been allowed to spread?

c) Have these inexactitudes and errors been corrected or refuted by proper authority?

If you have answered these questions, you can come to your own decision on what the condition of church music is in your area, ten years after the 1967 *Instruction* was issued. As with most matters decreed by the Second Vatican Council, when the will of the Council Fathers is carried out, the renewal and blossoming of the Faith will be achieved. But too many things ordered by the Council have not as yet had a chance to be implemented, because too many false ideas and practices have been foisted upon the Church by individuals who would have their own way. The Church, through the Council and the various *Instructions* that have followed, has shown us the way. It only remains for us to put the decrees into effect.

Monsignor Richard J. Schuler
(*Sacred Music*, Vol. 104, no.3, Fall 1977, p. 3-12)

NOTES

1. The *Constitution on the Sacred Liturgy*, Art. 112; *Instruction on Sacred Music*, Art. 4.

2. *The Place of Music in Eucharistic Celebrations*, Part III.

3. Article 4b.

4. Article 4a.

5. Cf. Richard J. Schuler, "Preparation of the Diocesan Clergy in Church Music." *Sacred Music,* Vol. 101, No. 3 (Fall 1974), p. 3-8.

6. Article 28. An interesting set of letters between the author and the associate director of the Bishops' Committee on the Liturgy, Reverend Thomas A. Krosnicki, S.V.D., on the subject of the distinction between solemn, sung and read Masses was published in *Sacred Music,* Vol. 100, No. 3 (Fall 1973), p. 41-43.

7. Article 41.

8. One place is the author's parish, the Church of Saint Agnes, Saint Paul, Minnesota, where Vespers in the full Gregorian setting have been sung every Sunday for the past three years by a *schola* of men. Since the new chant books for the Office have not as yet appeared, the group still uses the arrangement given in the *Liber Usualis.*

9. Recently, however, Cardinal Baum has urged parishes in the Archdiocese of Washington to schedule Mass in Latin.

10. Article 47.

11. Article 52.

The Reform of the Liturgy (1948-1975)

The Reform of the Liturgy (1948-1975) by Annibale Bugnini,
tr. by Matthew J. O'Connell. Collegeville, Minnesota:
The Liturgical Press, 1990. 974 pp.; hardback.

Recently, Archbishop Rembert Weakland of Milwaukee, one of a handful of American reformers responsible for the present state of the Catholic liturgy in the United States, expressed doubt about the reform, its organization and its results. Well he might, with the debacle visible on every side and the results of the liturgical "renewal" that continue to add daily to the devastation of the Church, its discipline, its teachings, its schools and religious life – in a word, every aspect of ecclesiastical life.

If one wants to see how the process began and developed, Archbishop Bugnini's book provides a detailed and complete account of the years preceding the Council and on until 1975. In reading the sad story, one wonders whether the reaction of incredibility or the passion of anger or the emotion of sorrow with tears should dominate. What so few did to so many prompts unbelief; that a thousand-year tradition should be destroyed causes anger; that a sublime means of prayer should be swept away brings tears.

Bugnini tells all, and not without openly expressing emotion and opinion. For a mine of information concerning the characters involved in the various preconciliar study bodies, the prelates and *periti* who constituted the various commissions and committees, the book is excellent. The account of the meetings and the developments in liturgical matters before, during and after the Council is a carefully documented record. The politics and misunderstanding, the scheming and quarrelling, the alignment of sides and the ultimate emergence of what today is called the reformed liturgy of the Second Vatican Council do not edify anyone.

Of course, there are "good guys" and "bad guys" according to Bugnini's story. The "bad guys" are the church musicians and those wishing to retain some use of the Latin language, conservatives who evoke the anger and sarcasm of the author because of their efforts to defend the heritage of the Church in its liturgical texts and the musical settings from Gregorian chant to modern compositions. Bugnini attributes bad will to many of those sitting with him on the various commissions, especially the members of the Consociatio Internationalis Musicae Sacrae. Among those singled out for special objection are Monsignor Iginio Anglès, president of the Pontifical Institute of Sacred Music in Rome, and Monsignor Johannes Overath, president of the papally founded Consociatio Internationalis Musicae Sacrae.

On the other side were the "good guys" who promoted the same agenda as Bugnini. Among them were Johannes Wagner of Trier, Frederick McManus of Washington, Joseph Gelineau, Pierre Jounel, A.G. Martimort, Cipriano Vagaggini, Rembert Weakland and Godfrey Diekmann. That there existed an international conspiracy among these liturgists has often been suggested but never proved, least of all from what is recorded in Bugnini's accounts. According to the original plan of procedure to be followed by the Council, the treatment of the liturgy was to come after the consideration of the Church. *Lumen gentium* should have been clearly established before *Sacrosanctum concilium* could be logically taken up and its decrees ordered. Indeed, since the Church is the living presence of Jesus Christ, then the actions of that Church (its liturgy) must flow from the divine Person, its very head. With the rejection of the initial documents of the pre-conciliar committees, to occupy the assembled bishops while the documents were rewritten, the discussion of the liturgy was illogically thrust into first place without adequate theological consideration of its very nature, the salvific action of Jesus Christ. Little wonder that the externals became so important and, in the minds of many, continue to constitute the main work of the Council.

This massive volume, written by Bugnini during his "exile" in Iran, with almost infinite detail, is divided into ten parts. The first part, called "The Main Stages," gives a brief account of the beginning of the reform, the preparatory commissions, the *Constitution on the Liturgy*, its fundamental principles, the *motu proprio, Sacram liturgiam*, and the

Sacred Congregation for Divine Worship. It continues to recount the "First Accomplishments" including the shift from Latin to the various vernacular languages, changes in the missals, and concelebration. Also considered in the first part, under the subtitle, "Two Areas of Activity," are the meetings themselves, the observers, and the conferences with various national liturgical experts, the question of translation, the establishment of the journal *Notitiae*, the phenomenon of experimentation with the liturgy, and finally a most interesting section on the opposition to the plans of Bugnini, where the author fully reveals himself.

Part II treats the new liturgical books and the calendar. Part III is on the *Missal*, the lectionary, Eucharistic prayers and Masses with special groups including children. Part IV considers the Liturgy of the Hours and Part V, the sacraments. Part VI has to do with blessings, including religious profession, funerals, the ritual and the pontifical. Part VII undertakes the simplification of pontifical rites both papal and episcopal. Part VIII accounts for special documents, including the *Instruction*s for carrying out the *Constitution on the Sacred Liturgy*, the subject of liturgy in seminaries, the worship of the Eucharistic mystery and finally veneration of the Blessed Virgin. Part IX is on sacred music and the 1967 *Instruction, Musicam sacram*, again another struggle between the liturgists and the musicians. Part X is called "*Varia*." The finale is Bugnini's *apologia pro vita sua*, "We tried to serve the Church...."

The effects of the Second Vatican Council will be felt for many years to come. This book is a useful compilation of data on the specific area of liturgical reform. Unfortunately, it is marred by the personal opinions and prejudiced position of its author who never ceases to grind his knives against those who had every right to express their opinions in the halls of the Council committees. One continually has the feeling that full sincerity is not present in sections dealing with musical matters. Too often organizations such as Universa Laus and such persons as Joseph Gelineau are employed to circumvent the established and traditional positions of the majority of church musicians represented by the Consociatio Internationalis Musicae Sacrae and the Pontifical School of Music in Rome. In this country, the work (conspiracy?) was carried forward by the actions of Rembert Weakland, Godfrey Diekmann and Frederick McManus who controlled the process of implementation of the decrees recorded by Bugnini, largely through their positions on the American bishops' committees for implementing the decrees of the Council. The results are the sad state of the Catholic Church in this country today, so sad that even those who set it in motion are beginning to have doubts.

The translation from Italian reads well. The book is attractively printed and well indexed. It is an important compilation of facts and materials, but always there remains throughout, the presence of Bugnini, his bias, his anger, and his prejudice, making one continue to ask the unanswerable question, "Why?"

Book Review by Monsignor Richard J. Schuler
(*Sacred Music*, Vol. 117, no.3, Fall 1990, p. 25-26)

Archbishop Annibale Bugnini

With the publication of the English translation of Archbishop Bugnini's *The Reform of the Liturgy (1948-1975)*, the wounds and rancor of the Council years are revived. The book recounts the battles and misunderstandings between the reforming liturgists and the church musicians. Bugnini himself said that the first ten years following the close of the Council were no more than continual fighting with the musicians.

It is never right to impute motives or to attribute ill will, but occasionally such things surface in the records. Surely Bugnini's opposition to the classical heritage of sacred music and the Latin language shows in this work. True, it is disguised under the need for participation of the faithful, understanding of the texts, and simplification of the rites, truly noble objectives of the Council Fathers. But after devastating the traditions and heritage of a thousand years of musical and liturgical development, there cannot be much remaining on which to encourage any kind of true participation, and understanding and simplification have little left to build on or work with.

An anti-Roman spirit, manifest especially in attacks on Latin as the language of the universal Church, constantly raises its head. One always wonders why Latin was considered to be competitive with the vernacular. Surely the creation of a repertory of vernacular choral music demands that it be constructed on the foundation of the treasury of Latin compositions.

The mere simplification of church music results in the abandoning of music as an art especially in its polyphonic developments, eliminating the masterpieces that have adorned the liturgy for a millenium. A rationalism that demands understanding of every word as essential to active participation, forgetting the moving of man's spirit by the mystery and beauty of music, drives the text into an unreasonably prominent position in liturgical celebration, almost to the total elimination of the art of sacred music, which must be united to the text to form the artistic whole that liturgical music must be. The impoverished translations of the Latin texts into English added an enormous burden to the effort to promote participation of the people as well as understanding of the vernacular texts.

Basic to the conflict between the liturgists and the musicians is a failure to understand clearly the meaning of *actuosa participatio populi* that the Council called for. If, indeed, singing of pieces by everyone constitutes the epitome of participation, then the art of music in the service of the liturgy is destined for extinction. In 1965, the Fifth International Church Music Congress, meeting in Chicago and Milwaukee, considered the meaning of that concept. A paper by Father Colman E. O'Neill, O.P., (*Sacred Music and Liturgy Reform after Vatican II, Rome*, 1969, p. 89-108) clearly distinguishes between internal and external participation, and indicates that singing is only one of many means of external participation, not to mention listening.

Just as basic to the struggle between the liturgists and the musicians was a false sense of ecumenism, a problem that surfaced not only in the liturgical discussions but in many other areas considered by the Council Fathers. Efforts made to restructure the Catholic liturgy into Protestant-like services grew out of this error and met with opposition from many Catholic sources. Even Bugnini takes up this criticism with reference to the activity of the Protestant monks of Taizé whose influence in preparing the reforms remains a mystery.

The conflicts that began in the Council commissions and continued in the years following are not dead. Church music lies in a shambles not only in this country but throughout the world, largely as a result of the work of Bugnini. The church musicians have withdrawn from the fray; as a result, hardly anything of any value has been forthcoming in the last twenty-five years in composition or performance. The liturgists, for their part, have produced nothing but an ongoing series of vaudeville acts, experiments and novelties; liturgy has become associated with entertainment (dancing, combos, even costuming), so each week must be different, a new act.

When one considers the great hope that the Second Vatican Council initiated and how we looked forward to the promise of new music for the vernacular languages, the integral part that music would have in the liturgy (*pars integrans*), the freedom to use all styles that were truly art and truly sacred, the call for new music for both Latin and vernacular liturgical texts, the demand that music be written both for congregations and for choirs, the extension of the permission to employ all serious instruments, the encouragement of musicological studies and particularly the advancement of Gregorian chant with the publication of new chant books – all this is what the Council Fathers ordered and the church musicians hoped to implement. The preservation of tradition along with a natural development of means for active participation and the use of the vernacular were the contribution of the church musicians to the Council documents, especially *Sacrosanctum concilium*. They fought against Bugnini and his allies to keep the art of music in its centuries-old role in the liturgy. They fought to maintain it in the writings of the post-conciliar period, especially in *Musicam sacram* of 1967, and the fight continues as liturgists continue to insert themselves into the field of sacred music. Cooperation between liturgists and musicians is still a state to be fondly hoped for, but it was not the spirit of Annibale Bugnini as his book shows so clearly.

Editorial by Monsignor Richard J. Schuler
(*Sacred Music*, Vol. 117, no.3, Fall 1990, p. 3-4)

Conciliar Constitution: *Sacrosanctum concilium*

This essay was given as a lecture at the University of Dallas,
October 1, 1992.

The first document of the Second Vatican Council to be publicly
promulgated was the *Constitution on the Sacred Liturgy, Sacrosanctum
concilium*, on December 4, 1963. It was the fruit of many years of
study and debate, the keystone of the liturgical reform that, in its
origins, stretched back into the 19th century. It was the specific work
of a pre-conciliar commission that was assembled in 1959, a conciliar
commission that functioned during the days of the Council, and all the
Fathers in their general meetings during the days of the first session of
the Council.

A detailed study of the *Constitution* must surely investigate the
politics that were intimately involved with its production. These matters
are dealt with in Fr. Ralph Wiltgen's book about the Council, *The Rhine
Flows into the Tiber*, and Archbishop Bugnini's autobiographical work,
The Reform of the Liturgy (1948-1975). While these matters are surely of
interest and do indeed tell one a great deal about the preparation of the
Constitution, it is not the concern of this paper to revive those dramatic
and often inflammatory confrontations between the participants with
different views. We must accept the document as it is, written under
the inspiration of the Holy Spirit, promulgated by an ecumenical
Council and the reigning Holy Father. Our interest is not in where it
has come from, or how it was arrived at, but rather where it is going
and how it is to be implemented now.

A conciliar *Constitution* is a very prestigious document. It rests on
the consensus of the bishops assembled in Council and its promulgation
by the Holy Father. It is binding on the universal Church. It rejoices
in the quality of infallibility which rests in the pope and the bishops in
union with him, assembled in general Council.

Sacrosanctum concilium is a lengthy document, consisting of an introduction and seven chapters, along with an appendix, all contained in 131 paragraphs. Published officially in Latin, several editions in English are available. A very convenient book, *Documents on the Liturgy (1963-1979)*, contains the *Constitution* and all other papal, conciliar and curial texts issued until 1979. Documents issued since then will shortly be gathered into another invaluable reference work.

At the outset of the *Constitution*, the Fathers of the Council begin by explaining their purposes in publishing the *Constitution*: 1) "to impart an ever increasing vigor to the Christian life of the faithful; 2) to adapt more suitably to the needs of our own times those institutions that are subject to change; 3) to foster whatever can promote union among all who believe in Christ; 4) to strengthen whatever can help to call the whole of humanity into the household of the Church" (Para. 1). They make clear that they wish to preserve and foster all lawfully acknowledged rites, but revise them carefully in the light of sound tradition to meet the circumstances and needs of modern times (Para. 4). And among the "lawfully acknowledged rites" one must include the Roman rite!

Chapter One gives the principles underlying the reform. It has five subdivisions and is contained in 41 paragraphs. These ideas are the foundation of all that will be proposed for implementation in the practical order, and therefore they are of the utmost importance and demand an accurate statement and careful interpretation. It was learned shortly after the promulgation of the *Constitution* that problems were arising concerning its meaning, and thus a pontifical commission for the interpretation of the *Constitution* was established by the Holy See. There are some who have maintained that a looseness of language was deliberately sought by some of the Fathers so that later on, opportunities to introduce radical changes into the liturgy might be arranged and credited to the *Constitution* itself.

The Church is the mystical Person of Jesus Christ, who before His Ascension into heaven said that He would be with the Church until the end of time. Christ lives on in His Church, and we are members of that Body, members indeed of His mystical Person. The chief activity of that Church is to carry out the priestly, kingly and prophetic offices of Christ Himself. It is through the liturgy that the priest acts *in persona Christi* in order to sanctify all the members of the Church who thereby participate in His priestly office.

It is that participation in the liturgy as the primary source of divine life that the *Constitution* is especially concerned with. "The Church earnestly desires that all the faithful be led to that full, conscious, and active participation in liturgical celebrations..." (Para. 14). "This full and active participation by all the people is the aim to be considered before all else" (Para. 14). "A prime need...is that attention be directed, first of all, to the liturgical formation of the clergy" (Para. 14). This is necessary so that they might bring to their people what the Church wishes. It is not permitted for anyone to add, remove or change anything in the liturgy, even a priest; it belongs to the Apostolic See, or in some matters to the local bishop, to determine liturgical usage (Para. 22). There are to be no innovations unless the good of the Church requires them, and care must be taken that any new forms in some way grow organically from forms already existing (Para. 23).

A basic principle of liturgical law requires the proper observance of individual roles within the liturgical action, each having a genuine liturgical function: e.g., priest, servers, singers (Para. 28, 29). To achieve active participation, people should be encouraged to take part in acclamations, responses, psalmody, antiphons and songs, as well as actions, gestures and bodily attitude (Para. 30). More must be said later about the meaning of participation (*actuosa* and *activa*), how it is achieved and in what it consists. But a general simplification of the rites is urged, and a more extensive use of Scripture readings is ordered (Para. 35).

One of the most controversial and most misunderstood general principles is that concerning the use of the Latin language and the place to be given to the vernacular tongues (Para. 36). It states clearly that the use of the Latin language is to be preserved in the Latin rites. This is one of the sections that has been the subject of debate, misunderstanding and error. The extent of the use of the vernacular is clearly circumscribed by the *Constitution*, which lists the sacraments, readings, instructions and some prayers and chants as being legitimately put into the vernacular tongues (Para. 36). More must be said on this subject a little later.

Recognition is given by the Fathers to the variety of cultural and social traditions that exist throughout the world, especially in mission lands; but the unity of the Roman rite must be maintained even when it is properly adapted to local customs by the authority of the bishops (Para. 40). Commissions on liturgy, art and music should assist the bishops; they should be made up of experts in their fields (Para. 44-46). Unfortunately many of these commissions are populated by people of less than "expert" qualifications.

Chapter Two of the *Constitution* is concerned with the Holy Eucharist. Chapter Three takes up the other sacraments; Chapter Four, the Divine Office; Chapter Five, the liturgical year; Chapter Six, sacred music; and Chapter Seven, sacred art. Each of these chapters could well constitute a series of lectures, but now I will limit my remarks to Chapter Six, on sacred music.

There are three basic problems that have surfaced on the subject of sacred music since the close of the Council: 1) the meaning of active participation; 2) the use of the vernacular; and 3) the qualities of "sacred" and "artistic" as applied to music for the liturgy. A proper understanding of these questions will assure the true implementation of the wishes of the Council Fathers, and will, indeed, overcome most conflicts that have arisen over these subjects both among church musicians and the laity.

1. No greater misunderstanding of conciliar orders in liturgical matters has arisen since the Council than that concerned with *actuosa participatio* (Para. 14). To begin with, it must be clearly understood that this is not something invented by the Second Vatican Council; Pius X uses the term and promotes the concept in his famous *motu proprio* of 1903, *Tra le sollicitudini*, which began the liturgical movement. It is spoken of in all papal documents on the liturgy during this century. Its essence lies in the interior life of grace, begun in us in baptism and increased throughout life by the sacraments, prayer, almsgiving, keeping the commandments, etc. The primary source of this supernatural life is, of course, the Holy Eucharist, especially as it is brought to us in the Sacrifice of the Mass. The Council Fathers, as all the popes of this century, are most anxious that all of the faithful have access to an increase of that grace by their taking an active part in the liturgy.

The Latin term used to describe this participation in the liturgy is *actuosa*. This is distinguished from the Latin term, *activa*. The distinction, unfortunately, does not exist in English which translates both words as "active": *Actuosa* carries the connotation of an interior action; *activa* has the meaning of external action. Only a baptized person is capable of *actuosa participatio* in the liturgy; anyone may have *activa participatio*. *Actuosa participatio* may be aided by *activa participatio*. Thus singing, speaking, walking, kneeling and many other actions that are *activa participatio* may increase and foster *actuosa participatio*, but in themselves they are not necessarily *actuosa participatio*.

Let me give you an example. A baptized woman who is blind and deaf comes often to church, sits to the side, never sings or prays aloud or moves from her place. She knows that the Mass is the renewal of Christ's sacrifice on Calvary and she receives Him in Holy Communion, maintaining always a reverent, prayerful silence. Present in the church at the same time is a Jew who is acting as undertaker at a funeral. A most cooperative man, he wishes to carry out the rites of the Church and help his clients to participate in the rites. He sings, answers the responses and takes part in the procession. Which person can be said to be practicing *actuosa participatio*? The baptized woman who neither says nor does much externally or the unbaptized Jew who eagerly sings and does many external actions? The answer is the blind old lady. The key to the problem lies in the fact of baptism which marks the soul and gives one the right to share in the divine life of grace. All external activities aid that; they do not create participation. The blind and deaf woman is indeed participating, while the Jew, since he is not baptized, cannot participate.

In the rush to bring about active participation in the liturgy, many false ideas were adopted in the United States. It was announced that choirs were to be disbanded, since they interfered with participation of the people, preventing them from singing. Everyone was urged (even forced) to sing hymns at Mass, although singing was not to his liking or within his talents (salvation depended on singing!). One had to use the "liturgy aid" that was handed out at the door, and one was not to read from an old hand missal or (God forbid!) say the Rosary. Standing replaced kneeling; hand shaking and hand holding were required for participation. The notion that true active participation must first of all be interior was not grasped. The distinction between *actuosa* and *activa* was not made clear. The treasury of sacred music that the Council ordered to be preserved and fostered was abandoned, because a congregation could not sing a six-part Mass of Palestrina nor even a unison Gregorian Gradual. And since all singing had to be done by all members of the congregation, according to these opinions, only the simplest hymns could be used. The famous Father Gelineau declared that perfection in music and its performance in the liturgy was not what musicians should look for. He allowed for religious art in concert form, but the great classical liturgical works were not to be used within the liturgy. The current erroneous idea that the treasury of sacred music is to be "preserved and fostered" in concert halls and not within the liturgy probably can be traced back to Gelineau.

Among the erroneous ideas that have found great circulation is the notion that listening is not active participation. Yet one of the most demanding of all human actions is that of listening. It requires strict attention and summons up in a person his total concentrative effort. It is possible, for example, to walk without really knowing that one is walking or advert to where one is going. It is possible even to sing, especially a very familiar tune, and not be conscious of actually singing. But one cannot truly listen without attention. Especially in our day of constant radio and TV broadcasting, we are able to tune out almost every sound we wish. For proof of this, ask any college professor or high school teacher! To listen attentively demands full human concentration. Listening can be the most active form of participation, demanding effort and attention. Truly, as the scriptures tell us, faith demands hearing, *fides ex auditu*.

Surely the baptized Christian who listens with care to the proclamation of the Gospel or the singing of the preface at Mass truly has achieved participation, both *activa* and *actuosa*. The Church does not have the entire congregation proclaim the Gospel text, but rather the deacon or the priest does it. It is the duty of all to listen. The Canon of the Mass is not to be recited by everyone but all are to hear it. Listening is a most important form of active participation.

There is a variety of roles to be observed in the public celebration of the liturgy. There is the role of priest, deacon, reader, cantor, choir and congregation, among many others. Because each office has its own purpose and its own manner of acting we have the basic reason for a distinction of roles. If the reader or the cantor is to read and sing, certainly the role of the others is to listen. If the choir is to sing, someone must listen and in so doing participate actively in the liturgy, even if during the period of listening he is relatively inactive in a physical way.

Every age has participated in the liturgy through baptism, as members of the Church and part of the Mystical Body of Christ. All ages have shared in the right and duty of *actuosa participatio populi.* If, as St. Pius X insists, the liturgy is the primary source of the Christian life, everyone must take part in it to achieve salvation. Active participation is not an invention of our day; the Church through the ages constantly shared the life of Christ with its members in the Mass and the sacraments, the very actions of Christ Himself working through His Church and His priesthood. For each age, the activities deemed by it to be useful in promoting that participation have varied according to the needs and ideas of the period. One cannot say that because the Medieval period developed a chant that was largely the possession of monastic choirs, the congregations who listened were not actively participating. Perhaps not according to post-Vatican II standards, but one must carefully avoid the error of judging the past by the present and applying to former times criteria that seem valuable in our own times. Because Palestrina's polyphonic Masses require the singing of trained choirs, can one assume that non-choir members in the Renaissance period were deprived of an active participation in the liturgy? No age could permit such a thing to happen and thus be deprived of the primary source of the spiritual life. The sixteenth-century baptized Roman did participate through listening along with other activities, as no doubt an eighteenth-century Austrian did when he heard a Mozart Mass performed by a choir and orchestra.

We must then carefully consider the role of each individual, and we must consider the cultural and personal conditions of each one who must find in the liturgy the primary source of his spiritual life. A variety of opportunities for liturgical activity is needed, and good pastoral direction will supply the need. The Church herself does so by the very rubrics of the liturgical books, directing what is to be done. The Vatican Council taught the need of various functions and various roles to carry out completely the liturgical actions. What is useful for a university community may not be workable for a mission parish, or what might be possible in a large urban church might not be feasible in a rural setting. In my parish, we are able to sing the orchestral Masses of the classical period with a choir of sixty voices, soloists and twenty or more instrumentalists, a practice that we do on thirty Sundays of the year. But I don't for even a moment think that such a program can be imitated very widely, and yet for the congregation that assembles on Sundays at Saint Agnes Church in Saint Paul, Minnesota, this is a form of participation in the liturgy that meets their needs. Surely the spoken and sung responses and acclamations in the liturgy are the right and duty of all present. One must never exclude the congregation totally from participation by singing, but the variety of methods allows for many possibilities for participation by singing or by listening to singing.

Important, too, for any participation in the liturgy is the elevation of the spirit of the worshiper. Ultimately, liturgy is prayer, the supreme prayer of adoration, thanksgiving, petition and reparation. Prayer is the raising of the heart and the mind to God as Creator, Redeemer and Sanctifier. The means to achieve such elevation of the spirit in prayer involve all the activities of the human person, both spirit and body. Such means produce true *actuosa participatio*. Thus beauty, whether it appeals to the sight, the ear, the imagination or any of the senses, is an important element in achieving participation. The architectural splendor of a great church or the sound of great music, or the solemnity of ceremonial movement by ministers clothed in precious vestments, or the beauty of the proclaimed word – all can effect a true and salutary participation in one who himself has not sung a note or taken a step. But he is not a mere silent spectator as some would say; he is actively participating because of his baptismal character and the grace stirred up in him by what he is seeing and hearing, thinking and praying.

With many false ideas about participation spread abroad, the true wish of the Council, which was based on a century of continuing efforts to accomplish *actuosa participatio*, was not achieved. The means became the end, and destroyed both the end and the means (cf. "Participation" in *Sacred Music*, Volume 114, No. 4, Winter 1987).

2. One of the great privileges granted by the Second Vatican Council was the permission to use the vernacular languages in the liturgy. The *Constitution* grants a limited use, intended chiefly for the benefit of the laity. Thus the readings, the acclamations and responses, as well as the administration of the sacraments, were able to be done in the people's language. I was in Germany in 1963 and had an opportunity to read the draft of the *Constitution* being considered that summer by the Council Fathers and the *periti*. I found the plan for

the introduction of the vernacular very interesting and most practical. Those who wrote the chapter on sacred music proposed to keep the solemn sung Mass in Latin, allowing the vernacular exclusively for the spoken liturgy. This would have made possible the preservation of the great treasury of church music, and at the same time it would have helped those missionary countries, where musical composition was not widely practiced, to borrow music in Latin from countries, such as Germany, France, the Slavic countries, *et al.*, where composers were active. Church music in Latin could be used all over the world, and it would be a unifying element amid all nations in the universal Church. Meanwhile in the spoken liturgy, the vernacular would be widely used. However, this solution of the question did not find its way to the final draft.

The final draft of the *Constitution* clearly states that Latin is the language of the liturgy (Para. 36). Latin it orders; the use of the vernacular it permits. The people are to be taught to sing in Latin those parts of the Mass that belong to them (Para. 54). But what unfortunately happened was that Latin was forbidden, even by bishops who wrote directions prohibiting its use, which was in direct contradiction to the *Constitution*. Much of the attack on Latin came from an anti-Roman spirit too often found among the clergy, even bishops!

Just as there was no conflict intended between the singing of the choir and the singing of the congregation, so there was no conflict foreseen between Latin and the vernacular in the minds of the bishops who wrote the *Constitution*. But a group of reformers, who had been defeated in its efforts to put its ideas into the *Constitution* itself, found after the publication of the document an opportunity to push its position on to the whole Church by interpreting the *Constitution*. As a result, Latin died, and with it the treasury of sacred music which the Council had ordered to be used and fostered. The abandoning of Latin was the second fatal blow, coming as it did on the heels of the first blow which was the misunderstanding of what true active participation is.

3. The third difficulty for the implementation of the Council's reform of church music lay in the controversy surrounding the idea of the "sacred"; it was popular to deny the existence of anything "sacred." The Church had long taught that there were sacred persons,

places and things, all sanctified by being set apart for the special use of the Deity. Included was sacred music. Musical sounds, of course, of themselves are neither sacred or secular; they become sacred through their association with sacred words and by the style of musical writing that through connotation has come to be accepted by the community as sacred music. Music has many uses in life: military music, dance music, music for eating, for weddings, funerals and music for worshiping God. What we hear in church we don't expect to hear in a bar, and visa versa. What is played for a military parade cannot be used as an evening serenade. So, also, is there music for church, agreed upon over centuries, as for example, Gregorian chant.

Jazz, country, Western, ballads, opera arias, folk-songs, art songs, the vast repertory of the modern secular symphony orchestra are not meant for church use. They are intended chiefly for the entertainment of the community. The purpose of church music is the glory of God and the edification of the people. It is not intended for entertainment, even at weddings. Our American advisory committee on music, appointed by the bishops, declared that the purpose of church music is "to create a truly human experience"; but the Council, echoing a thousand years of tradition, said that the purpose of church music is to glorify God and to edify the faithful. By denying that premise, the dike was opened to the admission into the church of all secular music and the abandoning of the treasury of sacred music.

Instruments that have a history of secular use only were brought into church: the piano, guitar, drums, combos of winds, all regarded as entertainment instruments, playing profane compositions, performed by vocal quartets and accompanied by dancing. Church music had become a "truly human experience"; which, of course, is just what musical entertainment is, a human experience. But the glory of God, the Council's stated reason for music in church, had been replaced by the pleasure of man. The pipe organ was singled out by the Council as the instrument of high esteem, and other instruments that are suitable for sacred use were allowed to be brought into the church too if they contributed to the dignity of worship (Para. 120).

The introduction of secular music into the liturgy did more than any other element to destroy the sacredness of the liturgy, the spirit of reverence, indeed the very devotion of the people. Music, in fact, is so closely united to the liturgy, particularly in its close connection to the liturgical texts, that the Council calls it *pars integrans* (an integral part) of the liturgy. When secular texts replaced the sacred liturgical texts, the liturgical year was destroyed in the process. An important sacramental which the Council was at great pains to promote, was lost. Pentecost and Christmas, a Marian feast and Epiphany, could hardly be distinguished from each other with the texts of the Proper of the Mass replaced by secular texts or even by the ubiquitous "four hymns": What was at first called "hootenanny music" and later elevated to "contemporary music" was nothing more than entertainment that had nothing at all to do with the liturgy of the Church. At best, these attempts at music for liturgy might have been pleasant at a picnic, a pow-wow, or a bus trip, but hardly suitable for the worship of the Triune God.

Closely connected with a denial of the sacred was the abandoning of the requirement that music for worship must be art. In abandoning Latin, the treasury of sacred music was pushed aside, from Gregorian chant to the compositions of the 20th century. With the insistence that participation of the people required the disbanding of choirs, the treasury of sacred music no longer had anyone to perform it. With the introduction of secular instruments, styles and texts, the creation of church music fell into the hands of those whose musical qualifications were poor and sometimes totally lacking. The quality of art demanded for the worship of God was beyond their ability. Those who had been devoting themselves to writing for the liturgy now gave up that labor of love, since the use of Latin, the singing of choirs, the writing for sacred instruments in a sacred style were all gone.

Within a short period, the great flowering of liturgy and church music envisioned by the Fathers of the Council turned into a catastrophic destruction of all that had been building for nearly two thousand years. The effort to destroy the Roman liturgy, and in particular the *Missa Romana cantata*, had succeeded. It was not the intention of the Council; it was not the work of the Council; it happened in spite of the Council. The natural thing is to ask "why"? As Pope Paul VI said, the smoke of Satan can be seen in the Church. It is an old axiom that when the Holy Spirit is active in the Church, the Devil is also very active. There has long been an anti-Roman hatred in the Church, often found among the clergy. The Council was an opportunity to bring to light some of the underground ideas called Modernism, long suppressed through the efforts of Pope Pius IX and Pope Pius X. During and after the Council, that heresy was spread by means of the great international assembly that the Council brought together in Rome and then sent forth to every continent. An international network of people in every area of church life, called IDOC [note: abbreviation for the International Center of Information and Documentation concerning the Conciliar Church] carried the ideas of Modernism into every land, infiltrating the religious life, seminaries, catechetics, schools, liturgy and church music. The same errors were found in all parts of the globe and at the same time. IDOC had all the earmarks of a conspiracy.

Need we be discouraged about the state of liturgy and church music in our country today? Well, it is not encouraging. With a very few exceptions, here and there around the country, church music in the United States today is in total collapse, a dire catastrophe, a complete failure. But we must attempt to correct that and put the wishes of the Council into effect. After all, when the Council of Trent closed in 1563, for a hundred years there was war and fighting in Europe, nations falling away from the Church, religious orders failing, heresy rampant. But then dawned the 17th century and with it a flowering of religion: new theology, new church music, new religious orders, new architecture, new saints and a spreading of Catholicism in Europe and in the newly discovered western hemisphere. The cause of all this was the Council of Trent and those who put it into effect. When it was finally put into practice, a great age dawned. So also will it come about in these times when the Second Vatican Council is finally given a chance and is put into practice. We may not live to see it in its full blossom, but we must begin and to the best of our abilities, lay the groundwork and put into effect here and now the will of the Church, the directives of the Second Vatican Council.

Monsignor Richard J. Schuler
(*Sacred Music*, Vol. 119, no.4, Winter 1992, p. 7-14)

Misunderstanding of *Actuoso Participatio*

At the recent meeting of the American bishops in Washington, D.C., one of the ordinaries made an observation on the quality of liturgy in this country. He told how he watched a video of a Mass with a stopwatch in hand and clocked the "active participation" of the laity. He registered 88 seconds of what he called "active participation" in a 59-minute Mass.

He said that participation at Mass is supposed to be full, active and conscious, but it is not working that way. The chairman replied that the Bishop had made a valid observation.

What a blatant example of misunderstanding of what *actuosa participatio* truly is!

First, it must be interior. A stopwatch is hardly its measure. There are several elements that allow the faithful to participate in the liturgy: some are spiritual and internal; others are external and sensorial. But it is faith and charity that are essential, uniting the Christian with the priest who is offering the Sacrifice.

Father Colman E. O'Neill, O.P., says this: "That *participatio actuosa* required by the Council may be defined as that form of devout involvement...which best promotes the exercise of the common priesthood of the baptized: their power to offer the Sacrifice of the Mass and to receive the sacraments. They take part in it by bodily movements, standing, kneeling or sitting as the occasion may demand; they join vocally in the parts which are intended for them. It also requires that they listen to, and understand, the Liturgy of the Word. It requires, too, that there be moments of silence when the import of the whole ceremonial may be absorbed and deeply personalized...It certainly does not imply uninterrupted observable activity."

Father O'Neill says that the precise form that participation takes in various circumstances varies. A parish church is different from a cathedral or a seminary. He says that on occasion a "silent Mass" is in order for a religious community, and participation of the whole Church, through the mysterious being of the Mystical Body, justifies Masses celebrated without a congregation.

Listening is a truly active participation. Listening both to the proclaimed Word and the performed music can be full, conscious and active participation. The same can be said for watching the ceremonial as it is enacted (*Sacred Music and Liturgy Reform after Vatican II*. Rome: Consociatio Internationalis Musicae Sacrae, 1969).

Only the baptized person can participate in the liturgy, and that is done through the grace of the sacrament. External activity may enhance that participation, but to attempt to measure it or assess it with a stopwatch shows that its essence is totally misunderstood

Monsignor Richard J. Schuler
(*Sacred Music*, Vol. 122, no. 3, Fall 1995, p. 6)

Participation

With the *Constitution on the Sacred Liturgy, Sacrosanctum concilium*, issued in 1963 by the Second Vatican Council, everyone became very conscious of personal participation in the sacred liturgy, particularly in the Mass.

But active participation in the liturgy was not a concept created by the Second Vatican Council. Indeed, even the very words *actuosa participatio* can be found in the writings of the popes for the past one hundred years. Pope Pius X called for it in his *motu proprio, Tra le sollicitudini*, published in 1903, when he said that "the faithful assemble to draw that spirit from its primary and indispensable source, that is, from active participation in the sacred mysteries and in the public and solemn prayer of the Church."

Pope Pius XI in his apostolic constitution, *Divini cultus*, wrote in 1928 that the restoration of Gregorian chant for the use of the people would provide the means whereby "the faithful may participate in divine worship more actively." Such participation was to be achieved both by singing and by an appreciation of the beauty of the liturgy which stirs the heart of the worshiper, who thereby enters into the sacred mysteries.

In his encyclicals, *Mystici corporis* in 1943, and *Mediator Dei* in 1947, Pope Pius XII used the term but carefully insisted that true participation was not merely external but consisted in a baptismal union with Christ in His Mystical Body, the Church. In 1958, the Sacred Congregation of Rites issued the *Instruction, De musica sacra*, which distinguished several qualities of participation:

The Mass of its nature requires that all those present participate in it, in the fashion proper to each.

a. This participation must primarily be interior (i.e., union with Christ the Priest; offering with and through Him).

b. But the participation of those present becomes fuller (*plenior*) if to internal attention is joined external participation, expressed, that is to say, by external actions such as the position of the body (genuflecting, standing, sitting), ceremonial gestures, or, in particular, the responses, prayers and singing.

It is this harmonious form of participation that is referred to in pontifical documents when they speak of active participation (*participatio actuosa*), the principal example of which is found in the celebrating priest and his ministers who, with due interior devotion and exact observance of the rubrics and ceremonies, minister at the altar.

c. Perfect *participatio actuosa* of the faithful, finally, is obtained when there is added sacramental participation (by communion).

d. Deliberate *participatio actuosa* of the faithful is not possible without their adequate instruction.

It is made clear that it is the baptismal character that forms the foundation of active participation.

Vatican II introduced no radical alteration in the concept of *participatio actuosa* as fostered by the popes for the past decades. The general principle is contained in Article 14 of the *Constitution on the Sacred Liturgy*:

> Mother Church earnestly desires that all the faithful should be led to that full, conscious and active participation in the ceremonies which is demanded by the very nature of the liturgy.
>
> Such participation by the Christian people as a "chosen race, a royal priesthood, a holy nation, a redeemed people" (I *Pet.* 2:9; 2:4-5) is their right and duty by reason of their baptism.
>
> In the restoration and promotion of the sacred liturgy this full and active participation by all the people is the aim to be considered before all else; for it is the primary and indispensable source from which the faithful are to derive the true spirit of Christ...

The word "full" (*plena*) refers to the integrally human fashion in which the baptized faithful take part in the liturgy, i.e., internally and externally. The word "conscious" (*conscia*) demands a knowledge of what one is doing on the part of the faithful, excluding any superstition or false piety. But the word "active" (*actuosa*) requires some greater examination.

A true grasp of the meaning of participation in the liturgy demands a clear understanding of the nature of the Church and above all of Christ Himself. At the basis of so much of today's problems in liturgy lies a false notion of Christology and ecclesiology. Christ, the incarnate Word of God, true God and true Man, lives on in this world now. "I will be with you all days until the end of the world." Even though He has arisen and ascended into Heaven, He lives with us. The Church is His Mystical Body, indeed His Mystical Person. We are the members of that Body. Its activity, the activity of the Church, is the activity of Christ, its Head. The hierarchical priesthood functions in the very person of Christ, doing His work of teaching, ruling and sanctifying. Thus the Mass and the sacraments are Christ's actions bringing to all the members of His Body, the Church, the very life that is in its Head. Participation in that life demands that every member of the Body take part in that action, which is primarily the liturgical activity of the Church. The liturgy is the primary source of that divine life, and thus all must be joined to it in an active way. Baptism is the key that opens the door and permits one to become part of the living Body of Christ. The baptized Christian has not only a right to participation in the Church's life but a duty as well. It is only the baptized person who can participate.

The difference between participation in the liturgy that can be called *activa* and participation that can be labeled *actuosa* rests in the presence in the soul of the baptismal character, the seal that grants one the right to participate. Without the baptismal mark, all the actions of singing, walking, kneeling or anything else can be termed "active;" but they do not constitute *participatio actuosa*. Only the baptismal character can make any actions truly participatory. Let us use an example. Let us say that a pious Hindu attends Mass, takes part in the singing and even walks in a procession with great piety. In the same church is also a Catholic who is blind and deaf and who is unable to leave his chair; he can neither sing nor hear the readings nor walk in the procession.

Which one has truly participated, the one who is very active, or the one who has confined himself solely to his thoughts of adoration? Obviously, it is the baptized Catholic who has exercised *participatio actuosa* despite his lack of external, physical movement. The Hindu, even with his many actions has not been capable of it, since he lacks the baptismal character.

Granting, then, the absolute necessity of baptism, it still is imperative for the Christian to take part in the liturgy actively by a variety of actions. This means that the internal *actuosa participatio*, which the baptismal mark empowers, must be aided by those external actions that he is capable of. He should do those things that the Church sets out for him according to his role in the liturgy and the various conditions that age, social position and cultural background dictate. He must join *participatio activa* to his *participatio actuosa* which he exercises as a baptized person.

What are those actions that make for true active participation in the liturgy? These must be both internal and external in quality, since man is a rational creature with body and soul. The external actions must be intelligent and understood, sincere and pious internally. The Church proposes many bodily positions: kneeling, standing, walking, sitting, etc. It likewise proposes many human actions: singing, speaking, listening and above all else, the reception of the Holy Eucharist. They demand internal attention as well as external execution.

One of the most active and demanding of human actions is that of listening. It requires strict attention and summons up in a person his total concentrative effort. It is possible, for example, to walk without really knowing that one is walking or advert to where one is going. It is possible even to sing, especially a very familiar tune, and not be conscious of actually singing. But one cannot truly listen without attention. Especially in our day of constant radio and TV broadcasting, we are able to tune out almost every sound we wish. To listen attentively demands full human concentration. Listening can be the most active form of participation, demanding effort and attention. Truly, as the scriptures tell us, faith demands hearing, *fides ex auditu*.

With that in mind, surely the baptized Christian who listens with care to the proclamation of the Gospel or the singing of the preface at Mass truly has achieved participation, both *activa* and *actuosa*.

The Church does not have the entire congregation proclaim the

Gospel text, but rather the deacon or the priest does it. It is the duty of all to listen. The Canon of the Mass is not to be recited by everyone but all are to hear it. Listening is a most important form of active participation.

There is a variety of roles to be observed in the public celebration of the liturgy. There is the role of priest, deacon, reader, cantor, choir and congregation, among many others. Because each office has his own purpose and its own manner of acting we have the basic reason for a distinction of roles. If the reader or the cantor is to read and sing, certainly the role of the others is to listen. If the choir is to sing, someone must listen and in so doing, participate actively in the liturgy, even if during the period of listening he is relatively inactive in a physical way.

Every age has participated in the liturgy through baptism, as members of the Church and part of the Mystical Body of Christ. All ages have shared in the right and duty of *actuosa participatio*. If, as Pius X insists, the liturgy is the primary source of the Christian life, everyone must take part in it to achieve salvation. Active participation is not an invention of our day; the Church throughout the ages constantly shared the life of Christ with its members in the Mass and the sacraments, the very actions of Christ Himself working through His Church and His priesthood. For each age the activities deemed by it to be useful in promoting that participation have varied according to the needs and ideas of the period. One cannot say that because the Medieval period developed a chant that was largely the possession of monastic choirs, the congregations who listened were not actively participating. Perhaps not according to post-Vatican II standards, but one must carefully avoid the error of judging the past by the present and applying to former times criteria that seem valuable in our own times. Because Palestrina's polyphonic Masses require the singing of trained choirs, can one assume that non-choir members in the Renaissance period were deprived of an active participation in the liturgy? No age could permit such a thing to happen and thus be deprived of the primary source of the spiritual life. The sixteenth-century baptized Roman did participate through listening along with other activities, as no doubt an eighteenth-century Austrian did when he heard a Mozart Mass performed by a choir and orchestra.

We must then carefully consider the roles of each individual, and we must consider the cultural and personal conditions of each one who must find in the liturgy the primary source of his spiritual life. A variety of opportunities for liturgical activity is needed, and good pastoral direction will supply the need. The Church herself does so by the very rubrics of the liturgical books, directing what is to be done. The Vatican Council taught the need of various functions and various roles to carry out completely the liturgical actions.

Surely the spoken and sung responses and acclamations in the liturgy are the right and the duty of all present. But the practice of calling the *Sanctus* an acclamation is without foundation; it is a hymn, found in the Old Testament and sung by the angels. It is not the exclusive prerogative of the congregation as it might be thought to be if it is labelled an acclamation. As a hymn, it can be given to a trained group and sung in a more elaborate setting. The same is true of the parts called the Ordinary of the Mass, including the *Credo*, which may be listened to and consented to with great faith without having to be spoken by the congregation. The Proper parts of the Mass, because of the great variety of texts and settings, fall of necessity to trained and practiced groups. One may, of course, never exclude the congregation totally from participation by singing, but the variety of methods allows for many possibilities for participation by singing or by listening to singing. The possibilities of participation are almost infinite.

Important, too, for any participation in the liturgy is the elevation of the spirit of the worshiper. Ultimately, liturgy is prayer, the supreme prayer of adoration, thanksgiving, petition and reparation. Prayer is the raising of the heart and the mind to God as Creator, Redeemer and Sanctifier. The means to achieve such elevation of the spirit in prayer involve all the activities of the human person, both spirit and body. Such means produce true *actuosa participatio*. Thus beauty, whether it appeals to the sight, the ear, the imagination or any of the senses, is an important element in achieving participation. The architectural splendor of a great church or the sound of great music, or the solemnity of ceremonial movement by ministers clothed in precious vestments, or the beauty of the proclaimed word – all can effect a true and salutary participation in one who himself has not sung a note or taken a step. But he is not a mere silent spectator as some would say; he is actively participating because of his baptismal character and the grace stirred up in him by what he is seeing and hearing, thinking and praying.

The Church has always promoted Gregorian chant. Especially during this past century, the popes have fostered the music of the Renaissance polyphonists. Pope John Paul II celebrated Mass in Saint Peter's Basilica with the Vienna orchestra and singers doing Mozart's Coronation Mass. Anyone who was present on that memorable occasion in that great church experienced true participation.

Thus to limit participation to singing impoverishes seriously the opportunity of the Christian to take part in the most essential means for his salvation. One does not have to sing to save his soul. But one must be active (*actuosa participatio*) in the liturgy, through baptism and other actions according to his ability, state, culture and disposition, in order to enter into the mystery of the redemption wrought by Christ, outside of which there is no salvation.

We can conclude with this definition of *participatio actuosa*:

> (It is) that form of devout involvement in the liturgical action which, in the present conditions of the Church, best promotes the exercise of the common priesthood of the baptized: that is, their power to offer the sacrifice of the Mass with Christ and to receive the sacraments. It is clear that, concretely, this requires that the faithful understand the liturgical ceremonial; that they take part in it by bodily movements, standing, kneeling or sitting as the occasion may demand; that they join vocally in the parts which are intended for them. It also requires that they listen to, and understand, the Liturgy of the Word. It requires, too, that there be moments of silence when the import of the whole ceremonial may be absorbed and deeply personalized (Colman E. O'Neill, "The Theological Meaning of *Actuosa Participatio* in the Liturgy," in *Sacred Music and Liturgy Reform after Vatican II.* Consociatio Internationalis Musicae Sacrae, Rome, 1969. p. 105).

Monsignor Richard J. Schuler
(*Sacred Music*, Vol. 114, no. 4, Winter 1987, p. 7-10)

COMMENTARY

Where Are We With the Liturgy?

When Dr. Virginia Schubert asked me to compose this brief essay in answer to the question "Where are we with the liturgy," I quickly said "Yes!" I am honored to be included in any work dedicated to one of the pre-eminent Midwest churchmen of the 20th century, and a tireless defender of the Church's treasury of sacred music. I was blessed to live in residence at Saint Agnes from 2008 until 2015, during which time I had the unmerited pleasure of celebrating many, many Masses while listening to the powerful sounds of the Twin Cities Catholic Chorale singing the priceless treasures of the Church's rich heritage of sacred music. To say it helped me to pray would be a shameful understatement.

But upon further reflection of what had been asked of me, my excitement turned to concern, as the answer to the overwhelmingly broad question "Where are we with the liturgy?" is not able to be delivered in any meaningful way in a 1,000-word essay. What is more, we live in deeply unsettled and unsettling times for those who have a love of the liturgical traditions of the Church. It is not controversial in the least to say the attitude of Pope Francis towards more traditional forms of worship is decidedly different than that of Pope Benedict. But I have no desire to add to that discussion.

And so perhaps the best answer to give on the state of the liturgy in the Church today is, "depends on the bishop, depends on the diocese." And in some sense, this is how it should be. As the chief steward of the liturgical life in his diocese, it is the bishop's solemn duty to be concerned about all things that touch upon the worship of God. In fact, it lies at the very heart of the burdensome task to which he has been called. We owe our bishops our prayers and not just our letters of protest, though there is, to be sure, a time and a place for those, too. People from a wide variety of points on the ideological spectrum can surely agree that to be a bishop is not an easy task, and it requires the shepherd's daily weighing of many competing goods to best pastor the flock entrusted to the earthen vessels of his own limited intellect and will, guided always, please God, by daily prayer and contact with the One who has loved him first.

As Pope Saint Pius X reminded us in *Tra le sollicitudini*, the promotion and protection of what the Second Vatican Council called "the treasure of sacred music" lies very much within the heart of those grave responsibilities given to bishops, including in a special way to the Bishop of Rome. The bishop does this in three ways. The first is by ensuring that the sacred music which accompanies the liturgical celebrations of his cathedral and diocesan ceremonies are in accord with the principles of sacred music enunciated by the Church, so as to serve as a model to his diocese and his priests. The second is by providing his pastors clear directives on sacred music. And the third is by ensuring that his seminarians receive at least the beginning of a formation in the Church's *authentic* understanding of sacred music.

It has been profoundly edifying to witness with my own ears a return to including the Proper Gregorian Introits, Offertory and Communion chants at many cathedrals within major diocesan liturgies, particularly when these assigned texts are not used simply as meditative pieces or as a prelude to Holy Mass, but as integral parts of the liturgical act for which they were composed. While still relatively uncommon, it is also the case that some diocesan liturgies now regularly feature the simpler Latin Mass settings. Robust congregational hymnody is also found in many cathedrals. Yes, it is true, not all cathedrals benefit from excellent music programs, as some bishops, like many priests, still unfortunately view music as mere window dressing to the Mass, and oftentimes their budget and personnel hires show it. Even more common is the practice of utilizing music in the diocesan liturgy to principally highlight cultural diversity, and often in a way that is less than inspiring. But I do see general progress in the area.

Providing direction to his pastors on liturgical music is another way in which the local bishop exercises his liturgical authority, and develops his people's capacity for that full, active, and conscious participation in the liturgical act that is their duty. But to be frank, I am sadly unaware of many contemporary bishops who have issued any substantial document on sacred music within their diocese.

One notable exception is Archbishop Alexander Sample of Portland, Oregon, a bishop whose own vocation includes, not surprisingly, Monsignor Schuler in a prominent way. I hope there are others, but I am not familiar with them. To be sure, the bishops of the United States released the text "Sing to the Lord" in 2007, but it has no legislative authority itself, beyond the legal weight of the individual documents from which its own provisions come.

Because most practicing Catholics receive the vast majority of their ongoing religious formation only at the Sunday Mass, it would seem to me to be of massive importance that the music utilized Sunday after Sunday manifest the qualities of holiness, beauty, and universality that are the defined features of sacred music. In a very visceral way, music communicates culture. Without a common culture, our faith becomes stripped down to presider preferences and is diminished to questions of mere validity. For all of these reasons I hope and pray that many more bishops will be inspired by Archbishop Sample's example and consider releasing norms for sacred music within their respective dioceses. Without this concrete act of leadership, parishes will continue to be a hodgepodge not only of various aesthetic quality, but indeed of Catholic identity itself.

Finally, in analyzing the state of Catholic liturgy and specifically sacred music, it is important to examine the formation that seminarians are receiving in sacred music within their respective houses of formation. While not involved in seminary work myself, I have plenty of friends who are, and the fact is that they are entrusted with a responsibility that is both exhilarating and crushing. The amount of material they are mandated to cover in the limited time allotted to them is next to impossible. And so it is understandable that in many houses of formation, rectors and formators don't consider sacred music to be a particularly pressing issue. Again, some notable exceptions should be acknowledged, such as the presence of the Catholic Institute of Sacred Music at Saint Patrick's in Menlo Park, thanks to the excellent leadership of the heroic Archbishop Salvatore Cordileone. But without a greater attentiveness to educating our young priests on the actual principles of sacred music, parishes will continue to be condemned to the aesthetic tastes of their passing-through-pastor and cultural limbo. Some guys like chant, some guys like guitars, some guys like drums, some guys like polyphony: Why is one better than another for the worship of God? This question can't be seriously answered without some education, and that education must be more than art appreciation. It must involve the study of the Church's actual teaching on this needlessly controversial topic.

The Second Vatican Council placed a great emphasis on a strong understanding of the theology of the local bishop and his role as the chief liturgical steward of the diocese entrusted to him. This was a great gift to the Church and an undervalued part of the Council's teachings. It is my fervent prayer that our beloved bishops will continue to strive to embrace their grave responsibility to truly shepherd, helping their people to pray and to offer fitting worship to the Almighty. May we assist them with our own prayers and sacrifices.

Reverend John Paul Erickson, Pastor
Church of the Transfiguration
Saint Paul, Minnesota

Introibo ad altare Dei

Photo: Neil Abbott

The Church of Saint Agnes, Saint Paul, Minnesota

Photo: Marlane Gallagher

Monsignor Richard Schuler and Paul LeVoir, director of the
Schola Cantorum at Saint Agnes Church.

Photo: Caecilia Lee

Monsignor Schuler directs the Twin Cities Catholic Chorale during a solemn
entrance procession at the Sunday High Mass at Saint Agnes.

Photo: Richard Graner

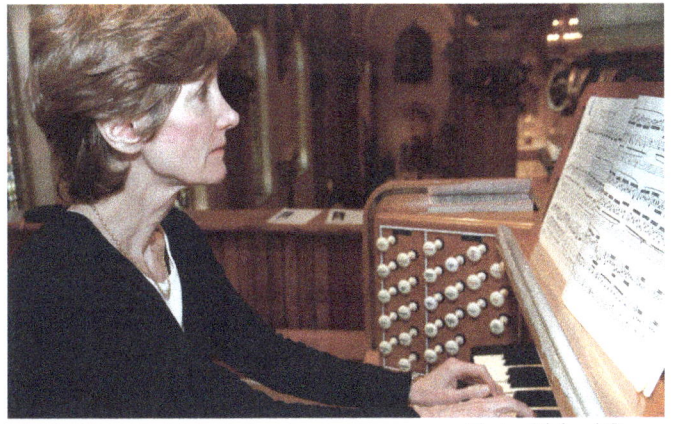

Music creates a sense of the sacred. Mary LeVoir has provided pipe organ accompaniment for Saint Agnes parish and the Twin Cities Catholic Chorale for many years.

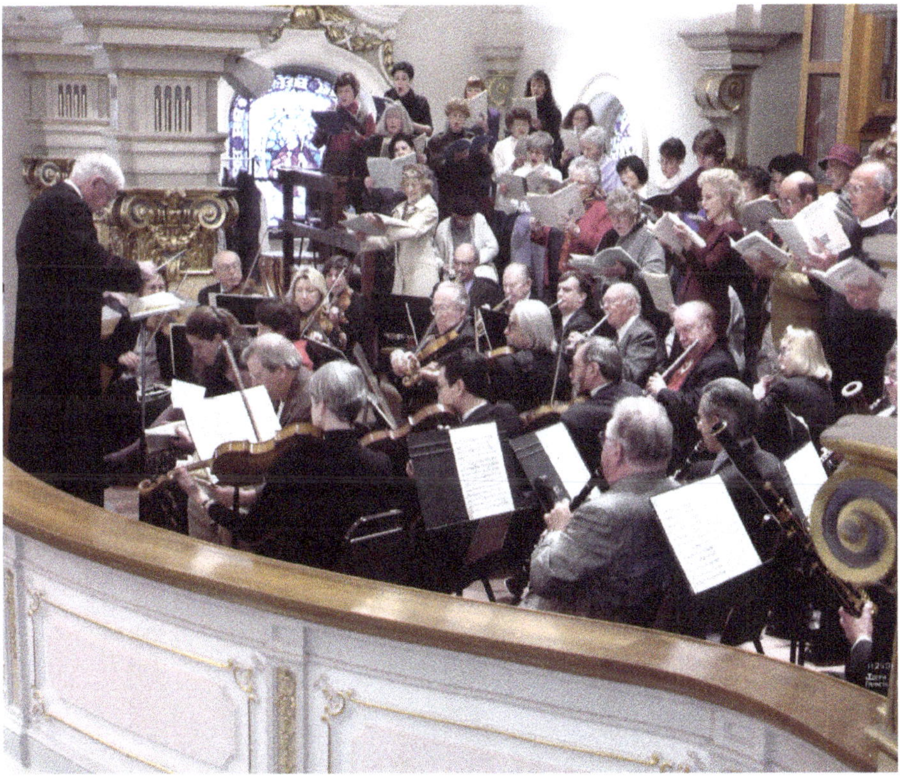

Photo: Joe Oden

Monsignor Schuler directs the Twin Cities Catholic Chorale and professional musicians through a spiritually uplifting polyphonic music arrangement that is both sacred and art as the Second Vatican Council required.

The choir loft in the baroque-style Church of Saint Agnes allows the music of the Chorale and orchestra to surround the congregation, thus assisting full participation in the Holy Sacrifice of the Mass.

Photo: Christine Grabow

Photo: Christine Grabow

Well-qualified Choirmasters are essential in fostering a sense of the sacred. Dr. Robert Peterson (top) became the assistant director of the Chorale under Monsignor Schuler in the 2002-2003 season and assumed leadership in 2007.

Photo: Neil Abbott

Dr. Marc Jaros is the third and current director of the Chorale, serving since 2019.

The use of solemn liturgical actions and symbols at Mass, such as the use of incense, reverent altar boys, and exquisite vestments, creates an overwhelming sense of the sacred presence of God in the Holy Sacrifice of the Mass.

Photo: Christine Grabow

Photo: Joe Oden

Monsignor Richard J. Schuler celebrating Mass on Palm Sunday

Photo: Neil Abbott

Reverend Mark Moriarty explains the symbolism of the intricate vestments used at Saint Agnes.

Corpus Christi procession before the imposing structure of Saint Agnes Church gives the presence of God a prominent place in the community.

Section Three
SACRED MUSIC

"We will never have a renewal of sacred music without faith; we will never have sacred music at all until the place of man in relation to God is established clearly. There will be no sacred music until the place of art in man's seeking for God is defined. There must be an affirmation of the sacred, and this must begin in the seminaries.... Two areas must be discussed: the prayer life of the seminarian himself, and the tools that he must acquire for the apostolate that will ultimately be his as a priest."

Monsignor Richard J. Schuler
"Preparation of the Diocesan Clergy in Church Music"
Sacred Music, Vol. 101, No 3, Fall 1974

What Makes Music Sacred?

This paper was given at the University of Wisconsin at Eau Claire, January 18, 1985.

A great debate has been underway for sometime about the sacred and the secular. There are some who wish to deny the very existence of "sacred." Others say all things are sacred, confusing the notion of sacred with good, as used by the Scriptures when God viewed His creation and "saw that it was good." This debate enters into all areas of life, including the field of art, and especially the art of music where the notion of "sacred music" has been almost a household term for years.

This debate between the sacred and the secular is felt, for example, in convents and monasteries, by monks and nuns who are attempting to adjust their consecrated, dedicated lives to their position in a modern world. It is met in theology, and especially in ascetical theology, where the term "world" was long taken to be the equivalent of evil. We find it in architecture, where it is hard to distinguish a sacred building from a secular one; in dance, where one may be at a loss to say that what is being performed is sacred or not; in clothing and vestments, even when associated with liturgical actions.

The *Oxford Dictionary* defines "sacred" as "consecrated, dedicated, set apart, made holy by association with a deity." It defines "secular" as "pertaining to the world as distinguished from the church and religion; with reference to music, not concerned with or devoted to the service of religion, not sacred, but profane."

What makes music sacred? What makes anything sacred? Things are not sacred in and of themselves. As the dictionary states, they are consecrated, dedicated, set apart; someone must do this for them. Here lies the key to determining what is sacred or not, but how this comes about involves the history of the human race; for us musicians, it involves the entire history of music, here in the west and in the east. The question of the sacred and the profane concerned the Fathers of the early Church, many of whom were convinced that the pagan influences so opposed to Christianity could creep into the Church through artistic and musical devices associated with the various pagan cults and lascivious practices. Instrumental music was particularly suspect and feared, as Clement of Alexandria (c.150-c.220), a very learned man with musical and poetical talents, warned. He rejected "the ancient psaltery, the trumpet, the timbrel and aulos, which those engaged in war and those who reject the fear of God make use of in the singing at their festivals."

In the Alexandrian tradition of allegorical interpretation of the Scriptures, Eusebius of Caesarea (c.260-c.340), the church historian, disapproved of instruments and substituted various allegories for the realities to explain his position. He wrote: "We sing the praises of God with a living psaltery." He called the body the cithara and the lyre of ten strings the five bodily senses and the five virtues of the soul in trying to explain references to the use of such instruments in the Old Testament. Saint Athanasius (c.298-373) followed in the same Alexandrian viewpoint.

In the west, Saint Jerome (c.340-420) was opposed to the use of instruments in Christian worship and made his influence felt on his friend Pope Damasus, in a period when much of the organization of the Roman liturgy was taking place. Saint Augustine (354-430) did much to achieve a synthesis between the learning of pagan Greece and Rome and the Christian faith, but he still accepted an allegorical interpretation of the use of instruments in Christian worship, chiefly because of the fear of the association connected with their use in pagan cults. It was, of course, always Psalm 150 that caused the problem for the commentators, since it so distinctly calls for the praise of God with instruments: "Praise the Lord with the sound of the tuba; praise Him with psaltery and harp."

After Saint Augustine, as the Church grew and its influence extended, less is found about the dangers inherent in the use of instrumental music or in the singing of women, because the association of these things with the pagan rites was gradually being forgotten as paganism waned and disappeared. At the same time, as the Church grew, it was able, little by little, to make use in its worship of those cultural, artistic and popular traditions of the Mediterranean basin that formerly had belonged in some part, at least, to pagan celebrations. The music itself was not pagan; it was the association it had with paganism that created the problem for the Fathers of the Church. Once that connotation ceased to be attached to instrumental music, to the singing of women and certain harmonies and melodies, the problem no longer loomed large. After the time of Augustine, the old fears were beginning to be lessened and the writers and preachers no longer are opposed to music. In the period when the Church and Christian influence are small and struggling and the dangers of the secular engulfing the sacred are great, we hear cries of alarm from the religious writers. When the influence of the Church is great, the danger of secularization is less, and we often find secular things being brought into religious use without fear of profanation.

Let us examine several periods in the history of music with these two points in mind: 1) connotation, and 2) the absorption of the sacred by the secular and vice versa, in periods of greater or lesser Christian influence.

First, the question of connotation. By connotation, we understand the meaning or significance attributed to something over a long period of time by the entire community. It does not change easily, but it can change. It is external to the thing itself, but use and tradition develop characteristic notions that seem to be inherent. In ancient Greece, the aulos and the cithara were instruments employed in the worship of Dionysius and Apollo, and for the converts to Christianity in Greek lands, these sounds recalled all the rites of pagan worship in their past lives and endangered their attachment to the newly embraced Christian faith. As paganism declined, generations grew up who had never experienced pagan rites and for whom the association of instruments with sinful festivities did not exist. In time, these instruments came to be used in Christian life and even in Christian worship. In a sense, they ceased to be pagan and secular and even became sacred, because the secular and pagan associations were no longer present.

One can see a similar pattern in much of the music that came to be the great corpus of Roman chant. A considerable bulk of it was derived from the folk music of the Mediterranean regions. These melodies lost their secular associations and acquired religious ones as the Church grew in influence on the lives of the people of the fifth and sixth centuries. We can see a similar thing happening in other artistic and cultural areas during those centuries also, when the Roman Empire was changing into the new Medieval order. For example, the old garments of the Roman patricians were retained as the vestments of the clergy; the very shape and structure of the Christian church building was borrowed from the ancient basilica which was originally a secular edifice, a law court or market; the political nomenclature of the ancient empire was accepted by the Church as she organized her dioceses, provinces, and prefectures, or sent out her legates and nuncios; the faldstool, the chalice itself, the bishop's garb, the use of the statues, mosaics and painting, were all found in pagan and secular culture. But as the Church spread and grew, connections that many things had with paganism and secular uses were forgotten, and they became fitting aids to Christian living and worship.

Through the Middle Ages, there seems to have been little concern for a distinction between the sacred and the secular. Today, we cannot easily detect the difference between the melodies of the troubadours and the *trouvères* and those melodies employed as hymns and sequences unless we examine the text, which we will see is a most important factor in determining if a piece is to be labeled as sacred or not. Even when Pope John XXII spoke out so strongly in the constitution, *Docta sanctorum*, in 1324, he was not so concerned about secular influences as he was with the proper use of the church modes, the intelligibility of the texts, and the general dignity of the service which he felt had been endangered by the novelties of the *Ars Nova*.

The early Renaissance period found no problem in employing profane sources – *chansons,* madrigals, *lieder* – for a *cantus prius factus* of a Mass composition, and even in entitling the work from the secular sources to identify its origins. These were not exceptionally profane or secular times. On the contrary, in addition to the fact that the secular connotations of a *chanson* or a madrigal *cantus* were lost in the complexities of contrapuntal treatment, we must remember that the times were such that religion was still strong in its influence on life and thus the sacred was able to absorb the secular. Only when the Catholic Faith began to weaken under the stress of the Protestant Reformation do we have this device of using a secular *cantus* for a religious composition forbidden by the Council of Trent. The composers indeed continued to write a *Missa sine nomine* where the secular *cantus* was still used but not identified, but no one objected because the association of the melodies with secular sources was not made.

The second point of our consideration is that when the Catholic Faith and religion are strong, the danger of the secular engulfing the sacred is much less, and thus we experience little outcry against the secular. Without repeating the history of each age, it should suffice to say that this was true in the early Middle Ages as instrumental music came to be adopted into the liturgy. The pipe organ, for example, was in its origin a secular instrument, but in the high Middle Ages it was so regularly found as a part of the church furniture that it became the sacred instrument *par excellence*. In the fourth, fifth and sixth centuries, the chant absorbed a great bulk of the Mediterranean folk music, as Christianity became an all-powerful element in European life. Throughout the Middle Ages, the sacred pervaded all life and dominated its secular aspects in every sphere. What we possess of Medieval music, painting, sculpture, and architecture demonstrates this again and again.

In music, the serious and lasting dichotomy between the sacred and the secular that we know today dates from the beginning of the baroque era, the early seventeenth century. It was then that the split in musical style between sacred and secular began, which led to the gradual decay of church music, a decline that musicians for the past one hundred years have been trying to arrest. The baroque era was very concerned with and conscious of style. The unity of style that had characterized the music of the Middle Ages and the Renaissance was lost when the new devices for the expression of the affections of the baroque were applied to the music of the Church as soon as they appeared in secular forms, particularly opera. They were judged by some to be unfitting for the music of worship. These new techniques were essentially devices for displaying the so-called affections through music. They were thought to be undignified and unworthy in connection with the sacred texts of the liturgy. Thus began the creation of a particular sacred style after the manner of Palestrina's compositions, a style of writing set aside as a sacred music. The new developments in composition were generally relegated to non-church music and were therefore considered all the more secular and unfitting for church use. The Church herself was on the defensive against the reformers, and the sacred was under attack also. It could no longer absorb and assimilate the secular. Thus, in the early 17th century, the very problem that afflicts us today was born, and we live to a great degree under the influences of the 17th century. We cannot easily push aside in a short time what has grown and become ingrained for nearly four hundred years.

To repeat, then, we can say that in times of great Christian strength and influences, secular music has been absorbed into the Church's life and worship without fear of secularization or profanation, but when the Faith declined in influence, great concern is shown for the dangers involved in such a process.

But is there any real distinction between sacred and secular in music? Is there something essentially sacred in a church style? Are certain melodies, rhythms or harmonies by their very nature holy or sacred and others secular and profane? Music is music; of itself it is neither sacred or secular, just as mathematics is neither sacred nor secular. But by association, by connotation, the consent of society, or the practice of the community, certain devices, harmonies, or rhythms – in a word, a certain style of composition and performance – has come to be called secular and another style sacred. In studies on the psychology of music, this is referred to by the term "connotation" or the "result of associations made between some aspect of the musical organization and extra musical experience."

Training and experience are necessary to establish such connotations, and once established they are hard to overcome. They are not merely individual, personal associations, but the common experience of a whole cultural group. We all know the difficulties involved in determining the emotions expressed by most Oriental music that we hear; we are unconditioned by experience or study to know if it is sad or joyous, religious or secular. Music in itself is not a language of absolute terms of communication. It differs from spoken language where sounds have absolute meanings agreed upon by the whole community. To express descriptive ideas, music must be dependent on outside means –words, pictures or onomatopoeic effects. Of itself it can convey only what experience and training have come to associate with certain sounds or devices. Thus we arrive at certain notions of what music for church should be by association and experience from our very earliest days. Some associations are entirely traditional. The pipe organ, for example, for the peoples of western culture is associated with church and evokes attitudes of piety, religion and faith. This is not true of the Oriental who lacks such experience. For him the gong, on the other hand, is a common sound lacking the westerners' connotation of the mysterious and the exotic.

Associations can develop and can cease to exist also. Life is constantly forming new connotations in everyone. Some ages have consciously developed a system of elaborate connotative devices in their music. By means of melodic, rhythmic or harmonic techniques, certain emotional states or even symbolic ideas have been expressed. The *leitmotiv* of Wagner or his pseudo-religious atmosphere created by shimmering strings and modal melodies are examples of such efforts. The baroque era, also, cultivated the use of dissonance to express the emotions contained in words such as "sigh" or "suffer" or "die." We today also have connotative music as the score of any film will demonstrate. We easily recognize the associations achieved by military music, by cowboy music, by the soap-opera theme played on an electronic organ, or the night at sea or a storm or a hundred other well-established musical devices that depict a scene or evoke an idea. And we have some ideas also about what we think is sacred music and what is not.

For times of great religious faith, we tend to say that the secular music of that age sounds like religious music, but for times of lesser faith and religious influence we tend to say that the religious music sounds secular. For example, the 16th century madrigals, performed without their texts, approach so closely to the motet writing of the same period that we might think of them as sacred. But the Mozart Masses remind us of his operas, only because the operas are better known to us. Had it been a different age, we would say that the operas sounded like Masses and the motets like madrigals.

Thus, there is nothing in the music itself – even in complicated rhythms – that by nature is sacred or secular. It is the connotation that makes the difference, and in a secular-dominated society, church music must beware of being submerged by these secular connotations.

But, to ask the question again, how do we determine a sacred composition from a secular one? There is a certain priority to be followed in judging. First, if the composition has a text, and if the text is sacred, coming from biblical, liturgical or pious sources, then one can say that it is a sacred piece. That does not mean that it is a good piece. Plenty of compositions with sacred texts are junk, unworthy of performance for any purpose. They are not good art and thus they have no place in God's worship or even for man's entertainment. They offend both.

If the composition has no text, then it is the style and the form that will help make a determination. What is the form employed by the composer? Is it a march or a dance? Or is it a symphony or perhaps a church sonata? Mozart's epistle sonatas are surely church music, even though the style employed is the same as he uses for his other works. *"Dove sono"* from the *Marriage of Figaro* is the same melody as Mozart used for the *"Agnus Dei"* in the *Coronation Mass.* One is considered a secular aria and the other a sacred, liturgical piece. Here the text is basic for the judgment. In the epistle sonatas, intended to be played during the silent reading of the Epistle at Mass in the old Tridentine rite, the purpose of the composer determined the decision to create a sacred composition.

Thus, the purpose of the composer is important in making a judgment. So is the experience of the audience. What does it connote to them? The famous hymn, *"O Esca Viatorum,"* is set to the melody harmonized by Heinrich Isaac as a German *lied*, *"Innsbruck, ich muss dich lassen,"* written as the composer was forced to leave that beautiful Alpine city when the court of Maximillian whom he served was departing for Vienna. Or the very religious tune that is so often sung as an *"Ave Maria,"* Jacob Arcadelt wrote as a *chanson*, *"Nous coyons que les hommes."* Liszt produced the *contrafactum.* He put the sacred words to the *chanson.* And there are many more pieces that one age used and loved as secular *chansons, lieder* or ballads that today we sing and love as religious hymns or motets. Thus the purpose is important, but so is the connotation.

How about style? We are conscious of this element today, a remnant of the baroque era when the break occurred and the *stile antiqua* and the *stile moderna* came into existence. The *prima prattica* and the *secunda prattica* set up a distinction between what was for church and what was for the theater and concert hall. It did not take long for the composers to grasp that the new devices in which they were especially interested could be used only in the theater, if they were to adhere to the distinction. As a result, the greater composers wrote very little for church, since they were not interested in merely imitating an earlier style. Those great composers who did write rather extensively for the Church wrote in their own style, making no distinction between the two. Thus Mozart wrote in a unified style: opera, symphony or Mass. Haydn, Beethoven and Schubert too. They distinguished the sacred and the secular through the purpose and by the sacred text. As we can look back at those years, it is only the music of those who practiced a unified technique that is considered today to be great art. The imitators, who used only the *stile antiqua* and the *prima prattica*, are not known today because of their church works. Both the great and the not-so-great wrote "sacred" music, but while "style" may have set it aside as "sacred," it was usually not of artistic significance, since it was too much of an imitation of the past. The greater composers used the style of their time, a unified style of their own, and determined a piece to be sacred by the text or by the purpose for which it was composed.

Another interesting point in the problem of sacred and secular is the question of performance. It is true that much sacred music was written for concert performance.

Surely all non-Latin texts were excluded from Roman Catholic liturgical use until the Second Vatican Council. The oratorio, the religious opera, *laudi*, and spiritual madrigals, for example, were intended for concert performance. But what about the Masses, Vespers, passions and spiritual concertos, church sonatas, trios and other choral and instrumental compositions? If their purpose was to adorn the liturgy, then in moving them to the secular setting of the concert hall are we not violating their very nature, the very purpose of the composer? Is not doing that, to some extent similar to moving the opera or the symphonic poem into the church service? We seem to have the problem of the sacred and the secular, but in a reverse arrangement. Connected closely with the place of performance is the very reason for composing or performing sacred music. Haydn wrote for the glory of God, *ad majorem Dei gloriam*. Liturgical music must be performed for that purpose. Secular music exists for the glory of man, his entertainment, his adulation and exaltation. That is why we can applaud for a concert, but applause in church for a liturgical performance is totally out of place. The distinction remains between sacred and secular: in composition, in performance, in purpose, in the very place in which it is done and in the manner in which it is received. Even in the manner of performance. A Haydn Mass, sung in a concert, crowds all the movements together in a short half-hour, the *Kyrie, Gloria, Credo, Sanctus-Benedictus* and *Agnus Dei* all following immediately on each other. In a performance within the Mass, in the manner intended by the composer, the parts are separated by time and by other music. It is not a concert piece, but an integral part of a liturgical action.

Still another area in which the distinction between sacred and secular impinges on the musician is the debate today about the use of sacred music in concerts in the public school, particularly around Christmas time. Surely it is the text that most often determines the sacred nature of a composition. Still, even an orchestra or band director has programming problems if he or she considers a medley of pieces that have become closely associated with certain sacred texts. Further, there are pieces written not for religious or liturgical use, but rather as a part of the secular observance of Christmas, for which the purpose of the composer should determine the nature of the piece; but can one truly separate the secular and the sacred nature of Christmas? In fact, can one really separate the secular and sacred parts of life? Of history? Of music?

The answer is, of course, no. It is, in fact, the very reason for the debate between sacred and secular. It has gone on from the beginning and will continue until the end. Some try to secularize our society, but our history and culture point the other way. Our very nature, created in God's image as the *Book of Genesis* says, is both spiritual and material, religious and worldly, sacred and secular. Thus we always express that in every facet of life, and not least, it is shown in our art, that expression of life that Dante called "God's grandchild"; since He made us His children and art is our child. The most that we can do is to recognize that music can be both sacred or secular. To deny that fact is failure to cope with reality. Then we must find means to determine which is which, not an easy task. Our tools for the decision rest first on the text, if there is one; secondly, on the purpose of the composer; thirdly, on the style of composition employed; fourthly, on the place in which it is to be performed and the musical forces to be employed.

Finally, we must never confuse the issue of sacred and artistic. Not all sacred music is, by any measure, artistic. Because a piece has a sacred text it is not necessarily good music or worthy of performance. As musicians, we must choose only those compositions that are good music. Then we may proceed to judge if they are sacred or secular. As church musicians we must then choose the sacred and truly fulfill the two requirements requested by the Vatican Council: sacred and artistic.

Monsignor Richard J. Schuler
(*Sacred Music*, Vol. 112, no. 2, Summer 1985, p. 8-12)

The Sacred

This paper was given at the Church Music Symposium
Christendom College, Front Royal, Virginia,
June 17-22, 1997

For more than twenty-five years, in this country, since the close of the Second Vatican Council, we have witnessed a disintegration of the Roman Catholic liturgy, a decline in church attendance, and a general erosion of the Faith, seen clearly by a drop in ordination to the priesthood, vocations to the religious life and the numbers of children and youth under instruction in Catholic schools. One logically asks what is the cause. Why has this happened?

Some erroneously would like to say that it is the result of the changes ordered by the conciliar Fathers. Others attribute it to a maturing of American Catholics who do not need the previous practices. Others deny that there is any problem and hail the present situation as a great success.

All of these are out of touch with reality. The general observer can see a falling off of Catholic life. Note the recent surveys of Mass attendance and the statistics on Catholic school enrollment. The facts are undeniable. We are part of a waning church, a disintegrating community, an eroding faith. And we must ask why.

My thesis is that the concept of "sacred" has been eliminated from Catholic life and practice. With such a denial, the corresponding reverence, which is the normal attitude in the presence of the sacred, has disappeared. All the arts which are sacred have suffered, not least sacred music. I would like to investigate the concept of "sacred," its existence and its essence, and its role in liturgical worship, especially in music.

We can begin by looking at ourselves. The union within man of the spiritual and the material – his body and his soul – is one of the mysteries of human life. The centuries are filled with philosophers and saints who by word and by act have attempted to reconcile the dichotomy. Manicheans, Iconoclasts and Puritans dot the records of Christian history in one-sided efforts to adjust the physical and the spiritual, just as Hedonists, Materialists and Humanists have falsely moved in an opposite direction. Only the Incarnation of the Second Person of the Blessed Trinity can provide the solution. Christ alone is the "light that illumines every man who comes into this world." In Him, the spiritual and the material, indeed the divine and the human, unite in perfect balance.

When God created man and all things, He saw that they were good. Every creature reflects the Creator who is Goodness. But man, through his gift of free will, brought disorder into creation, and his Original Sin continues to affect not only himself but all the created universe, which "groans and travails in pain," as Saint Paul says. The disharmony that man experiences within himself between the material and the spiritual extends to his relationship with the rest of earthly creation, which is material, and with his Creator, Who is a spirit. And even after the Resurrection, redeemed creation, rejoicing in the grace of Christ's victory over sin, bears the scars of Adam's fall. Burdened with the effects of Original Sin and yet still destined for an eternity in heaven, redeemed man has found the material world around him, and even within him, to be both his greatest friend and his worst enemy, his tool for salvation and his means of perdition, the reflection of the Creator and the lure of Satan. But since God made all things good, it can only be in man's misuse of these things that they become evil for him.

Man's noblest use of God's creation is art. In a sense, he here shares in God's creative power, for as God made man to His own image, so man in turn makes his art in the image of his own being or the world that surrounds him. Dante says that art is God's grandchild, the child of His child.

Unfortunately, human art shares in human weakness: Original Sin touched all of creation. Art, like the artist, is subject to death and sin. "Rapt of its own beauty, it can take itself for God," just as Adam and Eve desired to do. Nevertheless, God in His wisdom chose to use art in His relationship with man. He spoke to man in poetry through the prophets of the Old Testament; He inspired the song of the psalmist; He prescribed the architectural details for the building of the Ark, the Tabernacle, and the Temple; and He endowed man with an artistic spirit in imitation of His own creativity. Christ, too, came into close association with human art. He loved the beauty of the Temple; He preached in the literary forms and with the imagery of Jewish literature; He sang the canticles and the psalms and the hymns; He knew the choral and instrumental music and the sacred dance of the Temple.

Truly, art has been God's tool in dealing with man. Through it, He has materialized the spiritual and spiritualized the material. By art, the Infinite has been shown to the finite, the Creator to the creature, the Timeless to the temporal. God has been made known to man through the medium of matter in its noblest form. The Word was made flesh and His glory was made known, full of grace and truth. Indeed, the supreme art of the Father is the human nature of Jesus Christ.

But if art is God's tool in coming to man, so too must it be man's means of reaching God. Creation exists for the glory of God, and true art has its fulfillment only when it corresponds to the general purpose of all creation – the glory of God. (How right Joseph Haydn was to mark *Ad majorem Dei gloriam* at the top of his musical compositions!) Art, however, can fail in that purpose. It may be created only to give glory to man, or it may indeed be intended to give glory to Satan. But, as in all creation, evil lies in the perverse will of man, not in the creatures themselves. When an artist is able to make his medium reflect the beauty of the Creator and become a sign of eternal Beauty, then art is capable of lifting man, through God's grace, even into the life of the Trinity Itself. Art thus participates in the sacramental activity of the Church, but even when its effect is supernatural, it remains always a natural tool of religion. The harmony, truth and goodness of God seem to shine forth in it, and man is thereby attached to the reality that is represented here in matter. Man in that way experiences "the sacred."

On the other hand, art may fail to bring man to God. This results when the techniques and laws of the artistic discipline are absent or violated, or when the artist lacks the faith that sees in his work the reflection of the creativity of God Himself. In the first case, what is produced is not even true art, because nothing can substitute for a natural talent or for the training of that talent. This is salient, and perhaps it can be more quickly appreciated with reference to the practical arts than with the fine arts. Surely we are quick to detect the incompetency of a plumber or a TV repair man who does not have command of his craft. Actually, much of what may attempt to pass as art today is lacking in the basic requirements of the very discipline involved, and thus it does not even fall into the category of art. It cannot, therefore, bring man to God, since the false cannot achieve the True.

Pope Pius XII in his encyclical, *Musicae sacrae disciplina*, emphasized the need of these two basic requisites in an artist who will create true religious or sacred art: he must possess skill in the techniques of his discipline and he must have that faith in God which will give him the interior vision needed to perceive what God's majesty and worship demand. When either is lacking, the result is not satisfactory. The artist without faith cannot bring others to God, since no one can give what he does not himself possess. It may be true, of course, that subjectively one might be greatly moved by a work of an artist lacking that faith in God and seem to find in it a transcendental quality that reflects the Creator, when in reality such is not present. It is in this very fact that the danger of art for religion lies, and it is here that Satan can use art as a lure for man. On the other hand, a man who has great faith but lacks talent or skill or training in the techniques of his chosen medium can produce only a sham, since all the good will in the world will not make an artist. The work of art that the Church seeks will come from the trained and talented craftsman who has a vision of faith, is humble before the creativity of God in which he shares, and who has conceived in the depths of his soul a concept that he expresses in the material, but in which shines forth the majesty of God.

Pius XII tells us that the true work of art, secular or sacred, must be judged by the ultimate purpose of all creation, the glory of God. Theories of art or aesthetics do not determine the success of art. The successful artist must create something appropriate to the glory of God but at the same time capable of touching the soul of man. Religion must express itself, so that the spiritual can be made manifest; the invisible, visible; the unheard, audible. Christ is the mediator Who binds the material to the spiritual. He, the handiwork of the Father, is the bridge-builder, and human art in its way imitates and reflects Christ. It too, then, is a bridge-builder between the Creator and the creature.

The early Church was wary of art because of its connections and associations with pagan worship. There was always a degree of distrust of art in religion. Art is a danger to religion when it attempts to replace religion or substitute for it. Religion becomes a danger to art, when it attempts to regulate its inherent disciplines. But each needs the other: religion to inspire art to its highest expression; art to be the means of externalizing the spirit and truth of religion, the means of creating the "sacred" in human experience.

Art can be secular or sacred, depending on its purpose. Secular art exists to imitate nature, to entertain, to inspire, to create moods, to rouse passions, to engrandize man. It may have a hundred different purposes. Sacred art, on the other hand, as the Vatican Council has recalled, exists to glorify God and to edify the faithful. Art is true to itself when it fulfills its purpose. If its purpose is in accord with the eternal law of God, it is morally good; if it exists for an evil purpose, it is evil. The work of art itself is not evil; its purpose may make it evil. Such is Satanic art, or art intended to arouse the passions needlessly or promote eroticism.

Modern art has been almost totally secular; time alone will be its judge. If it fulfills its purpose and follows its own laws and nature, one may well affirm its value. But modern religious art in general has not been successful. In too many cases, contemporary attempts in nearly all the media have failed because the artist has lacked the techniques necessary for a proper handling of the materials to be dealt with: sound, paint, stone, wood, words. In other cases, the very purpose of sacred art has been wanting; the artist, even when he is a trained craftsman, cannot bring man to God if he himself lacks the necessary faith. The Middle Ages reached God through art; they have been called the ages of faith. The music, architecture, paintings and sculpture of those centuries still call forth in men's souls an enormous response toward God, as anyone who has entered the cathedrals of Chartres or Cologne or Amiens will attest.

In a practical way, the liturgical reform called for by the Fathers of the Vatican Council has so far failed because artists have failed. Liturgy, more than any other religious experience, needs to use the material. Its very purpose is to praise God by raising the minds and hearts of the faithful, through material things, to the Creator. This is accomplished only by the trained artist whose faith inspires him to create. When we survey the efforts of the past twenty-five years, one can only conclude that one or the other or both of these requisites is missing. Where is the sacred art in the translations into English? Do they transcend the material and carry man with their beauty toward the Creator? And the musical efforts, often produced by well-meaning amateurs who are totally unprepared to deal with the techniques of the art, fail to move the minds and hearts of believing and worshipping men. Where is the art that can serve to bring man to God in churches that have been whitewashed and made to resemble Puritan meeting halls? What has become of the art of sculpture or painting as handmaidens of worship?

Music that man makes for man is rightly and quite logically music for his entertainment, at whatever level of competency or sophistication it may exist. But music created and performed for the glory of God and the sanctification of the faithful demands quite different standards for judgment. Indeed, dignity, reverence and beauty are imperative for music directed to God, and when they are lacking in sacred art, it has not fulfilled its purpose. The denial of the sacred, or the substitution of the secular for the sacred, is the logical sequel that flows from humanism, the exaltation of man instead of God. "Sacred" by definition means the setting aside of something for the exclusive use of the Deity, particularly in the worship of the Deity. Something that is secular is what is employed for the daily use of man. Both are good; both are created by God; both indeed share in the effects of the Incarnation; both have perfectly legitimate purposes in man's life and salvation. But by common agreement, every society sets aside persons, places and things, including forms of art, that are pledged to the end of serving it in the endless effort to reach God. Obviously, these things are material for the most part, and they are closely connected with the senses of man, but through their sacralization, their sacramentalization and even their supernaturalization they are elevated to the highest possible level in man's relationship with God. Reverence, dignity and beauty will characterize these material things selected for such use, because man must seek the highest forms of expression of which he is capable in turning toward his God; his art provides that excellence and that perfection. It is sacred.

But when man assumes the place of God in the liturgy by an exalted humanism, the need for the sacred ceases. The need to dedicate material things to God by sacralizing them, even the need for the sacraments or the acknowledgment of the supernatural elevation of man through grace, ceases. The secular fulfills the purpose of humanism as well, if not better, than the sacred. Man has not then a need of God, and we have come to a kind of "practical atheism" which will never solve the eternal quest that man has to reach his Creator.

What must we do? What do we need? Everyone, not just the painter, the musician, the liturgical artist, but everyone must take part in finding again the path to God by means of the sacred. The Fathers of the Second Vatican Council envisioned a blossoming of holiness, and the liturgy was to be the chief source of that life. Liturgy is closely associated with art; music, indeed, is an integral part of liturgy. Liturgy is dependent on sacred art, and our relationship with God is dependent on liturgy. What, then, do we need to come to God and to holiness?

First, we need beauty of place. Our churches must not be mere meeting halls, stripped of all sculpture and painting, stained glass and rich vestments. The art employed must not be esoteric and so *avant-garde* that it is not easily grasped or appreciated. At the same time, it must be true art and not "kitsch." It must not be present as a kind of aestheticism but as a true servant of liturgy, made holy by its association with sacred ritual. The building and its appurtenances must inspire awe and reverence, a feeling of the presence of God, the first step in one's quest for Him. It must be a sacred place, set aside from the ugliness of the worldly, even removed from the goodness of every day life. While all that is used is material, the end result is the producing of an effect on the spirit.

Secondly, we need a beauty of movement within the holy place. Dignity, reverence, order and purpose must mark the sacred action. Celebrant, ministers, altar boys and all who participate must reflect the reason for the rite. It must be more than the creating of community; it must be greater than assembly of God's people to manifest love of each other. The purpose of the sacred rite must be the glory of God and the manifestation of man's continuing efforts to reach Him by giving Him all that the human race has, its best and greatest achievements. Over-familiarity, slovenliness, carelessness, the tawdry, the cheap, novelty and the secular have no place. What the chosen people knew about the conduct of the rites in the Temple in Jerusalem and what the era between the Council of Trent and our day should teach us is the mystical importance of the traditional, the ancient and the mysterious in ritual actions. The dignity of the Roman rite was assured through the careful observance of its rubrics and the use of the Latin language; the loss of dignity, reverence, order and even purpose can so easily be achieved by so-called "creativity" exercised by someone who lacks the requirements needed to produce true art.

Thirdly, we need beauty in sound, the sound of vocal and instrumental music, of church bells, of the voice of the lector and the cantor and the congregation. The iconoclasm following the Council banned from the liturgy the great art of the past by abandoning the Latin language to which church music has been inseparably united and by disbanding the musical organizations capable of performing it. In place of art music came a kind of do-it-yourself product that was unreasonably demanding of congregations incapable of any such effort. Congregational singing for the most part has been a failure, chiefly because more was demanded than the people are capable of. Choirs have disappeared, even when not intentionally disbanded, because the value of much of our contemporary composition has been so inferior that they have not found it worthwhile to continue. To revive choral singing in our churches will take many years and much prejudice has to be overcome first. But until art music, both in Latin and in the vernacular, is again fostered, our people will lack a means of grace that can bring them to God more effectively than any other liturgical art. Music is said to be an integral part of the liturgy; liturgical music is liturgy, and it must be worthy of so holy a thing. It cannot be music that is not quickly grasped or that belongs only to the initiated. The beauty of sacred music must be apparent and the text it adorns must be clearly understood. All styles that are true art are admitted if they are found to be effective and useful, but it requires competent artists to perform them. Listening is active participation just as singing is too. All take part in sacred music, both those who hear and those who sing or play. Very often it is the one who can listen who is moved to the highest degree of prayer, because he does not have to turn his attention to the demands of performance. He can afford the leisure that is needed to raise his heart to God in contemplation, inspired by the beauty of the sound that the artist has created for that very purpose.

The liturgy of earth is but a faint reflection of the liturgy of heaven, carried out by the choirs of angels and the saints of every class. It is the adoration of the Lamb, seated at the right hand of the

Father, in union with the Holy Spirit. Dante in his *Paradiso* describes it as the unfolding of the petals of a rose, while the great processions of the apostles, the martyrs, the confessors and the virgins move before the enthroned presence of the Blessed Virgin Mary. That liturgy is ceaselessly celebrated and is only palely reflected here on earth. The sacred art we employ is only a sensitive, prophetic anticipation of that glory which will one day outshine and overwhelm all human art and make it superfluous.

Monsignor Richard J. Schuler
(*Sacred Music*, Vol. 124, no. 2, Summer 1997, p. 12-16)

Sacred Music and the Liturgical Year

The church calendar, or the liturgical year, is a sacramental, i.e., it is a sign of a deeper reality and it is a means of grace. The deeper reality is the very life of Christ as it is relived by the Church, year after year until the end of time, for Christ is with us as He Himself told us He would be. The Church, the Mystical Body of Christ, is indeed the very Person of Christ living on for each succeeding generation, inviting us to live His life which He presents to us in the liturgy, especially in the Mass.

In Advent, by sacred sign, particularly through sacred texts, the Church offers us the centuries of waiting for the Messiah. The use of purple vestments, the absence of flowers on the altar, the silence of the organ and other musical instruments, and above all the words of the prophets foretelling the Incarnation – all teach us and move us to prepare to enter the redemptive action of the God-Man. His birth at Christmas, His manifestation at Epiphany, His life of mercy and wisdom during Lent, His suffering and death and resurrection in the Holy Triduum of Easter time carry us through to the glory of His ascension and the coming of the Holy Spirit at Pentecost. Then follow the many weeks that are a sign of His continuing life in this world, His living in the Church down through the centuries until the *parousia*. Then we return to begin again at Advent.

The life of the Christian must be pre-eminently the life of Christ, since it is only through Him that salvation can be achieved. Since Christ lives in His Church and the Church is indeed the very Person of Christ, then salvation can be found only through the Church. That life of the Church, the life of Christ, is presented to us chiefly in the liturgy, which Pope Pius X called the "primary and indispensible source of divine life." It is in the liturgy that we touch Him, "and grace goes out from Him." The liturgy is the representation of Christ's life and it is given to us by its annual sacramental renewal of the events that constituted His life in this world. They are the grace-producing mysteries that effect the redemption of the entire race from Adam to the end of time. The sacrament, which the liturgy is, employs sacred texts, sacred music, sacred signs, sacred ceremonies and sacred ministers. Most basic of all are the texts, which for centuries have made up the Mass and the various hours of prayer, most of which are from the Scriptures and some from the writings and works of the saints, the Fathers and Doctors of the Church. Selected for specific times of the liturgical year, they bear the burden of representing the mysteries being offered to us. The very Word of God brings to us the sanctifying grace of the mystery being commemorated. Adorned by music, proclaimed in a sacred setting, received by the people who are present, these sacred rites again join us to Christ re-enacting His redeeming life.

How close the church musician comes to all this! The opening words of Chapter VI of the *Constitution on the Sacred Liturgy* from the Second Vatican Council emphasize this:

> The musical tradition of the universal Church is a treasure of inestimable value, greater even than that of any other art. The main reason for this pre-eminence is that, as a combination of sacred music and words, it forms a necessary or integral part of the solemn liturgy.

But church musicians in this country have all but abandoned the liturgical year. Two practices war against the understanding and use of the liturgical year. One is the widespread custom of singing four hymns at Mass, replacing the texts of the liturgy, those Proper parts of the Mass in which the identity of the feast or season is particularly exposed. The other is the growing introduction of the so-called "general anthem," a composition with a very neutral text, some suitable for observances as far apart as Christmas and Easter.

The musical capabilities of most American congregations is minimal. Because very early in the reform, singing was declared to be the primary and foremost method of participation in the liturgy, music capable of congregational performance had to be found. The hymn was selected, and it replaced the Proper texts of Entrance Antiphon, Offertory and Communion pieces. Hymn texts were not intended to establish the liturgical season or set the tone for the feast, which are the function of the Proper liturgical texts. Given the limited selection of hymns in most missalettes, the church musician very quickly found problems. All the Sundays became alike and the seasons became indistinguishable. The liturgical year was taken away; grace was lost; the sameness of every Sunday produced a boredom that certainly has some connection with the decline in Sunday Mass attendance.

The general anthem is a boon for music publishers. It opens a market that can well include Roman Catholics, Jews and Protestants. Examine the texts of these compositions. No truly Christian theme or doctrine is stated. Texts from the Old Testament abound, worthy of use for nearly every occasion. Texts such as "Alleluia," "Praise the Lord," "Sing a New Song," "God is Love" are surely acceptable, but the church musician who uses these frequently can set aside the whole liturgical year for his congregation. Many times, too, the texts for the general anthems are not from Scripture or liturgical sources as the Council demanded them to be.

Composers will write the music that the Church wants. Publishers will offer the music that they can sell. The liturgists have indicated that the texts of the Ordinary of the Mass (*Kyrie, Gloria, Credo, Sanctus-Benedictus, Agnus Dei*) are not what they want or recommend for us. Thus we do not see new settings for these ancient texts that every generation but our own has set to its particular musical idiom. The texts of the Proper of the Mass (Introit, Gradual, Tract, Alleluia, Offertory, Communion and the Responsorial Psalm) are likewise forgotten by the composers, even though immediately after the close of the Council several efforts were mounted to set the Responsorial Psalms to music for both congregation and choir. With the Proper text replaced by hymns or general anthems, the liturgical year cannot be discerned. Every Mass and every season has become the same.

This certainly is not the wish of the Council. A whole chapter of the *Constitution on the Sacred Liturgy* is given over to the liturgical year. It is an essential element of the life of the Church, the sharing in Christ's life, the growth in grace that comes from the Mass and the sacraments. Church musicians should not be an obstacle to God's grace, to participation in the work of salvation, or to the sharing of the sacramental system through the reliving of Christ's life. We must work against the "four hymns," and the "general anthem" by restoring the use of the Ordinary and Proper texts of the Mass. If we want them, the composers will provide and the publishers will happily sell them to us.

Monsignor Richard J. Schuler
(*Sacred Music*, Vol. 118, no. 3, Fall 1991, p. 5-6)

Humanism and the Sacred

"The primary goal of all (Eucharistic) celebration is to make a humanly attractive experience." This is the statement of the Music Advisory Board of the American Bishops' Committee on the Liturgy, issued in 1968. And this is the expression of the real malady causing the deterioration of sacred music that is apparent on all sides in our country today.

Pope Paul VI has warned so often that the sin of our age is one of atheism, not indeed a theoretical, academic denial of God, but rather a *removal* of God from life in its everyday, actual practice. Man has put himself into God's place, and thus he has no real need for God any more. Man has himself become God, and little wonder then that we have "God is dead" theologians.

The evidences of this are numerous, and we need not turn to the marvels of technology to find the reasons for man's pride. Strangely enough in this "age of the moon," it is not the astronauts who would deny God's role in human life, but knowingly or not, those who would consider themselves most in His service. Let us observe only the reformers of the liturgy, where one might expect to find expression of man's dependence on his Creator, acknowledgment of his own sinfulness, and hope in a life of eternal happiness in heaven.

In many subtle ways, one can see the exaltation of man. Someone has pointed out that the Canon of the Mass in Latin begins with the word *Te* (*You*), but in its English translation, it begins with the word *We*. Elaborating its statement on the purpose of the Mass, the Music Advisory Board says:

"We assemble at Mass in order to speak our faith over again in community and, by speaking it, to renew and deepen it." One looks here in vain for God's saving grace, for any acknowledgment of the four great ends of all prayer: adoration, thanksgiving, reparation and petition. Indeed, can we ourselves directly increase any supernatural virtue in ourselves, if they are gifts of God, Who alone can give them or increase them?

Or again, for example, we can examine the whole effort to turn the altar *versus populum*, something that one can search the documents of the Vatican Council and not find even a reference to. It is an exaltation of man by thrusting the face and the person of the *man* who is a priest into the place of the *alter Christus*, whose face one does not need to see. With the celebrant facing the people, the human element is so greatly exaggerated with all the facial and bodily gestures which necessarily attract the attention of the congregation toward a certain, particular man who stands there, not toward an *alter Christus*, a priest who is Christ. Even Father Jungmann, to whose credit a great responsibility for the turning around of altars can be given, now says that he has second thoughts on its pastoral advantage; there never was any historical or artistic basis for such a "reform."

And again, consider the current insistence on the educational dimensions of the liturgy. A kind of rationalism, a form of humanism, it demands that every single word be immediately understood, which is perfectly logical if liturgy is man-directed, but not really a total necessity when liturgy is God-centered and the general ends of prayer are grasped. And, so too, with music. If the purpose of any art in the service of worship is to give glory to God and to sanctify the faithful, then dignity, beauty and reverence are imperative marks of such art, for sacred art would not fulfill its very purpose if it lacked any of these characteristics. But let one make the purpose of art and music in liturgy be rather the "creating of a humanly attractive experience" and immediately both art and music descend to the level quite logically of music for his entertainment, at whatever level of competency or sophistication it may exist. But music created and performed for the glory of God and the sanctification of the faithful demands quite different standards for judgment. One can easily grasp that the present use of so-called folk music and various forms of instrumental combos within the liturgy is nothing more than entertainment by merely attending such a service. One who does not attend can reach the same conclusion by simply noting how often such musical presentations must be changed, indicating that in a short time they bore the audience, who is no longer entertained by them. Like any show, they must be constantly "updated" or "renewed."

Humanism is at the root of the trouble in our liturgy today. How can an art that is dedicated *Ad majorem Dei gloriam* exist when man has replaced God, when a "humanly attractive experience" becomes its purpose for being?

One cannot, of course, deny that man is master of his universe and the center of his own activity in his world, even in his efforts to reach God. But one must hasten to point out that the world and all that is in it, together with all man's efforts and talents, have been raised up through the Incarnation to a supernatural level as they share in the redemptive grace of Christ. All of these created and redeemed materials, talents and efforts, however, must be used to carry us beyond matter to God the Father, who "dwells in light inaccessible," as Saint Paul says.

Art is the product of both the spirit and the body of man, and it can lead him to God. Indeed, art can sometimes lead him away from God, when it is not true art, for Satan can sometimes use material things in artistic garb to lead us astray. But when art is true and noble and directed toward God, man can expect that through it, he will reach Him. But when art is aimed only toward man, then even if it be true and beautiful, it will not serve as a means of reaching Him. Rather, ultimately, man will flounder in his own materialism; he will seek art for art's sake; he will turn to it for his own glorification.

The denial of the sacred, or the substitution of the secular for the sacred, is the logical sequel coupled to humanism. Sacred by definition means the setting aside of something for the exclusive use of the Deity, particularly in the worship of the Deity. Something that is secular is what is employed for the daily use of man. Both are good; both are created by God; both indeed share in the effects of the Incarnation; both have perfectly legitimate purposes in man's life and salvation. But by common agreement, every society sets aside persons, places and things, including forms of art, that are pledged to the end of serving it in the endless effort of reaching God. Obviously these things are material for the most part, and they are closely connected with the senses of man, but through their sacralization, their sacramentalization and even their supernaturalization, they are elevated to the highest possible level in man's relationship with God. Reverence, dignity and beauty will characterize these material things selected for such use, because man must seek the highest forms of expression of which he is capable in turning toward his God; his art provides that excellence and that perfection.

But when man assumes the place of God in the liturgy by an

exalted humanism, the need for the sacred ceases. The need to dedicate material things to God by sacralizing them, even the need for the sacraments or the acknowledgment of the supernatural elevation of man through grace, ceases. The secular fulfills the purposes of humanism as well, if not better, than the sacred. Man does not then need God, and we have returned to the "practical" atheism about which Pope Paul warns us.

The problems of sacred music today do not lie in selection of repertory or the encouraging of congregational participation. The disputes over Latin and the vernacular, the choir, the use of various instruments besides the organ are not the essential points. The problems are not musical; these, musicians could solve. It is not a question of composers or performers or even of money to encourage them. The problem is one of Faith, as it is in every other area of the Church today – Catholic education, religious vocations, celibacy for the clergy, birth control, or the authority of the Holy Father.

As early as during the preparation for the Fifth International Church Music Congress in 1965, one could see that there were those who would deny the existence of the sacred or the place of sacred music in the liturgy, despite the clear statement of the Vatican Council itself that sacred song forms a necessary or integral part of the solemn liturgy. Both the Pope and the Council frequently refer to "sacred" music, and the *Instruction* of 1967 begins with the very words, *Musica sacra*. The malady that afflicts the Church today was first seen in the liturgy and in sacred music. But it is apparent by now that what ails music in the service of worship is only a ripple on the surface of the sea; beneath there is a churning, seething, boiling ferment of error and disbelief. We will never have a renewal of sacred music without Faith; we will never have sacred music at all until the place of man in relation to God is clearly established. There will be no sacred music until the place of art in man's seeking God is defined and the affirmation of the sacred in art is maintained.

Atheism is the sin of our day. The music of our day has become its tool by abandoning its sacred function. The secular forms of art will never serve for worship of God, but they will continue to exalt man, as they have always done throughout human history. If we seek only man and place him at the center of a life restricted to time and to earth, then we have indeed found through art the proper means of exalting, entertaining and even worshiping him. But if we wish to obey the Vatican Council in its efforts to renew sacred music and to continue two thousand years of Christian teaching, then we must restore God to the center of our worship, re-establish the position of the sacred arts as a means of communication with God, and fall on our knees in belief, in hope and in love before the Creator, the Redeemer and the Sanctifier of sinful man, who comes to us through material things – things that man through art has dedicated to Him as sacred.

Monsignor Richard J. Schuler
(*Sacred Music*, Vol. 96, no. 4, Winter 1969, p. 3-6)

The Attack on the Church Musician

Almost as old as the sacrament of Holy Orders itself, and almost as venerable in the service of the Church, the role of church musician goes back to the beginning of Christian times, and indeed, before that, for the musician played a great role in the Jewish synagogue and in the Temple of Jerusalem. Music has always been intimately connected with the worship of God in both Christian and non-Christian communities. The composition and the performance of music as part of the divine service produced some of the greatest musicians to be found in the entire history of the musical art. The choirmaster and organist and cantor were persons of distinction and authority in their communities, learned in their art, respected in their professional positions. They served in the courts of emperors, kings, dukes, popes and bishops. They worked in cathedrals, in churches of great size and in chapels that were not so large. The musician knew his role and strove to fulfill it. Truly, Heaven must be filled with saints who came to that celestial reward for their earthly service of and loyalty to the Church in the apostolate of music. Pope Pius X promised them the reward of the apostles for their faithful work in the service of the Church.

But for the past thirty years, since the close of the Second Vatican Council, the church musician has been under attack, chiefly by some who have claimed to be fulfilling the decrees and demands of the conciliar Fathers. But nowhere in any of the documents given to the world by the Second Vatican Council can one find the cause of what has befallen the art of music and its place in the sacred liturgy. Far from ordering what has happened, the Council clearly praised and extolled music, declaring it *pars integrans in liturgia sacra*. It proclaimed sacred music to be "a treasure of inestimable value, greater even than that of any other art." It ordered that "the norms and precepts of ecclesiastical tradition and discipline" be maintained. It repeated the age-old purpose of sacred music, which is the "glory of God and the sanctification of the faithful."

Then who has destroyed our choirs? Who has imposed on us the claptrap that today is heard in our churches? Who has denied the sacred and introduced all manner of secular compositions into the liturgy? Who has forbidden the use of music with Latin texts? Who has replaced the pipe organ, held in so high esteem by the Council, with instruments never intended for use in church? Who has taken over the selection of music to be used in church and reduced the choirmaster to a subordinate role? Who has in fact disregarded the solemn decrees of the Council on music and in their place set up standards and practices quite contrary to the "norms and precepts of ecclesiastical tradition and discipline" ordered by the Council?

What has happened to the role of organist? Where are the musicians of professional level who once served the Church along with their work in secular schools of music? Where today can one go to study serious church music, including Gregorian chant? Why is it not possible to hear chant, the style of music given primacy of place by the Council, in our seminaries, abbeys and motherhouses? In our cathedrals and parish churches?

In a word, why has the Council not been put into practice in the United States? Why instead is there open and widespread disobedience to clear orders from the Council Fathers and the documents that came from Rome following the close of the Council?

Clearly there was a conspiracy to destroy the sacred. This effort was already present in the days of the Council. An attack on the *Missa Romana cantata* was launched then, but it did not succeed in getting its way into the conciliar document, the *Constitution on the Sacred Liturgy, Sacrosanctum concilium.* Again in 1967, when the *Instruction on the Implementation of the Constitution on the Sacred Liturgy* was issued with the title, *Musicam sacram*, there was bitter opposition to the use of the word "sacred." There is certainly a connection between this denial of the sacred and the efforts promoting the secularization of the world. But liturgy by its very nature demands that persons, places and things be set aside for use in the worship of God, things that thereby become "sacred" or set apart. The Catholic Church is a sacramental religion, using all of the beauty of God's creation, in every art, to bring glory to God by employing only the best and highest examples of God's creation and man's art.

The Roman Mass for centuries was hailed as the greatest

expression of divine worship, using every art to manifest externally man's adoration of God: music, painting, architecture, literature, silver and gold craft, and sculpture among many more. Why should this be attacked? What for centuries attracted converts to the Church, what was hailed by non-Catholics as the glory of Catholicism, what filled the pages of art and music history books, what both the peasant and the scholar knew and loved – why was it swept away?

This catastrophe following the Council, which was so filled with hope to bring the liturgical renewal begun in the mid-nineteenth century to full bloom, occurred in many countries at the same time. The same errors and novelties appeared simultaneously in Germany, France, the United States and several other lands, and from there soon to be spread over the whole world. The first stirrings of this movement can be detected at the Fifth International Church Music Congress which met in Chicago-Milwaukee in 1966. (See "A Chronicle of the Reform" in *Sacred Music*, Vol. 109, No. 1, 2, 3, 4 [1982] and Vol. 110, No. 1, 2, 3 [1983]). They were not musical problems that were surfacing at the first international meeting of church musicians following the close of the Council, but much deeper theological issues, including a denial of the sacred. Musicians could have coped with musical questions, but they were not what was troubling the Church.

Pope Paul VI himself referred to the "smoke of Satan" coming into the Church. It was not only in music and liturgy that the attack on the Church was launched. Education, the religious orders, catechetics, seminaries, the priesthood, theology, morality, indeed every area of church life was subjected to the same desacralization process. And always the destruction was proclaimed in the name of the Council or in the "spirit of the Council." One is led to the question, if there was indeed a conspiracy, where was it organized and from where was it controlled? It is not politically correct today to suggest the influence of Satan in the world, but clearly it is present and cannot be denied. Attacks on the Church and her sacred liturgy are to be expected.

To destroy the liturgy, which Pope Pius X said is the chief source of the spiritual life, would be the first target in any effort to destroy the Church. How many Catholics no longer attend Mass? How many receive the Holy Eucharist unworthily because they have been taught that there is no longer any serious sin? What percentage of the fifty million so-called Catholics in the United States today are lapsed and non-practicing? It is not just the loss of our ancient heritage of liturgical music that we mourn. It is the loss of souls that have suffered from being deprived of the source of supernatural life and who have been truly driven out of their spiritual home by what has been foisted on them wrongly as the reformed Liturgy ordered by the Vatican Council.

What should we do? As church musicians we have always done as the Church has asked. Obedience to our pastors was a hallmark of the true Catholic musician. We considered the liturgy and the rubrics to be sacred and to be carried out as the Church ordered. But today demands are being made of musicians that lead us astray from the path ordered by the Church. We can no longer acquiesce. We must fight for the truth as ordered by the Church, especially as it is clearly taught in the documents of the Council. We can no longer be dominated and intimidated by the liturgists who promote the secularism of the age, whose study of the liturgy is peripheral and even erroneous, who at best are ignorant and at worst inimical toward the Church, the liturgy, sacred music, the art of music and the conciliar reforms.

Too often in the past, the musician has just quietly retired, or in a stronger word, quit. Now we must take a stand and speak openly. It is not too late. Expose the errors, object to the abuses, proclaim the truth, stop supporting the pseudo-composers and the venal publishers who have no care for the sacred liturgy and its music. We have fallen into the hands of the *piccolomini*, the "little people," who are not trained for music and liturgy, who lack the knowledge and often times even the faith needed to create the true sacred music that the Church demands.

Archbishop Bugnini, the chief architect of the liturgical debacle, said that the first ten years of his reform were spent fighting the church musicians who alone withstood him. But then we quit, and what has happened is catastrophic, devastating, unbelievable. But we cannot simply bewail the state of affairs. We must renew the battle, fight and begin to rebuild. What the Church wants will ultimately come about, but we are the agents to cause it. *Ad ramos* — to the oars!

Monsignor Richard J. Schuler
(*Sacred Music*, Vol. 119, no. 4, Winter 1992, p. 3-5)

The Training of a Church Musician

Only when the goal is clear can the proper course be charted. An uncertain trumpet cannot proclaim an advance. So, too, with the preparation necessary for any trade or profession, when the goal is doubtful, the means are not effective.

The Church in our time has suffered from a decline in the numbers of young men entering the priesthood. Among the chief causes of the problem is a confusion among theologians about the very nature of the priesthood. When the *terminus ad quem* is not readily and clearly understood, the *via* toward it will be uncharted and few will set out, and many of those who begin will falter and fail to arrive at the end. If the priesthood is not the intimate sharing of a man in the life and action of Jesus Christ Himself, so that the priest acts *in persona Christi*, then who will assume the sacrifices inherent in preparation for it or continue throughout life in its practice?

And to a lesser degree, one might say the same for the church musician, who in a certain sense also has a vocation. Just what music for the Church should be today quickly provokes debate, anger and a great display of ignorance, even after the extensive treatment of the subject by the Second Vatican Council, which accorded a greater exposition on the subject of music for worship than ever before given by an ecumenical Council. As there is a shortage of those preparing for the priesthood, so there is a shortage of young persons seriously preparing for professional service as church musicians: composers, directors, performers both vocal and instrumental. Why? The end is disputed; the way is uncertain; the future questionable.

Never before has the opportunity been greater for prospective church musicians in this country. Times are affluent, when compared to previous decades; the conciliar documents have declared the position of sacred music to be *pars integrans in liturgia*, giving it a security never before enjoyed; a freedom for composing and performing has been assured by the Council; the official position of the Church has never before given such encouragement to sacred music. But why has so little of value developed since the Council, and, in fact, why has church music declined and even decayed in the last quarter century?

Why? Because it is not certain today just what church music is. What is sacred? What is art? For some, church music is hymn singing. For others it is the folk group, the combo and the guitar. For others it is a sweet and sentimental vocal or instrumental performance, mood music, like piped-in elevator sounds, intended mostly to cover noise, without any real value in itself.

True, hymns are part of music for worship, but in no way do they constitute the total treasury of sacred music that the Council speaks of or history records. The instruments used in today's combos hardly constitute the complement of instruments fittingly used in the Roman liturgy during the centuries of its development. Sacred music is not necessarily soft or sweet, prepared to be "seen but not heard."

The scope of the repertory we identify as church music is vast, covering centuries, the product of many nations, wed to many languages, composed by the greatest musicians of human history, making up the proudest heritage of the human race. It is both instrumental and vocal; it embraces a multitude of forms; it displays a variety of styles; it is truly an ecumenical art, finding a purpose in many religions and sects; when good and true, and therefore sacred and artistic, it constitutes the noblest of man's work, because its purpose is so high: the glory of God and the edification of the faithful.

With such characteristics, why do so few undertake to study and practice church music? Chiefly because so few know what it truly is. When the end is unknown, who will seek it? Education in church music begins in the home as all Christian instruction does. What parents inculcate at an early age begins the direction that the youngster will follow. Then come the primary grades in school where the earliest efforts are made to participate with others in the liturgy. As good music is introduced to the elementary and high school students, the proper understanding of the value of the artistic and the sacred is taught. An appreciation for the good and, ultimately, a desire for the beautiful will be a great treasure for students so fortunate as to be exposed to correct music for worship. It is the reward of good teaching and liturgical direction by qualified and dedicated teachers. All Catholics should be brought to understand and to appreciate the treasury of church music, both by performing it and by listening to its performance. The Council clearly directs that the treasury of sacred music be known and fostered by all.

In time, if God has given a special musical talent, a student who finds an attraction to liturgical music will seek to perfect the talent through study. Private instrumental lessons, membership in parish or community or school choral groups, and eventually formal training in college will bring him into a professional position as performer, composer or director. Such talent needs sound, professional training, both theoretical and practical. The basic undergraduate college music major course is essential for the training of a church musician who plans to make his life work the service of the Church.

Beyond the B.A. degree, for those who would seek positions of importance (cathedrals, seminaries and larger churches), graduate work in church music should be undertaken. It should be a furthering of instrumental and vocal techniques, further study in composition and theory, and especially a deepening of knowledge of the history of music and liturgy.

But where can this be done? About twenty-five years ago, this matter was discussed by the Bishops' Advisory Board on Music. Since the Vatican Council called for opportunities for such advanced musical and liturgical study, the American Bishops were anxious to supply such a need. I was asked to present some ideas on the graduate education of a church musician who could return to his diocese and further the implementation of the decrees of the Council in the parishes and schools. The program envisioned by the Council was clear and within the reach of everyone.

I was asked how I thought this could be implemented in the United States. I replied that the establishment of a new graduate school of church music, as some desired, was an expensive and impractical idea in the 1960s. The very assembly of a distinguished faculty, the cost of a building, the funds for expensive musical equipment and library, all showed that the solution to the Council's call for education on a superior level did not lie in the establishment of a new school of music. A better program would be to use the existing excellent schools of music in this country: Juilliard, Eastman, Curtis, Indiana, Michigan, California, among others, where graduate study of the highest quality was already organized. The establishment of an endowed chair of Catholic church music in several of these schools would be a solution to the problem of training well-qualified graduate students. Those who finished the course of study would be recipients of valued and respected degrees. The cost of such a program would be much less than that involved in establishing and maintaining a separate graduate school of church music. An endowed chair of church music and the assurance of a certain number of students with grants to cover their education would certainly be of interest to four or five graduate schools. With a master's or doctor's degree, musicians from a variety of collegiate backgrounds, occupying positions in major churches and schools in dioceses and religious communities spread across the country, the work of advancing the role of music as an integral part of the liturgy could be achieved. A salary commensurate with the musician's academic preparation would assure the Church that there would be no shortage of church musicians, well-trained and properly prepared.

The training of those responsible for the making of music is the basic element of success in carrying out the wishes of the Council Fathers on every level within the Church. Without it, we will continue as we have been going for the past twenty-five years – downwards.

Every institution knows that its success as well as its future depends on the training of its leaders. Church musicians need preparation. Just as with candidates for the priesthood, preparation is imperative, but those providing that preparation must know what are its goals in order to present the means toward the end. When the goal is uncertain, the preparation will be inadequate and the candidates few and inferior.

Monsignor Richard J. Schuler
(*Sacred Music*, Vol. 117, no. 3, Fall 1990, p. 18-20)

Preparation of the Diocesan Clergy in Church Music

Paper delivered at the Sixth International
Church Music Congress, Salzburg.

If this paper had been prepared for the Fourth International Church Music Congress in Cologne or even for the Fifth Congress in Chicago-Milwaukee, it would have taken an entirely different direction than at present. In 1961 or in 1966, one would have dealt with the renewal and improvement of the training of seminarians in the field of church music. However, unfortunately and tragically, in 1974 we must speak not of renewal but rather of a beginning, a re-introduction of a program to teach the seminarian the role of music in the prayer life of the Church and prepare him to carry out a sung liturgy so that he can function in the role of priest.

In 1961, one could point to several Roman decrees relating to the subject of liturgical music training for the candidate for the priesthood. There was the *motu proprio* of Pius X of 1903; the various *Instruction*s issued for the seminaries and religious houses of the city of Rome; the *Apostolic Constitution* of Pius XI (although very brief in its reference to seminaries); the encyclicals *Mediator Dei* (1953) and *Musicae sacrae disciplina* (1955). To be sure, these documents were very general and really did little to specify what even the most fundamental requirements should be. The candidate was to study music, both in its Gregorian and polyphonic forms; he was to learn hymns for use with the people; music was to be a means of prayer for himself and a tool for use in his apostolate. But compared to the detailed courses of instruction issued by secular educational agencies, these guidelines were far from adequate or specific. Nevertheless, one could say that *poco a poco*, progress in the musical education of the clergy was evident in 1961, even yet in 1966. Bishops were more willing to consider the subject seriously; seminary authorities were more ready to cooperate in giving time for musical instruction, although it was far from being considered a major area of study; more and more, the men assigned to roles as teachers of music in seminaries had been provided with higher studies in preparation for their work, although, in most cases, far from adequately.

Yet, in 1961 and in 1966, one could safely have said that the music reforms of Pius X had not been effectively accomplished. The reason for that failure lies with the lack of proper instruction musically of the clergy. The reason for this lack of instruction of the clergy can be traced to the failure of the seminaries to give adequate training to their students. And one can easily assign the chief reason for that: the teachers of music in most seminaries training the diocesan clergy were woefully uninstructed and lamentably deficient themselves in musical knowledge and method. *Nemo dat quod non habet.* Still at that juncture, 1966, one might have hoped for a continuing progress, a gradual brightening, even perhaps the dawning of a new age, as the impetus of conciliar decrees on church music forced action in this area of priestly training.

However, in 1974, we know that this is not the case. Today the picture is far gloomier than it was a decade ago, even perhaps than it was when Pius X began his pontificate in 1903. We still have the Roman *Instructions* from the pre-conciliar days, and in addition we have received others: the *Constitution on the Sacred Liturgy*; the *Instruction on Music in the Liturgy* in 1967; the comprehensive *Instruction on the Liturgical Formation of Seminarians* given by the Sacred Congregation of Seminaries and Universities in December, 1965. Why is it, then, that even with these further directives from the highest authority in the Church, the situation has so far deteriorated that even the minimal training in the forms of music ordered by the Council has almost disappeared in many seminaries? Two reasons can, I think, be advanced to explain this situation. First, there exists a general disrespect for authority in society, and this is reflected in the Church where an attitude can be detected that regards Roman documents as mere opinions to be read and set aside if they are not in agreement with one's own particular viewpoint. Perhaps the events that followed the issuing of the encyclical *Humanae vitae* promoted the opposition to authority within the Church to a great degree. Secondly, the widespread denial of the sacred, as it pertains to the means of worship, has upset the very position of sacred music as an integral part of liturgy, despite clear affirmations of the Council to the contrary.

It is evident that lack of respect for ecclesiastical authority and the denial of the sacred are not problems peculiar to church music and the training of seminarians. These phenomena are to be found through the whole Church and must be dealt with directly before it will be possible to renew the musical formation of diocesan seminarians and to implement the conciliar liturgical and musical reforms.

I. Let us consider the problem of the sacred. In 1968, the Music Advisory Board of the American Bishops' Committee on the Liturgy issued a statement in which it was proclaimed that "the primary goal of all Eucharistic celebration is to make a humanly attractive experience." Here is the expression of the malady that is causing the deterioration of the sacred. Human pleasure is the ultimate goal to be achieved. Liturgy no longer deals with the relationship between man and God, but rather that of man to man or even to oneself. Pope Paul VI has warned repeatedly that the sin of our age is one of atheism, not indeed a theoretical, academic denial of God, but rather a removal of God from life in its every day, actual practice. Man has put himself into God's place, and thus he has no real need for God any more. Man has himself become God, and little wonder then that we have "God is dead" theologians. How can sacred art exist in such a milieu, when the very purpose of sacred art is to lead us to God, who "dwells in light inaccessible"? This denial of the sacred as it exists in a person, a place or a thing exclusively dedicated to God, follows logically on the enthronement of man. Such humanism leads to secularism.

For those who have allowed the secular to replace the sacred, "God is dead." When man, in a sense, assumes the place of God in the liturgy by an exaggerated humanism, then the need for the sacred ceases. The need to dedicate material things to God by sacralizing them, even the need for the sacraments or the acknowledgment of the supernatural elevation of man through grace, ceases. The secular fulfills the purposes of humanism as well as, if not better, than the sacred. This would account for those who say that the duty of church music is to establish "community" or "togetherness" – both humanistic ideals. But when man does not feel a need for God, we have returned to the "practical" atheism about which Pope Paul warned us.

The problem today in the musical and liturgical training of seminarians is not essentially a musical one. If it were, musicians could solve it. The difficulty is one of faith, as it is in every other area of the Church today – Catholic education, religious vocations, celibacy of the clergy, divorce, birth control, or the authority of the Holy Father. It is useless to speak of a course of study for music in the seminary until the seminary and its professors are convinced of the fundamental truths of the Roman Catholic Faith. Sacred music cannot live, nor can liturgy itself survive, in a milieu that not merely questions but often denies what is Catholic dogma and morality under a thin veil of speculative, process theologizing. At least in the United States, seminaries have been in the forefront in promoting much that has led to a secularization of Catholicism. Comment on this is well expressed in a book, *American and Catholic* by Robert Leckie (New York: Doubleday and Co., 1970):

> Montesquieu once predicted that Protestantism would wither away, after which Catholicism would become Protestant. Bearing this in mind, recalling also how liberal Protestantism's attempt to Christianize secularism resulted in a secularization of Protestantism, it may be suggested that in its new emphasis on the social gospel, in its preoccupation with sex, its dissolving discipline, its abdication of moral authority and its own attempt to accommodate modernity, the American Church has already taken on much of the protective coloration of its environment. It is now thoroughly American, apparently riding the crest of the religious wave of the future, but whether or not it will still be Catholic remains to be seen.

As early as the preparations for the Fifth International Church Music Congress in 1965, one could see that there were those who would deny the existence of the sacred and the place of sacred music in the liturgy, despite the clear statement of the Vatican Council itself that sacred song forms a necessary or integral part of the solemn liturgy. Both the Pope and the Council frequently refer to "sacred" music, and the *Instruction* of 1967 actually begins with the words, *Musica sacra.* The malady that afflicts the Church today was first detected in sacred music and liturgy. But it is apparent by now that what ails music in the service of worship is only a ripple on the surface of the sea; beneath there is a churning, seething, boiling ferment of error and disbelief.

We will never have a renewal of sacred music without faith; we will never have sacred music at all until the place of man in relation to God is established clearly. There will be no sacred music until the place of art in man's seeking for God is defined. There must be an affirmation of the sacred, and this must begin in the seminaries.

II. But what is taught today in our seminaries? One cannot here take up what are the specific problems of the courses in dogmatic or moral theology, nor can one argue here about the questions of seminary discipline or the life patterns of clerical students. While all of this impinges directly on the liturgical and musical formation, there is not time to consider it. However, two areas must be discussed: the prayer life of the seminarian himself, and the tools that he must acquire for the apostolate that will ultimately be his as a priest.

First, his prayer life. Obviously this must begin long before the major seminary. In the home and in the elementary school a sense of reverence toward what is holy must be cultivated. By participating in the parish liturgy, the future seminarian can come to have a love of divine worship and an acquaintance with the means of worship: music, ceremonial, art, architecture – not merely as external phenomena but as the expression of the deep internal action of the baptized Christian taking part in the redeeming mysteries of Christ's Church. In the development of religious vocations, the contact with the holy and the beautiful is essential. By experiencing the sacred, the seed of a priestly vocation is planted. The deeper theological and ascetical foundations of a flourishing prayer life should be taught in the seminary, but even then the liturgy remains the primary source of all spiritual life, as Pope Saint Pius X said. A full and active participation in the liturgy demands on the part of the seminarian an ability to take his proper active role in the liturgical life of the seminary: to sing, to read, to fulfill the functions of the ministry or order according to the rank that he has achieved. To deprive him of training to sing or to read or to know the very role of sacred art in liturgy is to restrict him in his prayer life which should be centered in the liturgy as the primary source of grace. Seminaries that have abandoned Gregorian chant, the solemn Mass and the sung Office are hindering, not fostering, the development of the spiritual growth of their students.

Recently, a seminarian came to me to ask if he might take part in the solemn Mass on Sundays in my parish, because his seminary did not have a sung Mass. He was attracted by the ceremony and the music that stirred up within him a love for the sacrifice of the Mass. It is sad that in the institution that is training him to be a priest he cannot find what is the very essence of priestly work, the performance of the sacred, solemn liturgical action. Other seminarians have not even heard of what it is that they are missing. In such a training ground, can one expect to find a deep spiritual growth? It is not the mere specialist in modern thought or social welfare workers that a seminary is commissioned to prepare; the first obligation is to establish holiness upon which to build all else. Liturgy and sacred music are essential for this development.

Secondly, liturgy and sacred music are the tools of the future apostolate of the cleric. So much is written and spoken today about "special ministries." We have attempts such as the worker-priest, the priest-politician, the priest-sociologist, and all manner of secular gimmicks that do not achieve the true purpose of priesthood which is to stand as mediator between God and man, offering the perfect sacrifice to atone for sin. The real ministry lies in the liturgy with the art that serves as its handmaid. The sacred liturgy has attracted the human spirit for centuries and will today continue to exercise the same magnetic pull on men if its truly sacred character is allowed to shine forth. The redeeming action of Christ which is the essence of the liturgy needs external, visible and tangible means of expression. That central, transcendental, spiritual and sacred purpose of the Mass and the sacraments which Christ left us is to bring the fruits of His Redemption to each succeeding generation. The ceremonies, music, painting, architecture and all the other arts that surround the central kernel are the Church's means for presenting these mysteries of Redemption; they are the tools of the apostolate of the priest. To deprive a priest of a knowledge of these tools with their power to attract mankind and their significance as symbols transcending this world is like training a physician without teaching him the use and the value of medicine.

It is essential that the young cleric be taught to sing those parts of the liturgy required of the ministry or order he possesses; further, he should be given an appreciation of the role of sacred music in liturgy and a respect for the work of the professional church musician; beyond this, the seminary has an obligation to provide him with a sufficient knowledge of music in general that he may find in music a source of recreation and pleasure as it is expected an educated man will do. Recently, I had a fine young priest tell me that he could not and would not sing. He refuses to celebrate a *Missa cantata* or sing any service. I asked him if he had not been taught music during his six years in the preparatory seminary and another six years in one of the important major seminaries of the United States. He told me that he had not been trained to sing, but that he had been given instruction in how to direct the congregation or a choir! This, of course, reflects the level of competency of the instruction to which he was subjected; but it also shows how he has been cheated and how the people to whom he ministers have likewise been cheated out of one of the means of God's grace – the solemn liturgical actions which demand liturgical singing from the priest.

No one has ever proposed a training of clerics as professional musicians, except in those extraordinary cases when exceptional talents are discovered and a diocese has the good fortune to have a young priest whose gifts can be developed in order that he might instruct others. Most people can be taught to sing or play an instrument without having a special musical talent; long and intense study is not demanded for ordinary musical achievement, either vocal or instrumental. But musical training is imperative for the young cleric so that he can undertake his proper role in the liturgy, appreciate the roles of others, whether singers, instrumentalists or directors, and then oversee the general direction of the sacred liturgy in his charge, with a knowledge of its theology, its history and its art. A training in these minimal fundamentals should be given every student; he has a right, in justice, to it.

Connected essentially to the study of liturgical music is a knowledge of the Latin language. Seminaries that do not foster the study and use of Latin are promoting a kind of iconoclasm directed against the heritage of sacred music that the Council ordered to be promoted. There seems to be little doubt that the abandoning of Latin in direct disobedience to the decrees of the Council is connected closely with the decline of the sacred. Some weeks ago I invited a young deacon to exercise his newly acquired Order at a solemn Mass in my parish. The choirmaster came in before the ceremonies to inquire concerning what *Ite missa est* the young man wished to sing.

He did not know what the *Ite* was, and said that he would sing only in English. He had been taught nothing about Latin chant. Young priests today have been systematically and deliberately trained to despise the Latin tongue and all that has been associated with it for centuries, theologically and artistically.

III. Priestly vocations today in many countries are on the decline. The shortage of priests in some areas is becoming critical. Seminaries are depleted and many have even closed because of lack of students. Could the condition be caused by the abandoning of the sacred? Is it perhaps that the substitution of so many humanistic and secularist concerns has failed to attract the young who truly are seeking God? Religion is the sum of all doctrine, institutions, customs and ceremonies through which the human community expresses and organizes its relationship with the Creator. Subjectively, religion is an inclination of the whole man toward a transcendental Creator in Whom he believes, to Whom he feels obligated, on Whom he depends, and with Whom he tries to communicate. Man's need for outward communication with God results in his use of art in religion. Religion must express itself, so that the spiritual can be made manifest; the invisible, visible; the unheard, audible. Thus religion needs art for teaching, for missionary purposes, for its very existence. Is not the Word made flesh the perfect art of the Father, the most perfect revelation of God's glory and the center of all Christian religion? He is the Mediator which binds the material to the spiritual. Human art in its way imitates and reflects Christ; it is the bridge between Creator and creature. Is not the abandoning of the traditional Christian art in its musical, pictorial and sculptured forms, coupled with the failure of so much of modern art which has left its sacred connections, to be seen as one of the reasons for emptying our seminaries – indeed, emptying of the ranks of the priesthood too?

The young are looking for religious experience, but they fail to find it in the secular, humanistic forms now offered them. Some even say that drugs become a means of spiritual elevation as the young strive almost wildly and yet vainly to escape the material things that have surfeited them. Eroticism, drugs, and the restlessness of contemporary society only more deeply submerge man in matter rather than freeing him from it, so that his spirit might soar toward his Creator. It is only in such freedom of the spirit that a vocation can be nurtured; in the proper use of matter and in particular by the sanctifying of the material through sacred art, the souls of the young can be attracted to God and to His priesthood.

Monsignor Richard J. Schuler
(*Sacred Music*, Vol. 101, no. 3, Fall 1974, p. 3-8)

Where Are We Now With Sacred Music in the Parish?

> "The kingdom of heaven is like a mustard seed that a
> person took and sowed in a field. It is the smallest of
> all the seeds, yet when full-grown it is the largest of
> plants. It becomes a large bush, and the birds of the
> sky come and dwell in its branches." (*Matthew* 13:31–32).

One could indeed describe a contemporary movement in Sacred Music and the Sacred Liturgy in the United States as one in which many birds are flocking to dwell in the branches of a fruitful bush, sprouting from the seed Our Lord sowed in the heart and mind of Monsignor Schuler, a seed which Monsignor cultivated by his patient teaching and prophetic witness.

Three important qualities of Monsignor's example and writings form the basis for this growth: fidelity to tradition and its sources, fidelity to the Church of Jesus Christ, and the building up of community based on charity and friendship.

Gregorian chant, classical polyphony, the Viennese orchestral Masses – the whole of the Church's treasury of Sacred Music throughout history enriched Monsignor's life as a Christian and as a musician, forming him to take seriously the effect of the Incarnation of Christ on this world, the source of all Christian art. By taking up human nature into hypostatic union with the Godhead in the person of Jesus Christ, the Incarnation ennobles the entire created order, making it possible for the material of this world to proclaim the world to come. As a spiritual father formed by the Church's musical tradition, Monsignor exercised a fidelity to these sources not out of an aesthetic preference – which few in his later decades shared – but because these sources were a gift handed on through the Holy Spirit's providence for His Church to be given as a birthright to every

Catholic. Monsignor knew that beautiful music, the gems of the Church's musical tradition, is an effective and important connection to God. It is capable, especially in the modern time which has become hostile to the truths of the Faith, of drawing souls to Him. This fidelity to the sources was not only musical, but woven into a whole cloth of beauty in the Sacred Liturgy, encompassing the entire artistic canon handed on by the Church. Exquisite sacred vestments and vessels, aromatic incense, well-ordered and purposeful ceremonial, artful rhetoric in preaching, the noble poetry of the *Roman Missal* in a language consecrated to the worship of God, edifying art and architecture – all the sacred arts for him combined in a symphony to bespeak the presence of the Almighty so that "while we recognize God visibly, we may be drawn by Him to love of things unseen." Being steeped in the sources of tradition, Monsignor was capable of seeing the events and artistic production of his time with clarity, compelling him to embrace that which was worthy of the worship of God and lay aside that which was lacking, handing on to his flock the richest foods and choicest wines.

This formation compelled incisive writing and an extraordinarily visionary commitment to projects which, in our current time, seem more obvious and normative, even if still not ubiquitous. The well-celebrated liturgies of St. Agnes are becoming a reality in many parishes nationwide where *scholas* chant the Proper of the Mass, build up their repertory of polyphonic masterpieces, and occasionally even mount a Mozart *Mass*. This is happening not only at celebrations of the Traditional Mass, but also at Masses celebrated in the *Novus Ordo* in use since 1970 (e.g., Saint Vincent Ferrer in New York City, the Pittsburgh Oratory of Saint Philip Neri, Saint John Cantius in Chicago, Saint John in Stamford, Connecticut, and Saint Thomas Aquinas in Palo Alto, California).

Hundreds of parishes are now regularly incorporating chanted and polyphonic Ordinaries from the Gregorian and polyphonic treasury of the Church, along with various combinations of Gregorian and vernacular-language adaptations of chant for the Proper of the Mass (e.g., the Basilica of the Assumption in Baltimore, Maryland, the Co-Cathedral of the Sacred Heart in Houston, Texas, the Cathedral of Saint John the Baptist in Savannah, Georgia, and Holy Family in Saint Louis Park, Minnesota). Saint Mark in Highlands

Ranch, Colorado, has a "Learning to Love Latin" video on their parish website! Parishes such as these usually have teams of well-trained servers, a sacristy replete with beautiful vestments, and are undertaking major renovation projects to restore the artistic beauty of buildings whitewashed in the vicissitudes of history. Classical architecture firms are being established or expanding. Ecclesiastical tailors are swamped with business. New organs are being built and dedicated, and others, abandoned by dying congregations, find new homes in churches such as Transfiguration in the Archdiocese of St. Paul and Minneapolis.

Many, many parishes are starting to hire music directors with backgrounds in organ and sacred music. Singers with fine conservatory training as well as amateurs are discovering the beauty of the Church's music as they find a home in choir lofts across the country. Cathedrals, such as in Saint Paul, Minnesota, are hiring directors who are Doctors of Musical Arts with special organ training to direct the music repertoire in those sacred spaces. In addition, some seminaries are requiring training in the Church's treasury of sacred music – how to sing the Mass, the history and principles of sacred music, etc. (for example, Saint Patrick's in Menlo Park, California, Saint Joseph's in Yonkers, New York, Kennrick-Glennon Seminary in Saint Louis).

The number of sacred music training events has exponentially expanded during the past decade, and the events are full with Catholics seeking a formation in the sources of the Church's musical treasury. The Church Music Association of America (CMAA), to which Monsignor dedicated so many of his efforts, has made available tens of thousands of pages of music and resources for free online to musicians, sparking a Renaissance of Sacred Music. More than just reprints now, the CMAA is commissioning new compositions, new repertoire and pedagogical books, and new electronic resources to make the Church's music even more accessible and possible. And the journal which Monsignor edited, *Sacred Music*, is now in its 150th volume, publishing over 300 pages of scholarly and practical articles each year. Other organizations have been founded to contribute to the effort in their own way, such as Corpus Christi Watershed, the Catholic Institute of Sacred Music, the Benedict XVI Institute for Sacred Music and Divine Worship, and Southeastern Sacred Music.

Monsignor Schuler always contextualized these sources of tradition within the heart of the Church, receiving the Church's declarations with an open heart, and interpreting the Second Vatican Council with a sense of continuity shaped by his contact with the sources. This insight allowed him to distinguish between the liturgical changes actually required by *Sacrosanctum Concilium* and the newly promulgated *editio typica* of the *Roman Missal* and those ideological trends falsely disguised as Church teaching. This was an especially important distinction that he put into practice during a time when few had access to the original Latin texts of *Sacrosanctum concilium, Musicam sacram*, and the *General Instruction of the Roman Missal.*

Monsignor's careful understanding of this issue bore fruit in the fatherly mentorship he provided to seminarians asking questions during a particularly confusing time in the life of the Church. To them, he was a harbor of safety, providing them with a place where they could continue to love the authentically Catholic traditions which were being frowned upon in some parts of the Church. In the last twelve years, this approach has been particularly nourished by the promulgation of the new translation of the *Roman Missal*, itself a product of this hermeneutic of continuity that Monsignor espoused. This edition, with the text enriched through its fidelity to the Latin original, the celebrant's Gregorian chants ably adapted to the vernacular, and with the music integrated into the main body of the *Missal* rather than relegated to an index in the back, has formed the basis for a Renaissance in seminarian musical training. It has now become normative in American seminaries for men to be trained to sing the Mass either in required coursework or electives which many choose. Too, seminary *scholas* are regularly singing the Gregorian Ordinary and Propers or vernacular-language translations and learning masterpieces of the polyphonic practice. They are playing the organ at liturgies, and singing the music of a new generation of composers writing fitting sacred choral works in a refreshed harmonic language. First Masses are filled with Gregorian Propers, the Byrd *Mass for Four Voices*, and beautifully rendered motets sung by choirs which these new priests know they need to cultivate through structural and monetary support. For them, as for Monsignor, Sacred Music is an integral part of their worship and ministry, and they know that the dignified celebration of the sacraments – especially the Mass – lies at the heart of their vocations as priests of Jesus Christ.

Fittingly, Monsignor cultivated the seed planted in his heart with charity and friendship, allowing the seed likewise to sprout in the many souls he touched during his time on earth. Even having departed this life, his work lives on, teaching us in the many excellent essays in this volume, and in the lives and work of all those he taught to love Christ through the Church and Her Sacred Music. The example of the Twin Cities Catholic Chorale, an organization forged in the bonds of this charity and through a commitment to the continuation of the Church's sacred music repertory, has been emulated by other choral organizations. Conferences like that organized in the fortieth year of the Chorale, as well as many other events, together with the connections made possible through the internet, have connected souls who share a desire to preserve the Church's Sacred Music and renew the Sacred Liturgy. Two decades ago, the community in which those working to promote truly Sacred Music was one in which almost all doing so, across the country, were known to one another. Today, the number of people laboring in the vineyard of the Lord is one in which many have found a home, and the numbers are vast and dense, rooted in all parts of the country.

Certainly there is still much work to be done, but the many branches of the seed cultivated by Monsignor Schuler are sprouting, growing daily. May it continue to increase to the glory of God!

Jennifer Donelson-Nowicka, DMA
Saint Patrick's Seminary
Menlo Park, California

Section Four

GREGORIAN CHANT
AND LATIN LITURGY

"But the Council established clearly that music is an integral part ("*pars integrans*") of liturgy; it is Liturgy. Two requirements, not new to the Council because Pius X had reiterated them, were demanded: music for the liturgy must be sacred and it must be art. All the musical styles developed through the long history of Christianity that fulfill the requirements may be used if they are found to be fitting….It is through art that man comes to God."

Monsignor Richard J. Schuler
"Saint Agnes, Sunday Morning"
Sacred Music, Vol. 114, No. 3, Fall 1987

Gregorian Chant Since the Second Vatican Council

On December 4, 1963, the Second Vatican Council promulgated its *Constitution on the Sacred Liturgy, Sacrosanctum concilium*. Chapter VI was given over to the subject of sacred music and Gregorian chant in particular. This marked the first time that an ecumenical Council of the Church turned its attention to the ancient music of the Roman Church and ordered its use and preservation worldwide.

> The Church acknowledges Gregorian chant as specially suited to the Roman liturgy; therefore, other things being equal, it should be given pride of place in liturgical services.[1]
>
> The typical edition of the books of Gregorian chant is to be completed; and a more critical edition is to be prepared of those books already published since the restoration by Saint Pius X. It is desirable also that an edition be prepared containing simpler melodies, for use in small churches.[2]

The decrees are clear. The will of the Council is that both the practical use of and the theoretical research on Gregorian melodies should progress and increase. New editions presuppose musicological work as well as practical application of the new discoveries in the publication of new editions. If ever there was to be a practical use made of theoretical musicology it was in the plan of the Council that the editions of the ancient melodies once perfected should be ever more widely performed in all parts of the world.

But what is the state of the question twenty years later? Incredibly, at this writing, the use of Gregorian chant in the liturgy of the Roman Catholic Church has almost totally disappeared.[3] Instead of developing and finding a broader acceptance in all parts of the world, almost the direct opposite of the Council's decrees has occurred. New editions have recently been published incorporating much of the research of the past seventy-five years since the chant revival began in the late nineteenth century.[4] But the practical use of these editions in liturgical celebrations in monasteries, cathedrals and parish churches has not been widespread. Rather, with very few exceptions,[5] less chant is now sung in Catholic churches than at any time in the past century.

Basic to the reason for the disappearance of chant during the past fifteen years is the demise of the Latin language in Catholic worship. Chant and Latin are inseparably connected in a union that determines the rhythm and construction of the melodies and perhaps even the modal selection as well. The Vatican Council extended the privilege to use the vernacular languages in the official Roman liturgy, while still maintaining the position of Latin as the official language of the Roman liturgy and demanding its continued use in the Mass and the Hours.

> Particular law remaining in force, the use of the Latin language is to be preserved in the Latin rites. But since the use of the mother tongue, whether in the Mass, the administration of the sacraments, or other parts of the liturgy, frequently may be of great advantage to the people, the limits of its employment may be extended. This will apply in the first place to the readings and directives, and to some of the prayers and chants, according to the regulations on this matter to be laid down separately in subsequent chapters. These norms being observed, it is for the competent territorial ecclesiastical authority mentioned in Art. 22, to decide whether, and to what extent, the vernacular language is to be used; their decrees are to be approved, that is, confirmed by the Apostolic See. And whenever it seems to be called for, this authority is to consult with bishops of neighboring regions which have the same language. Translations from the Latin text into the mother tongue intended for use in the liturgy must be approved by the competent territorial ecclesiastical authority mentioned above.[6]

> In Masses which are celebrated with the people, a suitable place may be allotted to their mother tongue. This is to

apply in the first place to readings and the "common prayer," but also, as local conditions may warrant, to those parts which pertain to the people, according to the norm laid down in Art. 36 of this *Constitution*. Nevertheless, steps should be taken so that the faithful may also be able to say or to sing together in Latin those parts of the Ordinary of the Mass which pertain to them. And whenever a more extended use of the mother tongue within the Mass appears desirable, the regulation laid down in Art. 40 of this *Constitution* is to be observed.[7]

In accordance with the centuries-old tradition of the Latin rite, the Latin language is to be retained by clerics in the Divine Office. But in individual cases the Ordinary has the power of granting the use of a vernacular translation to those clerics for whom the use of Latin constitutes a grave obstacle to their praying the Office properly.[8]

Perhaps no part of the reforms of the Vatican Council has been more often and more widely misunderstood and rejected than its decrees on Latin. On the grassroots level, most of the clergy and laity alike were victims of propaganda that convinced them that Latin was forbidden and Gregorian chant eliminated. Without reading the documents of the Council, they depended on interpretations published by those, in all countries, who wished for a variety of reasons to destroy the use of the Latin language in the liturgy.[9] With Latin gone, chant was unable to survive, especially when the same propagandists warred against the continuation of choirs and *scholae cantorum* by proposing that they are opposed to the much-desired "active participation" of the congregation.[10]

In some dioceses in the United States, local legislation prohibited celebration of Mass in Latin, a direct contradiction by a lesser law-giver of the supreme authority of the Church as vested in the ecumenical Council and the Holy See.[11] Even now it is generally thought by the rank and file Catholic that Latin is outlawed and is associated only with the liturgy as it was celebrated before the Vatican Council. It is, therefore, often thought to be connected with schismatic movements for the restoration of the old manner of celebration, often called Tridentine because of its connection with the Council of Trent. It is not clearly understood by most clergy and laity that the concession of the vernacular made in 1963 by the *Constitution on the Sacred Liturgy* of the Second Vatican Council allowed the liturgy of the old books dating to the reforms of St. Pius V in 1570 to be celebrated in the vernacular. Subsequent reforms brought about by order of Pope Paul VI could be used in either Latin or the vernacular. Thus it is wrong to equate Latin with the old pre-Vatican books and the vernacular with the conciliar reforms, but with such misinformation abroad, Gregorian chant was doomed as pre-conciliar and because of its inseparable connection with the Latin language, no longer allowed.

Some little efforts were made in the United States to adapt the chant melodies to English texts. While some modest success may have been achieved in simple, syllabic chants, the idea itself is not a valid one. To adapt melodies to words is a doubtful procedure; the melodies must adorn the words and grow out of them. Especially in English, word order and sentence structure as well as frequency of monosyllabic words at the end of sentences prevented the proper distribution of the pre-existing Gregorian *neumes* over pre-determined English texts. Both the melodies and the texts were not subject to variation or adaptation according to Church law, which made the fusion of the two impossible.

The Holy See, in response to the Council's request for an edition of simpler melodies, issued a *Graduale Simplex*,[12] a work of doubtful value artistically and of no value practically, since its Latin text was rejected by the vernacularists and attempts to set its melodies to the various vernacular languages only displayed its poverty, musically speaking. The subject of adaptation of Gregorian chant to vernacular texts was extensively explored by German musicians, who concluded several decades ago, that it is not a possible solution for Germanic tongues, English included.[13] Further study has shown that even the Romance languages do not adequately mesh with the chant. If Gregorian chant is to be fostered and used as the Council demanded, then the Latin language must be employed as the Council also demanded.

Thus, in a mere twenty years, the high hopes of those who wrote Chapter VI of the *Constitution on the Sacred Liturgy* have been brought to nothing. It was their intention that the chant renaissance begun in the nineteenth century should be brought to its fullness. The efforts of the monks of Solesmes and the Caecilian societies of the German-speaking countries had introduced the chant into the living worship of the Church. This practical activity was based on the solid musicological research of the monks and other scholars. While a practical edition was published by the Holy See in the first decades of the twentieth century, research continued, especially in the area of rhythm. Various theories of performance were suggested and argued, but that of the Solesmes monks, particularly Dom André Mocquereau and Dom Joseph Gajard, was most widely adopted internationally, even though the German monasteries and churches were less than enthusiastic about using it. Unfortunately, minute disagreements over interpretation very often resulted in squabbles that lessened the true appreciation of Gregorian chant as worship music, and some theories of rhythmic performance caused the music to become impractical for most performers because of its artificial basis and its too precious approach to performance. Nevertheless, it was widely used in many countries, especially France, Netherlands and parts of Germany.

In the United States, development was slower, since most of the clergy before the 1930s were unfamiliar with chant and sacred music in general. Only with the training of the religious Sisters and their teaching of chant in the parochial schools did it finally become more generally used and eventually reach the ranks of the younger clergy who came through the system of parochial schools. By the time of the Second Vatican Council, Gregorian chant was in use, to some extent, in nearly all parishes in this country. It was taught in the parochial schools and cultivated seriously in seminaries, novitiates and monasteries. It was ripe for the final phase of development that the Council asked for. Those who have studied Gregorian chant have learned the beauty of the melodies, which have been a continuing source of inspiration for western music since the invention of polyphony. But the attraction of chant does not lie only in its antiquity or its pure melody or its free rhythm. Its attraction today is the same as it has been during the centuries of its use: it is religious music. It calls the soul and speaks to the heart in a language that all generations understand. Chant has suffered its greatest problems in the ages of rationalism when the text was held to be of greater importance than the melody, a situation that is prevalent today. But it is precisely the purpose of the melody to accentuate the text that it adorns. Texts without melody lose their impact, while the melody itself moves the hearer to a greater appreciation of the message contained in the text.

Many today are seeking to hear those ancient melodies, not only because of an interest in their musical heritage, but as an expression of the sanctity that chant conveys to the soul. In a world seeking the transcendental, Gregorian chant speaks to many of the supernatural and eternal.

True musicological research requires opportunity for performance. Perhaps that is why the studies made during the nineteenth century, resulting in a practical edition, were so successful. The scholars were motivated by the assurance of performance. That may be why research in chant has today fallen off, despite the request of the Council for continuing study and new editions. No one is singing it, so why produce new editions and why search for discoveries that remain sterile academic information? There is much in chant research that lies ahead. Until now, so little has been done on the manuscripts deposited in the monasteries of the Danube and Rhine basins. The reconstruction of the present edition rests chiefly on French and Swiss sources. The microfilm library at Saint John's Abbey in Collegeville, Minnesota, has brought to this country the opportunity to do original study on the tradition of chant that comes from the monasteries of Austria, Hungary and the other lands of the old Habsburg monarchy.[14] There is no reason that the chants sung in the liturgy must be restricted to those published in the *Graduale Romanum*. The very preface to the 1971 edition makes it clear that there are other melodies not included that may well form fitting compositions for the liturgy. Usually this is thought to mean works of polyphonic or modern composition. It means also those chants that remain in the Medieval manuscripts that have not as yet been explored, even when the texts may differ from those presently employed in the *Missale Romanum*. In fact, the preface to the new *Graduale Romanum* makes it very clear that the musician is free to find other texts and other melodies that are fitting, artistically and liturgically. A chant revival in practical performance could open for the musicologist a great field in providing melodies for Sunday use in parish settings. One could even dream of publishers looking for Medieval chant melodies as fast-selling items in their catalogues!

This, however, depends on the Latin language, so vitally and so intimately connected to a thousand years of liturgical music, both melodic and polyphonic. It brings up also the problem of the "sacred" in music, indeed in worship itself.[15] The post-conciliar years have seen the rejection of both Latin and the sacred, and the result has been music and ceremonies that have been widely rejected because of their banality, vulgarity and shallowness. Religion (from the Latin *religere*, to bind) binds man to God, and thus the arts used in its service must provide the means for that connection, elevating the spirit and heart of the worshiper to the Divine. When these arts are "of the earth, earthy," they cease to fulfill their function and are soon rejected, even though they may have some value as entertainment. True liturgical music must be good art; it must adorn and express the text to which it is wed; it must reflect the Creator to whom it is dedicated rather than the composer and the world from which it springs. Chant does this, and as the Church constantly insists, it remains the music of worship *par excellence.*

Latin also has its role in worship, even when all texts are not immediately understood by the worshiper. Periods of rationalism have always insisted on understanding every word in liturgical texts. Yet religion appeals to more than the intellect, as is clear by the very fact that music, incense, lights, flowers, etc., all form a part of ceremonial worship. Mystery is an essential ingredient in all worship. It is provided by such means as sacred language, signs and symbols, silence and darkness, vestments, processions and many other material things that have been given a new reality by being dedicated to transcending the world about us and carrying us to the world beyond. Latin is essential to that mystery in the Roman rites. When joined with Gregorian chant, its performance attracts the soul and speaks of the God, "who dwells in light inaccessible." Its appeal to youth, even to a generation that is immersed in secular forms so far removed from what can be called sacred, demonstrates the attraction that it holds and the message that it contains.

The decrees of the Second Vatican Council are only twenty years old. The Church moves in time with its eyes on eternity. The decrees of the Council of Trent (1545-1563) were not even promulgated in France for a hundred years after the close of that Council. Implementation of many of its orders still occupies the Church in many parts of the world. Thus one cannot expect that the decrees on Gregorian chant of Vatican II will be fully implemented immediately. Often, after a Council, a period of unrest and ferment occurs during which many opposing ideas and theories find free rein, but eventually disintegrate.

Probably the reaction against Gregorian chant, Latin, art music, a transcendental liturgical celebration and the formality of the historic Roman worship will pass, and there will be a return to the mainline of historical development in which Latin and chant will again have their true place. When the will of the Council comes to pass, then that place will be a prominent one, indeed chant will have "pride of place" as ordered.

Research on the manuscripts, now easily available in this country, may some day unlock the mysteries of the free rhythm of the Gregorian melodies. Transcriptions of the thousands of melodies that still remain in manuscripts and are not a part of the official *corpus* of chant today, can open a whole new world of Gregorian melody. Western music found inspiration for compositions in the treasury of chant from the beginnings of polyphonic writing. Further inspiration awaits composers in learning more of the limitless melody that is chant. Essentially, however, Gregorian chant is worship, and it will provide many generations to come with a means of finding the God whom they seek.

Monsignor Richard J. Schuler

(*Sacred Music*, Vol. 109, no. 3, Fall 1982, p. 17-21)

NOTES

1. The *Constitution on the Sacred Liturgy, Sacrosanctum concilium*, Article 116.

2. *Ibid.*, Article 117.

3. Cf. "*Investigatio de usu linguae latinae in liturgia romana et de missa quae 'tridentina' appellari solet*," *Notitiae*, No. 185, December 1981, p. 589-611. This survey was conducted officially by the Sacred Congregation of the Sacraments and Divine Worship through a questionnaire sent to all bishops in the world in 1980.

4. For the chants of the Mass, a new *Graduale Romanum* (Abbatia Sancti Petri de Solesmis, 1974) has been issued. For the chants of the Hours, a new *antiphonale* is in preparation.

5. The survey published in *Notitiae* No. 185, records only 33 instances of occasional Masses in Gregorian chant in Africa; 13 in North America; 2 in Central America; 22 in South America; 4 in Asia, 91 occasional and 55 frequent instances in Europe; and 4 in Australia and the Islands.

6. The *Constitution on the Sacred Liturgy*, Article 36.

7. *Ibid.*, Article 54.

8. *Ibid.*, Article 101.

9. Cf. Gary K. Potter, "The Liturgy Club," *Triumph*, Vol. 3 (May 1968), p. 10-14, 37; Richard J. Schuler, "Who Killed Sacred Music," *Triumph*, Vol. 4 (March 1969), p. 21-23.

10. Cf. Richard J. Schuler, "Latin," *Sacred Music*, Vol. 107, No. 2, p. 30; "Gregorian Chant and Latin in the Seminaries," *Sacred Music*, Vol. 107, No. I, p. 3-5; Colman E. O'Neill, "Theological Meaning of '*Actuosa Participatio*' in the Liturgy," in *Sacred Music and Liturgy Reform after Vatican II* (Rome: Consociatio Internationalis Musicae Sacrae, 1969), p. 89-108.

11. Cf. *Sacred Music and Liturgy Reform after Vatican II*, p. 22-23.

12. *Graduale Simplex in usum minorum ecclesiarum*, Typis Polyglottis Vaticanis, 1967.

13. For a listing of the literature published in German on the problem of adapting Gregorian chant to the German language, see Joseph Haas, "*Gestalt and Aufgabe*," *Der Allgemeiner Cacilien Verband* (Cologne, 1961), p. 81. In English, articles have appeared on the subject: Eugène Cardine, "A Propos of a 'Translation' of Gregorian Chant," *Musicae Sacrae Ministerium*, English Edition (Rome, 1965), Vol. II, No. 1-2, p. 19-22; Urbanus Bomm, "Address Delivered during the Congress on Sacred Music held at Bressanone, May 1964," *Musicae Sacrae Ministerium*, English Edition (Rome, 1964), Vol. I, N. 2, p. 5-9; G. Wallace Woodworth, "Latin and the Vernacular: A Parallel," *Sacred Music*, Vol. 94, No. 3 (Fall 1967), p. 8-9.

14. Cf. Julian G. Plante "The Hill Monastic Manuscript Library as a Resource for Musicologists and Musicians," *Sacred Music*, Vol. 105, No. 3 (Fall 1978), p. 7-11.

15. Cf. Richard J. Schuler, "The Sacred," *Sacred Music*, Vol. 107, No. 3 (Fall 1980), p. 21-27; James Hitchcock, "The Decline of the Sacred," *Sacred Music*, Vol. 100, No. 4 (Winter 1973), p. 3-9.

Gregorian Chant and the Vernacular

Interest in using the Gregorian melodies with vernacular languages continues to surface, especially in the United States, even though in Europe the idea is no longer seriously pursued. To a certain extent, the Vatican Council itself gave impetus to such experimentation, since it ordered the preservation and use of Gregorian chant and at the same time permitted the employment of vernacular tongues in the sung liturgy. In German-speaking countries, the movement for the use of the vernacular was underway much earlier than in other lands, and experiments and studies were undertaken as early as the 1930s to use chant with German texts. Serious reports were made about the feasibility of such efforts. Johannes Hatzfeld presented a memorandum to the German Bishops' conference in 1953, indicating that the combining of the German language and the Gregorian melodies was not possible. The Allgemeiner Cäcilien Verband published a compilation of studies on the matter in 1961, before the Second Vatican Council had even convened. Such authorities as Urbanus Bomm, abbot of Maria Laach, Ernst Tittel of Vienna and Father Eugène Cardine of Solesmes repeatedly wrote and spoke against such adaptations. The new liturgical books in the vernacular with their chant melodies for English texts are proof enough of the impossibility of the process.

Two important factors are involved in this question: 1) the need to preserve intact the *corpus* of Gregorian chant in its authentic melodies; 2) the necessity of creating new, truly artistic music to adorn the new vernacular texts.

First, the scholarly research into the manuscripts containing the ancient melodies undertaken in the second half of the 19th century, which continues into the present, is one of the greatest musicological projects ever brought to completion. The work of the Solesmes monks and the several efforts of musicologists in other lands, including Peter Wagner, are hailed by all as truly significant contributions to the art of music. Their work resulted in the restoration of the Gregorian melodies and the publication of the Vatican Edition, which spread the ancient chant of the Roman Church into all nations for universal use. To protect that research and its ancient heritage, the Holy See forbade strictly any change in the official melodies, since such would be a mutilation.

Secondly, in musical composition, notes are created to adorn a given text. Texts are not manipulated to fit a melody. The melody adorns the words, grows out of them and is closely united to them by the prosody, the meter, the quantitative and qualitative characteristics of the language, the tonic accent, the sentence structure and the very organic nature of the words themselves. A melody composed to a text cannot be separated from it and applied to another text or even a translation of that text without seriously altering the original. Chant melodies were composed to Latin texts and through the centuries they have come to be reverenced in a way analogous to the reverence paid to the Holy Scriptures. To adapt them is a violation.

Attempts at adaptation have failed. Even the efforts of the Solesmes monks before the Second Vatican Council to prepare chants for the new feasts which were introduced into the liturgy were not successful, and those were attempts using Latin texts. The vernacular languages are much farther removed. The new *Graduale Romanum* has eliminated all the ersatz centonizations that have been judged not to be authentic. The preface to the revised volume clearly indicates the principle of maintaining only authentic chants and eliminating all later inventions or modifications. The melodies must be preserved intact. If new texts for new feasts are introduced into the liturgy, then new melodies in a contemporary idiom must be found to adorn them. Here is the challenge of our time and the great opportunity of each age to create a new music in its own idiom for its new liturgies.

What, then, is the solution of this problem? How is the Gregorian chant to be preserved and fostered and given primacy of place? And how are we to have music for the new vernacular texts? It is simple. The Vatican Council has given the solution. Sing the Gregorian chant in Latin, since it is the official language of the Church and its use is mandated. But create a new music for the texts of the various vernacular liturgies. In that way, we will preserve intact and use the treasure of the centuries, and at the same time, we will create a new music that is truly art and not mere imitation or adaptation. When we try to adapt texts or melodies, we have neither the ancient treasure nor do we have a new art, but only a poor imitation.

Monsignor Richard J. Schuler
(*Sacred Music*, Vol. 112, no. 2, Summer 1985, p. 3-4)

Gregorian Chant in Today's Parish

This paper was originally presented at a conference on
Gregorian semiology, June 26-28, 1988,
at California State University, Los Angeles, in cooperation
with the Huntington Library.

Gregorian chant is different from all other music. It is essentially a sacred musical language whose origins lie in earliest times. Musicologists have established its relation with ancient Jewish and Greek music as well as with the folk music of the Mediterranean basin. It is the official music of the Roman Catholic Church and serves as a means of communication between God and man, useful and viable in every age and in every land. It is not a mere musical style to be superseded in a following age, nor is it an historic relic periodically to be brought back to life for aesthetic or academic interest. It is a living language. In a word, Gregorian chant is prayer.

We might define prayer as communication with God. Traditionally, prayer has four ends: adoration of the Deity, thanksgiving for His gifts, reparation for wrongs done, and petition for all that one needs. It has many forms: it may be vocal or solely mental; it may be formalized for repeated use or created new for each occasion; it may involve sound or silence; it may be private or public; it may be social or individual; it may be official or totally personal. Its purpose, regardless of its form, remains always the same: communication with God, a communication that is personal for each man, truly a manifestation of the omnipotence and infinity of God who knows and loves each one of us individually and personally.

Man, as a rational creature, made in the very image of God, communicates with his Creator in a manner dependent on his human nature, and thus involving his intellect and his will, most always in words, certainly always in concepts or thoughts. Christian prayer must, of course, be a human act stemming from human reason and free will. Inanimate prayer is not a possible option for the Christian; we cannot admit of a prayer-wheel or other devices that purport to carry one's prayers heavenward without any truly human expression that is based in mind and will. Thus, a recording of chant played over and over is not of itself a prayer unless the listener consciously makes it such in his mind and will. Further, prayer that is truly human does not omit emotion or passion or any other faculties of the human being. Prayer stems from the heart as well as from the head, and God's communication with the one praying may reciprocate in the same fashion. The essays of the mystics, the experiences of the saints and the explanations of spiritual writers of every age attest to this variety of response on the part of God.

Pope Pius X wrote of chant as "sung prayer." Thomas Merton said that chant is the voice of Christ. It is indeed the voice of the Church. Its connection with the liturgy sets it apart as music totally different from all other. Liturgy is the communing of Christ and His Church; its language is chant. Liturgy through its language is itself an act of Christ, offering His Father all the adoration, thanksgiving, reparation and petition that He and the members of His Mystical Body, the Church, daily extend heavenward. Chant is truly prayer, sung prayer.

Chant is a musical language united intimately and essentially to a textual language. Text and melody unite to create a means of expression that surpasses the power and meaning of each alone. Truly, the sacred texts from Scripture are the word of God, but united to the sacred melodies, the expression of the text assumes a purpose and power that makes chant the Church's official means of communicating with God, the very voice of Christ giving praise to the Father. The Church has always proclaimed the inspiration of the Holy Spirit in the writing of the texts of the Bible; the piety of the Middle Ages went further to express a certain inspiration that filled the melodies as well. United, they constitute the sacred song that has "primacy of place" in worship.

The Second Vatican Council expressed that connection between the word and the melody: "... as sacred song closely bound to the text, (music) forms a necessary or integral part of the solemn liturgy." The Council, in recognizing the existence of "sacred" song, reaffirmed the tradition that God is reached through material creation and human endeavor by setting aside elements of creation for the exclusive use of the Deity and communication with Him. The sacred and the holy are related through a mysterious human and divine interaction. The sacred is often described as tremendous, or dreadful, or fascinating. Rudolph Otto calls it the "numinous." It is God's intervention in our world and the reaction of each person to that mysterious divine invitation in his becoming holy, a reflection of the Creator. By means of the sacred, a bridge is built over the horizon separating the finite and the infinite. Through the sacred, that bridge, built of the material things so designated, becomes the means whereby God's holiness is transmitted to man.

Essential to the understanding of Gregorian chant is the admission of a "sacred song." In the rejection of the "sacred," the contemporary world has rejected Gregorian chant as well. The restoration of chant depends basically on the re-establishment of the existence of the "sacred."

Scripture tells us that God "dwells in light inaccessible." He is holiness; He is sanctity. As we approach Him we reflect that holiness, and the means we use for communication with Him must share in that holiness. Those things set apart for God's worship are, therefore, called sacred, because they are the means of holiness; they are dedicated to holiness. That dedication may stem from a formal ritual blessing or from the very purpose to which the thing is put. The very purpose of something determines if it is sacred or secular. It may be a person, a place or a thing. We consider a church to be a sacred place by reason of a ritual that constitutes it as a dedicated space, a sacred temple; a cemetery is considered a sacred place because of the very use to which the land is put, the resting place of those awaiting the resurrection; a Bishop is a sacred person because he has been ordained and anointed to that end, his special vocation. The list of sacred things is almost endless. It is always through the ongoing consent of the community and the ritual action of the Church that material things are recognized as "sacred," dedicated to God, set apart for a holy purpose. It is through these sacred persons, places and things that the holiness of God is transmitted to man, who becomes holy himself by reason of his contact with God through sacred things.

Some things, particularly some styles of art, may be thought of as sacred because through connotation the community over a long period has come to accept them as such. Connotation is an association, meaning or significance which attributes certain qualities to persons, places and things over a long period of time in the minds of a great number of the community. Such qualities are not essential to the object, but merely attributed to it through long usage; they may change, but only slowly and with consent of the majority of the community. For example, in ancient Greece, the *aulos* and the *cithara* were instruments employed in the worship of Dionysius and Apollo, and for the converts to Christianity in Greek lands, these sounds recalled all the rites of pagan worship in their past lives and endangered their attachment to the newly embraced Christian faith. But as paganism declined, generations grew up who had never experienced pagan rites and for whom the association of instruments with sinful festivities did not exist. In time, these instruments came to be used in Christian life and even in Christian worship. In a sense, they ceased to be pagan and secular and even became sacred, because the secular and pagan associations were no longer present.

One can see a similar pattern in much of the music that came to be the great *corpus* of Roman chant. A considerable bulk of it was derived from the folk music of the Mediterranean regions. These melodies lost their secular associations and acquired religious connotation as the Church grew in influence on the lives of the people of the fifth and sixth centuries. We can see a similar thing happening in other artistic and cultural areas during those centuries also, when the Roman Empire was changing into the new Medieval order. For example, the old garments of the Roman patricians were retained as the vestments of the clergy; the very shape and structure of the Christian church building was borrowed from the ancient basilica which was originally a secular edifice, a law court or market; the political nomenclature of the ancient empire was accepted by the Church as she organized her dioceses, provinces, and prefectures, or sent out her legates and nuncios; the faldstool, the chalice itself, the bishop's garb, the use of statues, mosaics and painting, were all found in the pagan and secular culture. But as the Church spread and grew, connections that many things had with paganism and secular uses were forgotten, and they became fitting aids to Christian living and worship.

It was the close connection of the chant melodies with the inspired sacred biblical texts of the liturgy that established the connotation of holiness for these melodies. They, as it were, absorbed the holiness of the text, and in that relationship themselves became holy.

Chant, then, is prayer, sung prayer. It is holy through its close connection with the sacred texts. But further, it is the voice of Christ, the voice of His Church, the voice of the members of that Church, the Body of Christ. Countless decrees of the Church establish chant as its official song and give it primacy of place in worship. Truly it is the voice of the Church, the voice of Christ Himself singing through His members. Chant had its origins in folk music. Is there any wonder why the documents of the Church on music constantly demand the singing of the people, the universal use of chant for that purpose, the repeated insistence that chant is the true song of the Church and its members? Not if one remembers that chant is truly folk music.

A useful distinction exists in the German language that in English is not as clearly expressed. The Germans speak of a *musik von das volk* and a *musik fur das volk*. (Music from the people and music for the people.) True folk music is from the people, going back to undetermined origins, handed on from generation to generation, a treasure of a particular culture. That is *musik von das volk*. The other is music created at a given moment for the people in whatever context and for whatever occasion it is meant. That is *musik fur das volk*. In English, this kind of music is often described as popular music. Chant has its roots in the true folk music, not our popular music, those melodies of the people used in the Mediterranean basin in the early centuries of the Christian era. They were, for the most part, secular or even pagan in origin and intent. But union with the Christian texts soon established them as "sacred." They were artfully joined, melody and text, and in addition to their "holiness" they were also art, the best of craftmanship, which set them high above the tawdry and cheap, the inept or puerile or amateurish, characteristics of much popular music. The chant, from its origins, thus demonstrated the two essentials of liturgical music: holiness and art. It was sacred and it was artistic.

Musicologists often point out that the church music of Joseph Haydn is based on the folk music of Austria. The melodies are not of themselves holy, but associated with the sacred texts of the liturgy they become holy. In the hands of the master, Haydn, they also become art of the first quality. That is why I think the Masses of Joseph Haydn are so much like Gregorian chant, not, indeed, in style or period of composition, but rather in purpose and in technique. Even the long melismatic passages of many Masses reflect similar treatment of texts in the *jubilus* sections of the Gregorian repertory. Both chant and Haydn's sacred music find their origins in folk music which a master musician has taken and molded to sacred texts. In Gregorian chant, connotation has a longer history and thus a stronger position establishing the "sacred" sounds, while in Haydn's Masses, too little time and use has been operative to secure firmly their universal acceptance as a true music of the people, holy and artistic.

Much of what contemporary commentators label as liturgical folk music fails on every score. It is not true folk music (*musik von das volk*); rather, it should be termed popular, not folk, music; it is certainly not "sacred" because of any present connotation; it is not true art, since it usually suffers from the musical incompetence of those who create it.

In summary then, we must affirm that all men must pray, since all are bound to acknowledge the Creator. We are limited to the material world around us, of which we ourselves are a part, for that communication expressing our adoration, thanksgiving, reparation and petitions. From the dawn of time man has set apart certain created persons, places and things to carry his prayer to the Creator. Music especially has had its role from the beginning in communicating with God, probably because music above all other arts is so ephemeral and spiritual, but at the same time, material and earthly in every way. From the earliest years of the Christian era, chant has been the music of the liturgy in spite of periods of decay and disuse. Interestingly, the very periods of least use were caused by the introduction of musical styles whose essence can be traced to the chant which they replaced; for example, the modality of the renaissance polyphony or the melismatic vocal passages of the baroque, reminiscent of the elaborate melismas of chant.

Two elements constantly warred against chant as the sacred music of the people: first, the ongoing desire to create a new style, the new replacing the old; and secondly, the tendency of the small group of singers to supplant the body of the faithful as more complicated compositions made the small group necessary for performance of more difficult music. But even in face of style changes and the substitution of small trained groups, chant persisted through the Christian centuries, encouraged by periodic reforms and revivals. Not the least of these was that which began in the mid-19th century and, blessed and encouraged by the Church, grew through the first half of the 20th century, until a misinterpretation of the Second Vatican Council brought it nearly to shipwreck.

Interest in chant, spurred by the scholarly and apostolic efforts of the monks of Solesmes, brought the revival of chant in France to classic proportion. The establishment of a *corpus* of the authentic melodies, the study of the theory of interpretation and the efforts, made worldwide by the monks, to introduce the people to singing Gregorian chant, proved that truly it is the authentic sacred music of the people. In France, the Gregorian melodies became household sounds, known to the vast majority of French people. It was sacred song; it was artistic in its composition and performance; it was truly folk music. In the United States, while not as advanced as the French scene, great progress had indeed been achieved by the opening of the Second Vatican Council. Especially through the efforts of the Catholic schools and the religious communities of women, Catholic grade school children across the land were learning and singing the sacred melodies. The Fathers of the Council intended to foster and increase the use of Gregorian chant, and they so ordered.

But a misinterpretation of the decrees of the Second Vatican Council wrought great harm to the chant revival, even when the Council Fathers had specifically indicated that the revival was to continue and be encouraged. First, a false understanding of the position of Latin in relation to the vernacular has all but eliminated the official language of the Church from any use in its liturgical worship, thus killing the melodies so closely united to the Latin sacred texts. Secondly, a misunderstanding of folk music and a confusion of the Council's demand for use of a true people's music with tunes written for a variety of secular purposes. And thirdly, a denial of a distinction between the sacred and the secular, resulting in an abandonment of Gregorian chant as a sacred music.

But another revival is at hand and has begun. What is the will of the Church will ultimately be achieved. New scholarship has brought to light many simplifications in performance practice, an aid to wider use of chant by larger groups. And a rejection of the secularization of liturgy has begun by the faithful who have suffered under experimentations and outright rejection of liturgical directives.

Among the young there is an avid interest in Gregorian chant as a truly sacred music. The Gregorian Congress in Paris in 1985 was the product of young French students who discovered what they had been deprived of – their inheritance. And they were asking "why?"

How can all this apply to an American parish in 1988? A pastor who wishes to implement the wishes of the Church, as they are expressed in the documents of the Council and those that followed afterwards, can turn to Gregorian chant and have his people singing again what is the official song of the Church. The objection against Latin is unfounded; why should this be an obstacle to the people of 1988 when it was no problem to the school children of the years before the Council? It is not impossible to learn the Ordinary parts of the Mass in Latin and understand what they are and what they mean. The Holy See itself has provided in a small booklet, *Jubilate Deo*, just recently reissued, the texts needed for a parish to sing chant. Teachers are in short supply to train both adults and children, but the new semiology makes it easier to train teachers since the method itself is less complex. *Scholas* of men or women can master the techniques of chant with a minimum of instruction. Once grasped, the unity of the Gregorian style makes possible the performance of the entire *corpus* of chants with growing facility. Their contribution to the sacred character and the beauty of the liturgy will be readily received by all who have not succumbed to false interpretations of the wishes of the Council and the Church.

In Saint Paul, Minnesota, at the Church of Saint Agnes, over the past twenty years since the close of the Council, a continuing use of Gregorian chant has established it in the various liturgical functions of the parish. The solemn Mass on Sunday has the Proper parts sung in full Gregorian settings by a *schola* of men using the new *Graduale Romanum* and the new principles of semiology. The Ordinary parts of those Masses are sung in Gregorian settings about half of the Sundays, while a Viennese classical orchestral repertory is scheduled for some thirty Sundays. We have a Gregorian Mass every Saturday, and our schoolchildren learn some Gregorian chants for their weekly sung Masses. For the past fifteen years, at the suggestion of the Vatican Council, we have sung Vespers each Sunday. Between ten and fifteen men use the new parts of the service that have been issued from Rome and make up the remainder from the old *Liber Usualis*. These are all volunteer singers who have found in the chant an expression of prayer and holiness that they seek for their own personal religious needs. The chant is not sung for its own sake, nor are the singers particularly conscious of performing a special style of music, a style which they have mastered and grown familiar with as a vehicle of expression, a means of prayer.

The Church recognizes Gregorian chant as its official music. In so doing, it does not make musical judgments about other styles, but simply acknowledges that since prayer is its chief function, i.e., communication with its Head, Jesus Christ, it is by means of Gregorian chant that this communication is most successfully achieved. The four purposes of prayer are most adequately accomplished: adoration, thanksgiving, reparation and petition. The classical balance of text and melody is found here. The balance between reason and emotion exists in chant. It is the most perfect form that has come down through the ages to allow man and God to commune. It is a treasure beyond all others. It is truly a sacred sound.

Monsignor Richard J. Schuler
(*Sacred Music*, Vol. 115, no. 2, Summer 1988, p. 13-17)

Vespers

The *Constitution on the Sacred Liturgy* from Vatican II (n.100) clearly states that "pastors should see to it that the chief Hours, especially Vespers, are celebrated in common in church on Sundays and the more solemn feasts. The laity, too, are encouraged to recite the Divine Office either with the priests, or among themselves, or even individually." And again, in *The General Instruction of the Liturgy of the Hours* (n.23), the directive is clearly stated: "Those in Holy Orders... must therefore see to it that the people are invited, and prepared by suitable instruction, to celebrate the principal Hours in common, especially on Sundays and Holydays. They should teach the people how to make this participation a source of genuine prayer."

But how often has this command been observed? Not even in cathedrals or in abbey churches can one participate in the Office of Hours on Sunday. With the revision of the Office as asked for by the Council, it was hoped that it would become truly the "prayer of the Church," used by both clerics and laity. With the privilege of using the vernacular, it was expected that all would take part. What happened was even the churches that may have celebrated Vespers before, now after the Council, have dropped the practice. Instead of nourishing the flock with the food of eternal life found in the Holy Scriptures, the opportunities for communal prayer have been significantly reduced or eliminated.

In my parish (Saint Agnes in Saint Paul, Minnesota), a group of men have sung Vespers every Sunday afternoon for the past twenty years. They are sung in Latin according to the order of the old *Liber Usualis*, since no new books have been issued with the music for the revised Office except for the *Liber Hymnarius* which has only parts of the Hour of Vespers. About fifteen men make up the choir, vested and seated in the sanctuary. The congregation is small, but about forty people attend, who are invited to sing the Office with the choir, but who mostly participate by following the English translation given in parallel columns with the Latin. The Blessed Sacrament is exposed during the singing of the Hour, and Benediction is given at the conclusion. Vespers has always been considered a Eucharistic celebration.

Many people tell me that coming to Vespers is a truly spiritual experience. In the late afternoon, the sun is setting and the west windows of the church shine with the brilliance of the setting sun. The mystery of the Gregorian psalm tones, repeated again and again, bring a peace to the church and to the souls of the congregation. The presence of the exposed Eucharist, the smell of the incense, the holiness of the texts being chanted, all make the hour of Vespers an attraction that brings one back week after week. This parish has had a great number of vocations to the priesthood (thirteen First Masses in the past twelve years). The vocation, given by God, is nurtured in the quiet of Vespers. The young man sings the praises of God, the official prayer of the Church, and God speaks to him. The setting is right; the words are the very Word of God; little wonder that God's call is heard in His house.

The easiest way to begin Vespers in a parish church is to dig out the old *Liber Usualis* or the *Saint Gregory Hymnal* which has Sunday Vespers. Choir lofts are probably full of books with the words and notes for Vespers. But if you would rather use the vernacular, then it is more of a problem. Where does one find the texts and the notation? How do you sing the vernacular psalms? What does one do with the hymns, the chapter, the responses? It is more difficult to begin in the vernacular than it is with Latin. Here is where our composers should provide us with suitable and beautiful music for singing the official vernacular liturgy of the hours. We don't need "music for a Vesper service" – music at Vespers. One should use the official texts, not a home-made service. We need the texts, the tones for the psalms, music for the other parts. It can be done, in English or in Latin, and be for our people what the conciliar Fathers wanted when they ordered Vespers for all parish churches on all Sundays and great feasts.

Monsignor Richard J. Schuler
(*Sacred Music*, Vol. 122, no. 1, Spring 1995, p. 4)

Saint Agnes, Sunday Morning

The Second Vatican Council gave us great liberty. In the field of church music, this was particularly true. Before the Council, the reforms of Pope Pius X with his *motu proprio* of 1903 had, in some quarters, been so narrowed and so restrictive that one could almost say that "music was to be seen but not heard!" The prevalent interpretation of the liturgical music reforms in the first half of the 20th century had indeed cleaned out much of the objectionable profane repertory that Pius objected to, but it had also thrown out the baby with the bath water. The great classical composers of the 18th and 19th centuries were not allowed, and in an effort to promote Gregorian chant, most polyphonic compositions were thought to be somewhat suspect in their liturgical propriety, even though such procedures were not to be found in official Roman documents.

But the Council established clearly that music is an integral part (*pars integrans*) of liturgy; it *is* liturgy. Two requirements, not new to the Council because Pius X had reiterated them, were demanded: music for the liturgy must be sacred and it must be art. All the musical styles developed through the long history of Christianity that fulfill the requirements may be used if they are found to be fitting. Thus today, in the light of the conciliar decrees, Mozart, Haydn, Beethoven, Schubert and many others are once again legitimized, since they have indeed produced compositions for the Church that are both sacred and true art.

However, instead of accepting the freedom offered by the Council, we have had a worse restriction imposed on our church music. Falsely, we were told that the Council had done away with the singing of choirs. Falsely, we were told that the Latin language was forbidden. Without a choir and without Latin, the classical composers remain just so many scores in a music library, "seen but not heard." Yet the Council said that the "great treasury of church music should be used and fostered."

Thus, we must once again encourage church choirs and urge them to sing for a Latin liturgy. This is what the Council ordered.

At the Church of Saint Agnes in Saint Paul, Minnesota, such a program has been underway for at least twenty years. Each Sunday, the solemn Mass (with two deacons) is celebrated in Latin. On thirty Sundays of the year, the music of the Viennese classicists (Mozart, Haydn, Beethoven *et al.)* is sung by the Twin Cities Catholic Chorale assisted by professional instrumentalists (usually about twenty). The choir of sixty voices, plus four soloists, has some twenty Masses in its repertory. The Proper is sung in Gregorian chant by a *schola* of men, and the congregation sings the responses and acclamations.

When the music is elaborate, it is important that the ceremonies also be carried out with solemnity. Thus, in addition to the celebrant and deacons and the lector, there are some fifteen altar boys from the parish high school and grade school who fill the various roles of thurifer, torch bearers, acolytes and masters of ceremonies. The *Missal* of Pope Paul VI is used, and the rubrics of the *Novus Ordo* are carefully followed. The celebrant sings the Canon from the *Ordo Missae in Cantu*, published by the monks of Solesmes. The readings are in English, but otherwise all is done in Latin. Books necessary for such a Mass are easily available from the Vatican bookstore: *Missale Romanum*; *Ordo Missae in Cantu*; and *Graduale Romanum*. While one could get along with the old *Liber Usualis*, the new order of the liturgy has moved many of the texts of the Proper, making it rather difficult to find the various pieces in the old books. The new *Graduale* has simplified the process. Adequate aids for the congregation are available, particularly one issued by the Leaflet Missal Company (419 W. Minnehaha Avenue, Saint Paul, Minnesota 55103), entitled *The Sung Liturgy*, prepared by Reverend Sheldon Roy of the Diocese of Alexandria. It contains all the parts to be sung by the congregation as well as the priest.

Recently the Solemn Mass from Saint Agnes was broadcast nationally on the program *Music in America*, which originates from Station WFMT in Chicago. Some two hundred public radio stations across the country aired the hour-long program, and the number of requests for copies of the broadcast led to the preparation of three 100-minute stereo tapes, entitled *Saint Agnes, Sunday Morning*. These were engineered by WFMT and marketed by Leaflet Missal Company. Included on each tape is the full Mass: Gregorian chant, organ music, readings, homilies and three orchestra Masses (Haydn's *Paukenmesse*, Beethoven's *Mass in C*, and Gounod's *Saint Cecilia Mass*).

Saint Agnes is a large church, constructed in the baroque style of south Germany and Austria by immigrants who came from the old Austro-Hungarian Empire at the end of the nineteenth century. It has an onion tower which rises to two hundred feet that would adorn the streets of Innsbruck, Vienna or Graz and be a tourist attraction in those cities. The interior has recently been refurbished in the rococo manner, making it very fitting for the music used. The pioneers who immigrated into Minnesota wished to recreate some of their homeland, and their church continues to give their descendants not only the architecture but the music that they brought with them. There is an ethnic connection, but the music is truly international. It is easily grasped by all and serves as prayer, because it is truly sacred and truly art. When Pope John Paul II invited Herbert von Karajan to conduct Mozart's *Coronation Mass* for the papal liturgy in Saint Peter's, it was made perfectly clear that the classical repertory of the Viennese School is fitting for the sacred liturgy; it is sacred and it is art.

It is through art that man comes to God. Music, architecture, painting, sculpture –indeed, flowers, candles, incense, vestments and ceremony – all can be the means of grace and prayer, provided that they are worthy of the Creator of all art and holy as He is. Jesus Christ is the supreme art of the Father. Our art must be a reflection of Him in whose image we are all made. Such liturgy is the aim of Saint Agnes, Sunday mornings.

Monsignor Richard J. Schuler
(*Sacred Music*, Vol. 114, no. 3, Fall 1987, p. 15-16)

The Young Will Discover Chant:
An Interview with Monsignor Richard J. Schuler

This interview, conducted by Thomas Woods, was first printed in
Christi Fideles, (March 1997)

TOM WOODS: What is your music program at Saint Agnes and how does it stand out?

SCHULER: We have five masses on the weekend. The evening Mass on Saturday is about once or twice a month, a sung Mass in Latin with a group which we call our Chamber Choir that sings mostly Renaissance things and Gregorian Proper. The 10:00 a.m. on Sunday is a Solemn Mass with orchestra (about twenty-five players) and the Twin Cities Catholic Chorale, which is about sixty voices. And we sing the Viennese classical Masses: Mozart, Haydn, Beethoven, and so on. There are about twenty-four Masses in our repertoire.

WOODS: I understand that the fruits of your work include a good number of vocations.

SCHULER: We've done pretty well there. In the last fourteen or fifteen years, we've had fifteen first Masses here. And at the present time we have ten kids from this parish in the seminary.

WOODS: Is there a connection between what you're trying to do at Saint Agnes and their own discernment of a vocation?

SCHULER: I think there's a connection, and many have said that. For the last twenty years we've sung Vespers every Sunday afternoon, and I find a good number of people who show up for that indicate a vocation, in time.

WOODS: Some of the most distasteful aspects of the ongoing liturgical changes have been advanced in the name of making the Mass more appealing and accessible to the young. Do your own people generally appreciate what you're trying to do at Saint Agnes?

SCHULER: I think so. In our high school, for example, the students are very interested in religious music. In fact, they've got a concert coming up tomorrow which is entitled, "A Survey of Religion and Music." Moreover, we have a lot of altar boys. We have about fifty servers out of the grade school. They're in teams, and for our Sunday High Mass, we always have fifteen servers. There's a lot of competition.

WOODS: You have argued that there is nothing inherent in music or in a particular instrument that makes it either religious or secular, sacred or profane.

SCHULER: Well, by sacred, we mean what man has over the centuries come to regard as that. We can't say that a flute is not sacred, or that it is sacred; or a violin or an organ. The organ has come to be thought of as a sacred instrument only because it's been used mostly in churches. It's the connotation of a thing that determines whether it's sacred or secular, and that connotation isn't built up overnight.

WOODS: Some people maintain that you go further and are willing to say that even in the realm of pop culture, for example, it is inadmissible to argue that a particular genre is inherently evil.

SCHULER: I think some of the stuff that comes out in hard rock is so totally associated with evil that there is something evil in it. I don't think you can have what you can call "Christian Rock."

WOODS: That was my next question.

SCHULER: I don't think that the text is going to baptize what is bad. There are some who would like or say that you can Christianize rock music. I don't think that you can. Music can't become holy because it's tacked onto a sacred text.

WOODS: What about the use of hymns in the Liturgy?

SCHULER: The hymn has not been a part of the Mass Liturgy. You don't find hymns in the *Missal*. There are hymns in the breviary, the part of the Liturgy of the Hours, but the use of hymns in Mass is tacked on.

WOODS: I understand that all the Masses you celebrate are in the new rite.

SCHULER: Yes.

WOODS: Where do you stand on the question of the Traditional Mass? I understand your view is that to fight to restore it would be to concede that the liberals have given us a Modernist Liturgy. And you refuse to do that. You want to present a sacred celebration of this new Mass.

SCHULER: Right. The *Novus Ordo* is given to us by the Church, and I think we're committed to accepting that. There may be things we'd like to see changed. For example, there's no Octave of Pentecost any more, no Octave of Epiphany. A few things are missing that I would like to see come back and they could be put back. But by and large, the changes that were put into the *Novus Ordo* are not bad. If we would do what is there and not make up our own rubrics, that could be a perfectly good thing, as I've hoped to have demonstrated at Saint Agnes.

WOODS: Do you think there is a role for the Traditional Mass movement to play in trying to restore a sense of the sacred to the Liturgy, or would you rather see the people who favor the Traditional Mass work simply toward reverent celebrations of the *Novus Ordo*.

SCHULER: The Church has allowed it (Traditional Latin Mass), there's no question about that. But I have the feeling that it's done because these people who ask for it were so appalled by the irreverence that was coming out in what was called the "new" Liturgy, that they said, give us back what we had. To save their souls, the Holy See said fine. But I think that the New *Ordo* is here to stay and that we should use it to the best of our ability. Work for certain changes, like that calendar change that I suggested. But I don't like to see two *Missals* in use.

WOODS: What would you say to somebody who notes that the introduction of the *Novus Ordo* seems to have taken place simultaneously with the introduction of bad music?

SCHULER: There is a term I use, the *piccolomini*, which in Italian means the little men. I claim that's who took over the whole liturgical reform. They got in the driver seat and they did it as they wanted, not as the Church has directed. What we have in most places is the operation of *piccolomini*. This was true in church music. The people who are writing so-called church music today are not the best-educated people in music or in liturgy. They're not trained, they have no notion of the history of this thing. They are the "little guys." That's in everything: art, architecture, church decoration, all that sort of thing.

WOODS: Are you claiming this is a powerful minority of the liturgical establishment?

SCHULER: I think it is the liturgical establishment.

WOODS: How is it that the *piccolomini* have had such a mind-boggling success?

SCHULER: I'm not a person who finds trouble under every rug, but there was undoubtedly some kind of organized effort or conspiracy. And this thing spread instantly, via some of these national groups, the Bishops' conference groups. They're full of what I call the "DP": dumb priests. They accepted this as if it were the documentation of the Council. I've got an article in the next issue of *Sacred Music* in which we show that Monsignor Frederick McManus, of all people, has admitted that *Environment and Art in Christian Worship* (the document that has been used to tear most of our churches apart) is no more than the opinion of those who wrote it. No legal status whatsoever, yet we've ruined the churches of our country, holding that document up as if it were the Bible.

WOODS: Have you encountered any hostility from anyone for what you're trying to do?

SCHULER: The Archbishop here in Saint Paul has been very friendly. But there have been the bureaucrats – some have asked about our Masses at the main altar *ad orientem*. They wanted to know what kind of permission I had to get to do what I was doing. I told them we are just fulfilling the law of the Church. I have a story to tell. I was at a meeting of some priests, for Confirmation, and I was seated across from the Archbishop, and down at the other end of the table a priest hollered up, "How's your Latin High Mass going?" And I said, "Oh, fine, we get a good crowd every Sunday." And the guy next to me said, "How can you have a Latin High Mass?" And the Archbishop looked at him and said, "Father, he doesn't have to explain why he has a Latin High Mass; but those who don't must explain why they don't."

WOODS: What happened to Gregorian chant? I know Vatican II said it should be given pride of place, but this has been ignored.

SCHULER: It seems to be a dislike of Latin. You chant in Latin, you can't put Gregorian chant in the vernacular. They outlawed the Latin, therefore they lost the Gregorian chant. We do Gregorian chant here for all the Latin Masses we celebrate.

WOODS: As we know, there are many perfectly good reasons to retain Latin.

SCHULER: Certainly, if only to keep Gregorian chant. I'm all for the vernacular, it was a great privilege given to us, but I think Latin ought to be retained for the sung liturgy. One of the difficulties in so many countries is that they don't have any composers and few musicians. With Latin, they could use what was composed in Germany, France and Italy and Yugoslavia, whatever, because it came out in Latin, and it could be used all over the world. But once the vernacular replaced the Latin, then what are you going to do with German vernacular? We don't want any of that here, we don't want any Hungarian music here. It is restricted to its own place. Chant, on the other hand, is universal.

WOODS: We're essentially asking this age to come up with a whole new *corpus* of Catholic music.

SCHULER: We don't have any composers, nor do we have any who can sing the music. Part of the problem with any kind of music creation and publication is that you've got to have somebody who can do it, perform it. With the disbanding of choirs, there was no one to sing it anymore. Then there was no one to buy it, therefore there was no one to publish it, and therefore there was no one to write it. So they've killed the whole system and all the previous repertoire we had accumulated over centuries by getting rid of the Latin.

WOODS: It occurs to me that it was relatively easy to abandon Latin.

SCHULER: We were forced to. I don't know if you've ever seen that book I put out called *Music and Liturgy Reforms After Vatican II*, but in there I took a survey of the bishops in the country and asked if they were maintaining Latin as the Church had asked. Practically every one of them said they had forbidden it. I can't understand how a diocese can forbid something that is ordered by a universal Church law of a Council.

WOODS: It's easy to abandon the Latin, it's much more difficult to bring it back.

SCHULER: Oh, yes, because they don't study Latin anymore. The seminaries, which are presumed to be on the graduate level of studies, are studying theology, and they don't know a word of Latin. One thousand years of Catholic theology in Latin, and these people who are studying it today don't understand it at all.

WOODS: There's also the problem that the laity, especially the rising generations, are entirely unfamiliar with even the most common church music.

SCHULER: That's true. There's nothing taught in schools. But it's a simple thing. You can teach a crowd of kids the *Kyrie Eleison* in Gregorian chant in a matter of ten-fifteen minutes. And the *Sanctus* is the same way. There was such a hatred of Latin among these *piccolomini* people. They don't want it, it's Roman, and you do away with the Latin. And of course, if you do away with Latin, you do away with what was most of the Roman Rite.

WOODS: It certainly wasn't the laity that hated Latin.

SCHULER: No, it was the clergy.

WOODS: The laity, though, does not put up much of a fight when changes are made.

SCHULER: We were trained all the way through to do what we were told, and this is what they played on. The laity would do what they were told.

WOODS: Perhaps that can work to our advantage, on the other hand, if Latin is to be revived.

SCHULER: I think so. Certainly nobody is trying to go back to where everything would be in Latin, spoken and sung. But once we get back to using it for special occasions, for one Mass out of three or four, and when Masses that are sung have Latin music, then there will be a swing back.

WOODS: As editor of *Sacred Music*, where do you see church music headed? Do you see signs of a revival in chant, for example?

SCHULER: Well, it can't be much worse, so it must go the other way. The young will eventually discover there is something they have been deprived of, and they're going to say, where is all this? And come back to it. There was a Gregorian chant congress in Paris about five years ago, and a young fellow came up and said, "We discovered this, we've been deprived of what is a thousand years of our country's musical history and we want it back; we want to know why we weren't told about it."

WOODS: I might add that no one expected the monks of Santo Domingo de Silos to sell eight million copies of their Gregorian chant recording.

<u>SCHULER</u>: Not far from where I live now is Saint John's Abbey, and we used to visit up there every summer when I was a boy. We always went to Vespers, which was sung in Latin, and while I didn't know what they were doing, still there was something about it that told me this was the way you got to Heaven. There was a connection with Heaven: the beauty of that music. We sat there for hours, and it had an effect on me. I think chant has something in itself that creates that peace, belief, all that we want.

<u>WOODS</u>: Thank you, Monsignor

Monsignor Richard J. Schuler
(*Sacred Music*, Vol. 134, no. 2, Summer 2007, p. 34-38)

Regarding Sacred Liturgy, Art, and Music
at the Church of Saint Agnes

> He said unto them: "Therefore, every scribe instructed in the kingdom of heaven, is like to a man that is a householder, who bringeth forth out of his treasure new things and old." (*Matthew* 13:52)

When a more traditionally minded priest is assigned as a pastor, he often helps the parish rediscover beautiful traditions from the past. A parish might have had a Corpus Christi Eucharistic Procession but previous pastors, for one reason or another, may have stopped those practices. The Church of Saint Agnes is one of those rare parishes where beautiful traditions, devotions and liturgical practices have continued from time immemorial either from the very beginning or for many decades. As Deacon Harold Hughesdon, of fond memory, was often known to say in his British accent, "We have *always* done it that way!" or "We have *never* done it that way!" For example, Saint Agnes has had a Sunday sung Latin Mass since 1887. Masses have also been *ad orientem* (facing the altar) since 1887. Other practices such as Forty Hours Eucharistic Adoration and Tuesday night Novenas to Our Lady of Perpetual Help have occurred almost as long. Obviously, Saint Agnes is very unique.

It has long been a part of Saint Agnes lore that the parish holds the distinct honor of having been the first parish in the United States to celebrate the New Mass from the first typical edition. Someone connected with the parish happened to be in Rome and bought the newly printed *Missal* from the bookstore as soon it was available, then flew back to Minnesota where it was used the very next Sunday at the Latin High Mass. All other parishes were using various experimental *Missals*. This episode captures how Saint Agnes has always treasured the new and the old.

Hermeneutic of Continuity

Monsignor Richard Schuler and his immediate predecessor, Monsignor Rudolph Bandas, shepherded Saint Agnes during and after a tumultuous time of rampant misinterpretation of the Second Vatican Council. The decisions they made in implementing the Second Vatican Council are a great example of what Pope Benedict calls the hermeneutic of continuity. This means a taking into consideration what has been done before as you interpret the changes of the Second Vatican Council. There should be an inclination for keeping things the same or similar as in the past unless the rubrics or *General Instruction* specifically state otherwise.

Allegedly, after the Second Vatican Council, a more progressive pastor confronted the then Archbishop (either Binz or Byrne) asking him how Saint Agnes "got away with having a Latin Mass?" To which the Archbishop replied that pastors needed his permission to have the Mass in the vernacular, whereas Saint Agnes needed no permission to have the Mass in Latin. The most obvious examples of the hermeneutic of continuity are in the use of Gregorian chant and celebrating Mass *ad orientem*. Both Monsignors knew the Second Vatican Council had given pride of place, in regards to music, to Gregorian chant. However, they also readily made use of the permission to have the vernacular in the Mass. They accomplished this by maintaining the principal Mass of the day as a sung Latin Ordinary Form Mass. This included singing the Latin Order of the Mass and Propers by either the priest celebrant or *Schola* while the Liturgy of the Word was read in the vernacular. Other Masses on Sunday and during the week used the new *Missals* in English. Herein lies the important principle that a sacred liturgical language builds a connection with others from the past and the present. One really senses being part of the Universal Church.

Practically speaking, increasing the amount of Latin and chant in a parish can be done in different ways: chanting the *Kyrie*, *Gloria*, *Credo*, *Sanctus* and *Agnus Dei* on select Solemnities and Feast days; seasonal use of Gregorian chant such as during Lent; chanting the *Pater Noster* more frequently at Masses that are otherwise in the vernacular; singing the *Introit* and/or the Communion Antiphon at the principal Mass of the day (these are often easier to learn than some of the Graduals). The Solesmes *Gregorian Missal* is a superb resource and worship aid for *Schola* and the faithful.

Read the Documents

Monsignor Schuler told me once that Archbishop Roach asked him, "When are you going to turn your altar around?" Monsignor retorted, "When you can show me where it says I have to." Neither Monsignor Schuler nor Monsignor Bandas were caught up in the confusion and propaganda that followed the Council. They could read and they did read the documents. Bandas was a *peritus* (an expert selected by the local archbishop to assist him) at the Second Vatican Council. Bandas wrote and spoke about the errors that were being multiplied in the wake of the Council but he was largely unheeded. In the July 7, 1968 Sunday Bulletin, Bandas wrote a veritable syllabus of errors that listed the common misinterpretations of the Council due to an erroneous "spirit of the Council." For example, he stated that the Council nowhere says: "That the Latin Mass, the High Mass, and choirs have been abolished." Bandas died unexpectedly in 1969 and was replaced by Monsignor Richard Schuler.

Monsignor Schuler supported the reforms intended by the Council but understood that they were limited and always in light of what had gone before. Monsignor Schuler, with his knowledge of Latin, could see that the rubrics of the new Latin Missal were written with the presumption that the Mass was to be celebrated *ad orientem*. At the end of the offertory the rubrics state: "*Stans postea in medio altaris, versus ad populum, extendens et iungens manus, dicit:*" Translated, it states that the priest is standing in the middle of the altar, "having turned to the people." *Ad orientem* is not just a matter of avoiding the barbaric destruction of beautiful high altars, but it represents the intent to communicate how the priest is praying *with* the people, *to* God.

There is no substitute for directly encountering the primary sources of the Second Vatican Council, particularly *Sacrosanctum concilium* and *Musicam sacram*, as well as the *General Instruction on the Roman Missal* and the rubrics of the Third Typical Edition. Careful reading by priests is an absolute must. A rudimentary understanding of Latin, or at least being able to look up the meaning of Latin words is not just helpful but should be *de rigueur* for any Latin rite priest.

Sacred Architecture, Vestments, and Vessels

Part of the experience of Sacred Liturgy at Saint Agnes involves not only beautiful music and the use of Latin, but also beautiful architecture, vestments, and vessels. The first thing one notices at Saint Agnes is the Austrian Baroque *façade* in white limestone. It is magnificent, to say the least. The general architectural design has been said to imitate Kloster Schlägl in Upper Austria. The church looks as if it was simply lifted out of Austria and set down in the Frogtown neighborhood. Noble architecture requires loving care and money. Millions of dollars have been raised and spent on the exterior and interior of the edifice so as to maintain its beauty and functionality. The people of God want a church which points to the transcendent and inspires them to meditate on the sacred. New, traditional churches being built in many southern and midwestern states are evidence the laity are ready and willing to invest in sacred beauty. Money follows mission, a mission that is good and edifying.

Vestments that are attractively adorned with sacred art and symbols are fitting for the Holy Sacrifice of the Mass. Many of the vestments used at Saint Agnes were rescued from other churches and institutions that did not share an appreciation for highly ornamented, traditional vestment design. Other vestments were donated to the parish as word spread throughout the nation and the world of Monsignor's Schuler's good taste. In fact, one gold set of vestments found its way to Saint Agnes after having been made for a Hollywood movie. New sets of vestments have been commissioned by donors – patrons who support the purchase of new and beautiful liturgical garb are easily found. Wear and tear, from even loving use, is bound to happen. For the past several years, Saint Agnes has undertaken the project of restoring chasubles, stoles, dalmatics, maniples, burses and chalice veils. Giving God praise and thanks in a manner that even slightly imitates His goodness, truth and beauty, seems to be a matter of justice.

Pastors can be understandably reluctant to have the parish's sacred vessels refurbished and replated with gold. It is always at least a four-figure expense if it is done well. In this area too, Saint Agnes has always been a good steward. Over the last decade, the parish has conducted multiple "old gold" collections of jewelry that are worn, broken or out of style. Silver jewelry, coins, gems and even gold fillings have been donated. These items are then resold or sold for scrap. The proceeds are used to refurbish and replate the parish's chalices, patens, ciboria and monstrances. Again, the laity want to honor God and worship Him using dignified sacred vessels.

Orchestral and Polyphonic Masses

The Latin High Mass with *Schola*, Chorale and Orchestra, has been one of the defining features of Saint Agnes for the last fifty years. The Twin Cities Catholic Chorale, accompanied by professional soloists and orchestra musicians, sings twenty-eight to thirty classical orchestral Masses every liturgical year. These are not performances. The music is in its appropriate setting, the Holy Mass. Renaissance polyphony is also sung many times throughout the year. During Advent, Lent and Ordinary time during the summer months, the *Schola* chants the Mass in Latin.

Although it is unlikely that this kind of sacred music can be duplicated at many parishes, priests should consider adding some of this music at the principal Mass of the day on select Sundays and Holydays. Utilizing an orchestrated or polyphonic *Gloria* and *Credo* is very doable. For example, Schubert's *Mass in G* can be employed in whole or in part at a Mass that is otherwise entirely in the vernacular. The investment of time and resources will reap the great benefit of increased reverence and devotion.

In conclusion, the vast majority of pastors will not come into a situation similar to the Church of Saint Agnes where the old and the new have been so gracefully integrated. However, the same basic principles and practices that guided Monsignors Schuler and Bandas can be used to reintroduce beautiful liturgy and sacred music in other parishes. Every priest and music director must start with a sense of sympathy for the state of liturgical confusion; the people of God are often not at fault for the liturgical abuses and undignified music to which they have been accustomed. Patience and charitable explanations, as well as prudent but limited introduction into the Mass of good music, will help Catholics to appreciate, as if anew, that which should never have been forgotten.

Reverend Mark Moriarty, Pastor
Church of Saint Agnes
Saint Paul, Minnesota

Appendix A

MONSIGNOR RICHARD J. SCHULER

Monsignor Richard J. Schuler
directing the Twin Cities Catholic Chorale.

Photo: Joe Oden, used with permission

A Biography of Monsignor Richard J. Schuler

By Charles W. Nelson

(Reprinted from *To Sing With the Angels*, by Virginia A. Schubert)

Richard Joseph Schuler was born in Minneapolis, Minnesota, on December 30, 1920, the third child of Otto and Wilhelmine Schuler. One of his favorite quips in later life was that all great people were born in December – including God! Following the deaths of his elder brother and sister, however, he was raised as the eldest son to his younger sisters, Catherine and Jeanne.

A part of his early years was spent working in the family business, the Schuler Shoe Store, where he learned two insights from his father which were to affect his pastoral approach in later years: you cannot serve customers if the store isn't open and you shouldn't change the familiar hours of operation.

He began his schooling in the Ascension Grade School under the tutelage of the Sisters of Saint Joseph of Carondelet who nourished and developed his Catholic faith. Father Schuler particularly remembered the time he spent in the classroom of Sister Anne Patricia Doyle who awakened his interests in literature and music. While at Ascension, he began his musical education taking lessons in the piano and flute which he played in the school orchestra. Richard also became an altar boy in the fifth grade and had many memories of his pastor, Monsignor Dunphy. At funerals, the good prelate delivered the eulogy standing next to the coffin and often laying his hand on the casket when he referred to the deceased. He also liked to bang on the bier while trying to make a point. Father Schuler and his fellow servers often wondered if someday the deceased might sit up and demand to know who was knocking on the coffin!

In 1934, Richard entered De La Salle High School, a Christian Brothers institution. While pursuing his secondary school education,

Father Schuler began organ lessons at the MacPhail School of Music where he did so well that he was hired as the substitute organist at the Basilica of Saint Mary in downtown Minneapolis. He often recalled the peculiarities of its Rector, Monsignor Reardon, who always insisted that services began on time – even if the hearse had not yet arrived. Father remembered beginning the Requiem Mass several times a full ten minutes before the appearance of the mourners and the body!

Richard graduated from De La Salle in 1938 and enrolled at the College of Saint Thomas, where he majored in English. Because he had taken summer courses at the University of Minnesota, he had a surplus of credits and, in 1940, with the encouragement of his pastor and priestly professors, he entered the Saint Paul Seminary. After his third year, he had finished the requirements for a Bachelor of Arts and was awarded an English degree from Saint Thomas. Because of World War II and the need for chaplains and more parish priests to take their places, classes continued all year at the seminary so that Father Schuler was ordained earlier than scheduled on August 18, 1945, and celebrated his First Solemn Mass the next day at the Ascension Church.

During his years at the seminary, his abilities as an organist had attracted the attention of Father Francis A. Missia, the Professor of Music, who appointed him the accompanist of the Seminary Choir. Father Schuler recalled Father Missia as an exceptionally talented, but demanding musician who had a formidable temper. One year, having arrived at the Cathedral to play for the Ordination Ceremony, Father Schuler realized that he had left the score for the *Ecce Sacerdos Magnus* (which happened to be the processional) back at the seminary. Father Missia had begun warm-ups for the choir while Father Schuler was desperately trying to find transportation back to his rooms. He finally appealed to the father of one of the other seminarians who raced back to the seminary and returned with the score in the nick of time, thus avoiding a liturgical catastrophe as the choir was not prepared to sing *a capella* or endure a tirade from its director!

Following his ordination, Father Schuler was assigned to Nazareth Hall, the preparatory seminary in the Fall of 1945, where he taught Music and History. He was also sent as weekend assistant to Holy Childhood Parish where its pastor, Father John Buchanan, was starting his choir school. The Archbishop felt that Father Schuler's musical talents could be put to good use in this endeavor, but Father Schuler was not favorably disposed towards boy sopranos as he preferred the real thing, and so devoted his time to training the altar boys, so that Holy Childhood became known not only for its music, but also for its flawless liturgy.

With the encouragement of Father Missia, Father Schuler began graduate studies at the Eastman School of Music in Rochester, New York, in the summers, earning his Masters in 1950. That same year, he was assigned as weekend assistant and Choir Director at the Church of the Nativity in Saint Paul whose pastor, Bishop James J. Byrne, wanted a choir to rival the Cathedral's. Following a year's study in Rome on a Fulbright Scholarship, Father Schuler returned to Nativity, but not to Nazareth Hall as Archbishop Murray appointed him to the faculty of the College of Saint Thomas, where, in addition to directing the Liturgical Choir, he also taught Music and Theology.

While he was in Europe, Father Schuler's friend and mentor, Father Missia, died and with him the Saint Paul Catholic Choral Society. Not wanting to lose such a valuable musical asset to the Archdiocese, Father Schuler drew on its former members and added new ones from his own choirs, to found the Twin Cities Catholic Chorale in 1955, which is the subject of *To Sing With the Angels*. He likewise became involved in the Guild of Catholic Choirmasters and Organists, an organization of parish choirs from throughout the Archdiocese. As a choir director with several ensembles at his command, Father Schuler introduced innovation and change in the choir loft including the extensive use of Gregorian chant and orchestral accompaniment for the sung Masses. In 1967, he completed work on his Doctorate in Music History at the University of Minnesota.

Because of his extensive work with parish and diocesan choirs, Father Schuler became more widely known in national and international Catholic church music circles. He wrote articles, gave invited lectures, composed, and participated in choral workshops and seminars such as those at Boys' Town and Christendom College. The fame of the Nativity Choir grew as Bishop Byrne got his wish. Father continued to expand its repertoire and embellish its performances. He was a demanding taskmaster and a stickler for excellence, but remained popular with his singers and the parishioners. On one of the interminable Sundays after Pentecost in 1960, a careless celebrant began the Collect when an authoritative voice proclaimed from the choir loft for all to hear: "There IS a *Gloria* today!" leaving the choir too much in hysterics to sing. On one Fall Tuesday evening, a prospective new singer came puffing up to the loft and gasped to Father Schuler that he would like to audition for the choir. After a brief pause, the choirmaster looked at the man and said that if he could still sing after making it up all those stairs, he was in! One of the director's favorite remarks during rehearsals was to look quizzically at the choir after going through a musical selection and say, "That was very interesting, but now let's try and sing it the way Schubert wrote it!"

In 1961, Father Schuler attended the Fourth International Church Music Congress in Cologne, Germany, where he met Monsignor Johannes Overath and became involved with the international church music establishment which led to his holding national and international offices and helping to organize two international church music congresses.

In the aftermath of the Second Vatican Council, many erroneous interpretations of its documents and wrongheaded applications of its directives took place which did irreparable damage to many aspects of the Church – especially to its treasury of sacred music. Due to a complete misunderstanding of the *Constitution on the Sacred Liturgy,* Monsignor Steiner, then Pastor of Nativity Church, was persuaded by one of his assistants that choirs were no longer needed as the congregation would be doing all the singing. As a result, the Nativity Choir was disbanded in May, 1966 and Father Schuler was assigned elsewhere. There were tears, tantrums, recriminations, and a rift in the parish, but the damage was done and the work of sixteen years undone. The rancor persisted for years.

Father Schuler was sent to the College of Saint Catherine as Chaplain to the community of Sisters who were already making dramatic changes in their Order. He tried unsuccessfully to caution them against the drastic actions they were initiating and warned of the havoc which would (and did) result. During this same time, Father Schuler got to know Monsignor Rudolph Bandas, Pastor of Saint Agnes Parish, who had been a *peritus* at all four sessions of the Second Vatican Council and had a clear and orthodox understanding of the intents of the Council Fathers. Because of his influence, his parish had implemented the changes recommended by the Council, but without the turmoil and controversy. With worsening relations with the Sisters of Saint Joseph, Father Schuler was happy to be assigned as weekend assistant at Saint Agnes, and, in 1969, following the death of Monsignor Bandas, he became its eighth pastor.

When he assumed the office of pastor of Saint Agnes, Father Schuler informed his congregation that he saw his responsibilities as threefold:

- to carry out the reforms of the Second Vatican Council carefully and correctly in keeping with the intentions of the framers of the documents;
- to encourage vocations to the priesthood and religious life; and
- to embellish the sacred liturgies with the treasures of the Church's rich history of sacred music.

Because his predecessor had maintained the traditional ceremonies and liturgies of the Church, Father Schuler found a solid basis already in place, and he immediately began to build on it through a vigorous recruitment and training program for the altar boys, instilling in them a true sense of the solemnity of the rites they were performing. He likewise focused his attention on the growth and improvement of the parish schools as the best incubators of vocations.

He began visiting, and even teaching, some high school classes to encourage and foster interest in the religious life, as well as initiating the practice of dialogue homilies with the elementary school students at school Masses. Finally, he gave funding and encouragement to the parish choir and its director, Sister Hermana Maurer, SSND. He also brought his own Twin Cities Catholic Chorale to Saint Agnes on occasion to sing the High Mass.

In 1970, Father Schuler celebrated the 25th anniversary of his ordination with a special Mass at Saint Agnes sung by the Twin Cities Catholic Chorale and the Dallas Catholic Choir under the direction of Father Ralph March, O. Cist., accompanied by organist Paul Manz. At that Mass, it was announced that the jubilarian had been named an honorary prelate (Monsignor) of the Church by Pope Paul VI. In spite of this honor, the pastor preferred the title of "Father" to "Monsignor." The first, he explained was conferred by a sacrament, while the second was bestowed by a piece of paper.

But all was not peaceful at Saint Agnes as the misunderstandings of Vatican II infected the Notre Dame Order as well as the diocesan Board of Education who demanded drastic changes in the teaching of the essentials of the Catholic Faith. Supported by a majority of the parents of the parish and many of the teaching Sisters, Monsignor Schuler held out for continued orthodoxy. They eventually were successful but, as a result, a rift developed in the parish and the School Sisters of Notre Dame began to withdraw from the Saint Agnes Schools. With the help of local educators, Monsignor Schuler began the hiring of lay faculty to teach with the few Sisters who remained so that the parish school continued uninterrupted in its mission of educating the Catholics of the future.

In 1974, Monsignor Schuler and Father March rehearsed their choirs separately in order that they could sing together at the Sixth International Church Music Congress in Salzburg, Austria. On their way to the conference, the two choirs sang a daily High Mass in many abbeys, cathedrals and parish churches. On August 15, the Feast of the Assumption, they sang Joseph Haydn's *Paukenmesse* in the Alte Peterskirche in Munich, accompanied by members of the Munich Symphony Orchestra. It was this extraordinary experience which led Monsignor Schuler to make Saint Agnes the permanent home of the Chorale accompanied by professional musicians aided by professional soloists which has made the parish famous around the world for the beauty of its music and the perfection of its liturgies. Three popes were familiar with Monsignor Schuler's accomplishments and one of them (Benedict XVI) sent condolences to his parish after his death.

When he first took over as pastor of Saint Agnes, Monsignor Schuler began the practice of praying for vocations every Sunday as the congregation asked God for "many priests, deacons, brothers and sisters for the Church." The prayer, augmented by the concentrated efforts and encouragement of the pastor, has yielded a rich harvest. As a result of his thirty-two years at Saint Agnes, twenty-eight priests were ordained, five permanent deacons were anointed, and two bishops and one archbishop were consecrated. All seminarians were welcomed to Saint Agnes to participate in the liturgies, to sing in the Chorale, and to benefit from the spiritual direction and canonical instruction of Monsignor Schuler.

In spite of his devotion to the Magisterium of the Church and his insistence on orthodoxy in all aspects of parish life, or perhaps because of these, Monsignor was often reviled, criticized, mocked, and insulted. Yet, through it all, he never lost his confidence and faith that all would eventually work out for the best. Father Eric Olson, a priest of the Diocese of Marquette, Michigan, who first met Monsignor at one of the summer workshops he conducted at Christendom College and knew him for the rest of his life, said of him: "He never grew bitter or angry as some of the clergy did. In spite of all the hardships and disappointments, he always remained a perfect gentleman and the ideal of a what a Catholic priest should be. He was an inspiration to all of us."

He also managed to keep his sense of humor and perspective which made him such a joy to work with. On several Tuesday nights, as he arrived in the Saint Agnes choir loft, he would complain that they had added steps to the staircase. Dr. Thaddeus Chao, a physician and long-time member of the Chorale, used to marvel at Monsignor's good health and strong constitution. He was sure it was due to his German genes! But even German genes eventually begin to age, and, in the new millennium, Monsignor's strenuous lifestyle began to catch up with him. As a result of his sixty years of arduous labor and busy schedules, Monsignor started to slow down, and in June, 2001, he stepped aside as pastor of Saint Agnes, but remained in the parish and continued as Director of the Chorale, although he did appoint Dr. Robert L. Peterson as Associate Director.

Monsignor continued to attend the Sunday High Masses, but Dr. Peterson now directed the Chorale. He likewise still worked with and advised seminarians so that the First Masses of newly ordained priests continued, and on May 28, 2006, Father Sean Magnuson celebrated his Mass of Thanksgiving at Saint Agnes in the presence of the Pastor Emeritus. The next day, Monsignor suffered a stroke from which he never fully recovered. He spent the rest of his days in assisted living facilities and nursing homes, where he continued to celebrate daily Mass and receive visitors.

In 2007, his health continued to decline, and on April 20, he died while listening to a Chorale recording of Beethoven's *Mass in C* – surely a preview of the angelic music he would soon be hearing in the Courts of Heaven.

Well done, good and faithful servant.

Et Erit in Pace Memoria Ejus:
Richard J. Schuler 1920-2007+

By Reverend Robert A. Skeris

(Reprinted from *To Sing With the Angels*, by Virginia A. Schubert)

"You would have been impressed by some of the young priests praying with him on his deathbed, singing Latin chants from memory! The Twin Cities Catholic Chorale even sang part of the '*Nos autem*' by heart."

"As far as church music goes, he is one in ten million."

"Had Monsignor Schuler's 10:00 Sunday High Mass been the one adopted by the universal Church after the Council it is unlikely there would have been such an urgent need for traditionalist counterrevolution."

"I will never forget the beauty of Holy Mass at Saint Agnes. He and the liturgy he promoted so beautifully were major factors in the rebirth of my Catholic faith."

"Palm Sunday 1992 was the first time I visited Saint Agnes church. I had been away from the Church, in no small part due to the banality of liturgy – though I didn't know there could be anything better. On a recommendation from a friend I visited the parish. I had never been to a Latin Mass. I had never heard a sung Mass. That day I felt like I was being introduced to my religion for the first time. That was my first Latin Mass. I returned for Holy Thursday and the Vigil before I had to return to college. I didn't understand then the Latin of the Mass, but it was clear that the faith expressed in those liturgies was total, and I needed to be there. I'd had it with half-way Catholicism. At Saint Agnes the Faith was on display gloriously. Here the Faith seemed as ancient as it did strong and vibrant. And from that Holy Week, I determined that I was going to learn and do my part to preserve the Gregorian melodies."

"It was during a visit to Saint Agnes Church on an October weekend in 1993 that my life was changed forever. A weekend of Monsignor Schuler's wonderful hospitality was crowned by Holy Mass with the Mozart *Missa Longa* as the musical offering. The seeds for the N.N. Catholic Chorale were sown that day. By the grace of God we are now in our tenth year and still growing. Suffice it to say that there would be no N.N. Catholic Chorale without the inspiration, guidance and prayers of our beloved Monsignor Schuler. He was of great courage and example in a bleak time. He was a good friend. May he rest in peace."

"It was a great privilege to have met Monsignor Schuler, albeit only once. He kept the flame of the Sacred Liturgy alight in a very dark age indeed and passed that light on to many others to whom he was a father and a guide. May Almighty God reward this disciple of the true liturgical movement – this pioneer of the new liturgical movement! R.I.P."

Even this small sampling of voices from the world wide web gives eloquent testimony to the enormous beneficial effects of Richard Schuler's priestly life and work. And what (we ask) was the vital force which sustained that life and impelled those achievements?

Surely it was his firm and lively faith in God, in God's Son become man, in the Church He established on the Rock of Peter. There can be little doubt that this is the key to understanding the four score and seven years of Monsignor Schuler's earthly sojourn.

It explains his path to the altar of God, who gave joy to his youth; his academic training and teaching career; his founding of the Twin Cities Catholic Chorale in 1956; his decades of notable collaboration in national and international church music organizations. That faith and loyalty to the church and the Vicar of Christ also marked his pastoral efforts at Saint Agnes parish from 1969 until 2001. Those efforts were best described in his own words.

> In every way, what is done at Saint Agnes is in perfect accord with the directives of the Holy See and the reforms of the Second Vatican Council. Liturgy at Saint Agnes is not a home-made activity. Rather it is the action of the Church, which is the Mystical Christ; and therefore, the liturgy is the very action of the Redeemer Himself. Only the Church, the Mystical Christ, can determine what that is to be. It remains for the priest and the people to carry it out as the Church prescribes it with as much care, reverence and solemnity as possible. From the beginning of the parish, this was the intention of the pastors, and nothing was spared to make the Eucharistic Sacrifice noble and beautiful, fully in accord with the ritual of the Roman Catholic Church.

In these words lies Richard Schuler's legacy, here his lesson for all who come after him.

How often have we heard it said that "no one is irreplaceable?" That claim may be true when it applies to certain positions in the life of men and society. But if the statement refers to the inner core of a person as an individual, to his originality and his personality – then "irreplaceable" is a rather superficial word.

To the extent that every person is a unique creation of God, every person is in himself irreplaceable, because one of a kind. But for others, a man can be irreplaceable if during his life, he was able to enrich others from the heart of his own personality, to form and shape and mould them. In that sense, for those of us who knew him well as fatherly friend and counselor, the late lamented Richard Schuler is indeed irreplaceable. For us, there will come situations in which we can no longer ask his advice because Richard Schuler has left us for a better place. Our sorrow is great because we no longer have him as a man, can no longer hear his voice or feel his friendly handshake, can no longer see his impressive priestly figure.

But he has built himself a monument in the hearts of those to whom he was priest, teacher, mentor, and friend. His image should remain in our memories and in our hearts, so that he continues to influence and inspire us.

Together with the company of comrades from the American Society of St. Caecilia (1956/64), the Consociatio Internationalis Musicae Sacrae, and the Church Music Association of America (1964 ff.), I say farewell to Richard Schuler with a word we so often exchanged after long evenings of conversation both serious and cheerful...on the Burgmauer or on Lafond Street, at Campo Santo Teutonico in the Vatican or at Father Siegfried Reh's hospitable rectory in Holzgau in the Lechtal: "I'll see you in the morning!"

Yes, indeed, in the morning...in the morning when that Morning Star arises which knows no setting – He, who returning from the grave serenely shone forth upon mankind, bringing to you, old friend, and to all of us redemption and everlasting life!

(First published in *Sacred Music*, Vol. 134, no. 2, Summer 2007, p. 3-5)

A Tribute to Monsignor Richard Schuler

By Reverend William E. Sanderson

This sermon was delivered on April 22, 2008 at the Church of Saint
Agnes, Saint Paul, Minnesota.

Reverend Fathers and Deacons, dear Sisters and consecrated Religious,
dear friends in Christ:

I am Father William Sanderson, pastor of Saint Mary's and
Saint Francis of Assisi parishes in south Omaha. It is a great joy and
privilege for me to be here tonight to celebrate this Mass with you to
commemorate the first anniversary of the death of Monsignor Richard
J. Schuler. Many of you may remember that Monsignor Schuler called
on me over twenty years ago to sing the parts of the celebrant for the
recordings of the Masses for Christmas, Easter, and Pentecost from
Saint Agnes that were produced by Leaflet Missal Company. After
that, whenever he introduced me to someone I had not previously
known, he introduced me as "the voice" on the recordings.

My first visit to Saint Agnes was nearly thirty years ago, in
October of 1978. I had just entered the Saint Paul Seminary and
became acquainted with a seminarian from Saint Agnes, Richard
Hogan. There was a memorial Mass for Pope John Paul I, the Mozart
Requiem, to which Father Hogan invited me to attend. I wept for joy
that night when I heard that beautiful music and experienced the full
beauty of the Roman Liturgy that I thought had been swept away in
the backwash of Vatican II. I was at the altar of God and Monsignor
Schuler brought me back, at least briefly, to the joy of my youth in that
High Mass.

I had come to know about Saint Agnes even before that. I had
attended Saint John's Prep School in Collegeville during the school
year 1968-69. Through the influence of some classmates, I started
to cultivate an interest in classical music. I kept in touch with these

classmates, who later would ride the bus from North Minneapolis on Sunday mornings to attend Mass at Saint Agnes. I vicariously came to learn about and purchase vinyl disk recordings of Haydn's *Paukenmesse* and *Lord Nelson Mass*, and Mozart's *Coronation Mass* which I would later come to experience, in person, in this very church.

I entered the Saint Paul Seminary in September of 1978, and in 1979, I entered Saint Agnes Seminary on Tuesday nights and began to cultivate a friendship with Monsignor Schuler that I will always cherish.

Tonight we will commemorate the first anniversary of the death of a great man, a great priest, a great musician, a great teacher, and a great friend. We reflect on the gift of his life, his faith, and his priesthood. As a young man Richard Schuler heard God's call to the priesthood and he responded, "Here I am." Having completed his studies at the College of Saint Thomas and the Saint Paul Seminary, on August 18, 1945, the day of his ordination, he was called by Archbishop Gregory Murray by name and he responded, *"Ad sum"* – "Here I am" – as he was ordained a priest. He sought to carry out God's will in his assignments at Nazareth Hall, College of Saint Thomas, and in his own advanced studies. In 1969, he began what I consider his greatest work: that as pastor of Saint Agnes.

What made Monsignor Schuler so great was his love for the Church and the priesthood. On the day of his ordination, he made certain promises as does every priest. He promised: with the help of the Holy Spirit, to discharge, without fail, the office of the priesthood as a conscientious fellow worker with the Bishops in caring for the Lord's flock. He promised to celebrate the mysteries of Christ faithfully and religiously as the Church has handed them down for the glory of God and the sanctification of Christ's people. He promised to exercise the ministry of the Word worthily and wisely, preaching the Gospel and explaining the Catholic faith. He promised to consecrate his life to God for the salvation of his people and to unite himself more closely every day to Christ the High Priest. And on that day, as he knelt before Archbishop Murray, he placed his newly anointed hands on a chalice and paten and, in the words of the Rite of Ordination, he "accepted from the holy people of God the gifts to be offered to him." He was admonished: "Know what you are doing, imitate the mystery you celebrate, model your life on the mystery of the Lord's cross." As

I see it, he never forgot those promises nor did he ever tire of living them out.

His greatest love was for the Holy Sacrifice of the Mass: protecting, preserving, and presenting the Roman Liturgy in all its splendor, even at a time it was being trivialized in the wake of Vatican II with the many liturgical and musical abominations that were wrongly foisted on the faithful in its name.

He understood with clarity the opening lines of Chapter VI of the *Constitution on the Sacred Liturgy* about sacred music:

> The musical tradition of the universal Church is a treasure of inestimable value, greater even than that of any other art. The main reason for this pre-eminence is that, as a combination of sacred music and words, it forms a necessary or integral part of the solemn liturgy (n.112).
>
> The treasury of sacred music is to be preserved and cultivated with great care. Choirs must be assiduously developed, especially in cathedral churches. Bishops and other pastors of souls must take great care to ensure that whenever the sacred action is to be accompanied by chant, the whole body of the faithful may be able to contribute that active participation which is rightly theirs (n.114).
>
> The Church recognizes Gregorian chant as being specially suited to the Roman liturgy. Therefore, other things being equal, it should be given pride of place in liturgical services (n.116).

He never forgot that the Council not only called for the "active" participation of the faithful but, as stated in paragraph 50 of the *Constitution on the Sacred Liturgy*, the "devout" active participation of the faithful.

Monsignor Schuler was an outstanding promoter of vocations to the priesthood and consecrated life. His parish and rectory were like a "little United Nations of the Catholic Church." The doors were open to any Bishop, priest, deacon, or seminarian in good standing – even liberals. I don't know exactly the number of first Masses celebrated at Saint Agnes during his tenure or the number of vocations he salvaged and sent to other dioceses when rejected by the seminary. I don't know the number of hours he spent with the "underground" seminarians, providing a safe haven where the Faith could be shared openly and presented unabashedly and heretical distortions corrected with clarity, charity and forthrightness. The Church, especially in this portion of the Midwest, has been greatly enriched by his willingness to share his faith and commitment to the Church so openly and generously with young men in formation.

In the *Acts of the Apostles* today we read,

> They proclaimed the good news to that city and made a considerable number of disciples. They strengthened the spirits of the disciples and exhorted them to persevere in the Faith, saying, "It is necessary for us to undergo many hardships to enter the Kingdom of God."

And so he offered encouragement, support, and whatever assistance was needed for any worthy candidate to the priesthood to accept whatever hardships he may need to endure along the way to the day of his ordination.

I would like to share with you, at least briefly, some of the correspondence I shared with Monsignor Schuler through the years. The memories I treasure the most with Monsignor deal with the production of the Leaflet Missal recordings and the program that preceded them. This all began with a radio broadcast in Fall, 1984 on National Public Radio's weekly program, *Lincoln's Music in America.* That program featured otherwise little known musicians, ensembles, and choirs throughout the country. Monsignor invited me to travel to Saint Agnes to be the celebrant for the Beethoven *Mass in C.* The broadcast featured many parts of the Mass and an extensive interview with Monsignor Schuler. It came to be the most requested rebroadcast of *Music in America.*

After the recording session and initial broadcast, Monsignor wrote to me on October 27, 1984:

> As I write this I am listening to you sing the *oratio super oblationis* and the Preface. Marvelous. The tape is enclosed. It is really fine, done in good taste and truly all I had hoped it would be. Did you hear it in Omaha? I had a call from someone in Jacksonville, Florida who heard it. I will let you know the reactions we get.

He also shared with me a copy of a letter he had received dated October 19, 1984 from Evans Mirageas, the man from WFMT in Chicago who recorded the Mass at Saint Agnes for *Lincoln's Music in America* on National Public Radio and conducted the interview. He wrote:

> Here are the finished tapes of the *Music in America* program on Saint Agnes. I hope that we have done justice to your efforts. I was mightily impressed with the dedication and spirit of your performers, both in the choir and the soloists. And to have the instrumentalists was a real pleasure. I cannot thank you and the other Fathers enough for the assistance and cooperation you extended before and during last Sunday. It was a pleasure to be able to carry your musical message to our audience. Your parishioners are very lucky to have you, Father.

Monsignor was kind enough to share a copy of a letter dated November 14, 1984, he received from a priest in Oklahoma City, a retired Latin teacher who wrote to him about the broadcast. He wrote:

> The October 28th broadcast of music from Saint Agnes Church on *Lincoln's Music in America* prompts me to write to you. I would like to express my sincere gratitude to you personally and to your musicians, professional and amateur, for your musical accomplishment and for the faith which so clearly motivates your efforts.
> I have never met you or even, I am sorry to say, heard your name, but please accept my expression of deep gratitude for the statement about Catholicism, worship and the interior life of humanity which your work is. It is a great joy to recall that there exists someone who is capable of dealing with the American Church's well-intentioned trivialization of the sacred; I cannot express how encouraging it is to know that this person is a priest.

Not quite a year later in a letter dated September 23, 1985 he wrote me another letter. I think it is important that I share this, because a priest so often becomes so wrapped up in the cares of his office and responsibilities that he sometimes may forget to acknowledge his gratitude to those with whom he works the closest. Even if this is not the case, I believe that if Monsignor were here tonight, he would say something similar to all of you tonight. This is what he wrote.

> Sunday, September 15th was a great day at Saint Agnes and a day I shall always remember. It was full of great surprises and so much that was beautiful and friendly. I don't know how I can possibly express my gratitude and my appreciation for all that was planned and carried out to observe the fortieth anniversary of my ordination to the holy priesthood. The presence of so many dear friends and parishioners, the wonderful music of the Twin Cities Catholic Chorale with the instrumentalists, the fine sermon by Father Hogan, the careful ceremonies of our altar boys, the exquisite reception, the many details and loving care all made the occasion perfect.

Monsignor Schuler taught us many lessons worthy of remembrance. About the proper approach to the Sacred Liturgy he always said: "It must be reverent and it must be dignified. Reverent so that it does not offend God; dignified so that it does not offend man." About music itself: "It must be sacred and it must be music." About keeping proper time with the music as written: "There must be NO toe-tapping and watch the conductor." About fidelity to the musical score especially when departures were being made: "That's very nice, but I don't think that's the way Schubert wrote it."

Yes, "Every high priest is taken from among men and made their representative before God, to offer gifts and sacrifices for sins. No one takes this honor upon himself but only when called by God" (*Hebrews* 5:1, 4). It was one year ago God called Monsignor one more time: After eighty-six years on this earth; after sixty-two years of service as a priest; after fifty-one years as Director of the Twin Cities Catholic Chorale; after thirty-two years as pastor of Saint Agnes, he set down his baton and the burden of years. With the strains of the Beethoven *Mass in C* playing softly in the background we can be sure he whispered in his heart one more time, "Here I am."

(First published in *Sacred Music*, Vol. 135, no. 4, Winter 2008, p. 54-58)

Epilogue

"With the dawning of the 17th century came a flowering of religion...a spreading of Catholicism in Europe and in the newly discovered western hemisphere. The cause of all this was the Council of Trent and those who put it into effect. When it was finally put into practice, a great age dawned. So also will it come about in these times when the Second Vatican Council is finally given a chance and is put into practice. We may not live to see it in its full blossom, but we must begin and to the best of our abilities, lay the groundwork and put into effect here and now the will of the Church, the directives of the Second Vatican Council."

Monsignor Richard J. Schuler
(*Sacred Music*, Vol. 119, no.4, Winter 1992, p. 7-14)

Contributors

John M. DeJak

John M. DeJak, an attorney and educator, is Headmaster of Chelsea Academy in Front Royal, Virginia. He practiced law and served on active duty as an officer in the U.S. Army prior to being named the founding headmaster of two private high schools in the Twin Cities area. He has taught Latin, Greek, literature, government, and theology in high schools in Chicago, Cleveland, the Twin Cities, Ann Arbor, and Front Royal. He is the co-editor of *With God in America: The Spiritual Legacy of an Unlikely Jesuit* (Loyola Press, 2016). A member of the Fellowship of Catholic Scholars, he is also an Adjunct Professor at the University of Saint Thomas and the Saint Paul Seminary in Saint Paul, Minnesota. His articles have appeared in *Chronicles*, *Gilbert Magazine*, *Homiletic and Pastoral Review*, the *Distributist Review*, *The Wanderer*, and the *Saint Austin Review*. He and his wife, Annie, and their eight children live in Front Royal, Virginia.

Jennifer Donelson-Nowicka

Jennifer Donelson-Nowicka holds the William P. Mahrt endowed chair in Sacred Music at Saint Patrick's Seminary in Menlo Park, California. Having worked in seminary and lay musical formation for over a decade at Saint Gregory the Great Seminary in Nebraska and Saint Joseph's Seminary (Dunwoodie) in New York, she has founded the Catholic Institute of Sacred Music at Saint Patrick's Seminary, which offers graduate-level coursework in Sacred Music to lay students across the world. She serves on the board of the Church Music Association of America (CMAA), is the managing editor of the CMAA's journal *Sacred Music*, and is a regular member of the faculty for the CMAA's annual Sacred Music Colloquium. As academic liaison of the CMAA, she has organized and presented papers at several academic conferences on Charles Tournemire (2012, 2013), the role of Gregorian Chant in pastoral ministry and religious education (2017), the life and work of William Mahrt (2023), the work of Monsignor Richard Schuler (2013). As sometime-president, she is currently a board member of the Society for Catholic Liturgy. Donelson-Nowicka serves as a consultant to the USCCB's Committee on Divine Worship and is an organizer of the Sacra Liturgia conferences. In addition to the coursework and musical formation she provides at the seminary, she teaches chant to the Benedictine monks of San Benedetto in Monte, located in Norcia, Italy.

Reverend John Paul Erickson

Father Erickson, ordained in 2006 for the Archdiocese of Saint Paul and Minneapolis, currently serves as pastor of Transfiguration Catholic Church in Oakdale, Minnesota. For ten years he served as the Director of the Office of Worship for the same archdiocese, living in residence at Saint Agnes for many of them. He pursued liturgical studies at Mundelein's Liturgical Institute, and taught for a time as adjunct faculty at the Saint Paul Seminary.

Paul LeVoir

Paul W. LeVoir is the systems administrator at a local title company in the Twin Cities area and has directed the *Schola Cantorum* at the Church of Saint Agnes in Saint Paul, Minnesota, since 1979. He has also contributed to *Sacred Music* magazine.

William Mahrt

William Mahrt received his PhD at Stanford University in 1969. After having taught at Case Western Reserve University and Eastman School of Music, he returned to Stanford, where he teaches Medieval and Renaissance music. Since 1972 he has directed the Stanford Early Music Singers; he was a founding member of the Saint Ann Choir and has been its director since 1964, singing Mass and Vespers in Gregorian chant and classical polyphony on Sundays and holydays. Dr. Mahrt is president of the Church Music Association of America and editor of its journal, *Sacred Music*, the oldest continuously published music journal in the United States. A collection of his essays, *The Musical Shape of the Liturgy*, was published in 2012. Dr. Mahrt traveled to Germany, Italy, and Austria in 1974 with the Twin Cities Catholic Chorale. An endowed chair in Sacred Music named after Professor Mahrt has been established at the seminary of the Archdiocese of San Francisco.

Reverend Mark Moriarty

After his ordination in 1999, Father Mark Moriarty served as an assistant pastor at Saint Hubert Catholic Community (1999-2000) in Chanhassen, followed by Holy Trinity and Saint Augustine Catholic Churches (2000-2003) in South Saint Paul, Minnesota. Father Moriarty then served for nine years as pastor of Mary, Queen of Peace parish in

Rogers, Minnesota. During that time, in addition to his role as pastor, Father Moriarty was chaplain to Providence Academy (2003-2006). In May, 2012, Father Moriarty was assigned as pastor of the Church of Saint Agnes and Superintendent of Saint Agnes School.

Charles W. Nelson

Charles W. Nelson was a member of the Boys' Choir, the School Choir, and the Senior Mixed Choir at the Church of the Nativity of Our Lord in Saint Paul, Minnesota, when the young Father Richard Schuler was the director of those choirs and weekend assistant at Nativity. Nelson is currently a lector at the Church of Saint Agnes and a member of the Board of the Twin Cities Catholic Chorale, where he serves as chairman of the Schuler Archives Committee. Dr. Nelson graduated with a BA from the College of Saint Thomas. He earned the MA and PhD degrees at the University of Nebraska in English Literature with specialties in Medieval and Renaissance Literature. He is Professor Emeritus from Michigan Technological University and is currently a Visiting Professor at the University of Saint Thomas in Saint Paul.

Reverend William E. Sanderson

Father Sanderson, now retired, was ordained in 1983 for the Archdiocese of Omaha, Nebraska, and served in many parishes in that archdiocese. Father Sanderson is originally from Sioux Falls, South Dakota, where he completed his baccalaureate degree at the University of Sioux Falls in 1974. He studied for the priesthood at the Saint Paul Seminary and during that period began his association with the Church of Saint Agnes in Saint Paul and Monsignor Schuler, who became an important mentor and a good friend. His First Mass was celebrated at the Church of Saint Margaret Mary in Omaha, but his First Mass in Latin was at Saint Agnes where he celebrated Mass on November 2 that year, the feast of All Souls, for which the Twin Cities Catholic Chorale sang the Mozart *Requiem*. In 1986 when the Chorale recorded the Masses of Haydn, Gounod and Beethoven in a format which included the full Mass, Monsignor Schuler asked Father Sanderson to be the celebrant for those recordings. He recounts that experience in chapter seven of *To Sing With the Angels*. Father Sanderson was invited to be the celebrant and preach on the first anniversary of Monsignor Schuler's death when the Chorale sang the Mozart *Requiem* in his memory. Father Sanderson was responsible for the installation of new pipe organs at two parishes, Saint Mary's and at Holy Ghost while in Omaha. He is already assisting in two local parishes in Florida.

Reverend Robert A. Skeris

Father Skeris was ordained in 1961 for the Archdiocese of Milwaukee. He has a doctorate in Theology from the Rhenish Friedrich-Wilhelms University in Bonn, Germany. He was Director of the Centre for Ward Method Studies in the Benjamin T. Rome School of Music and Chairman of the Administration Committee of the Dom Mocquereau Fund at the Catholic University of America for several years. He was previously Director of the Hymnology Section in the international Institute for Hymnological and Ethnomusicological Studies at the Abbey of Maria Laach in Germany and then Prefect of the Pontifical Institute of Sacred Music in Rome. Father Skeris has published widely on the theology of worship and its music, hymnology, and Gregorian chant. A founding member of the Church Music Association of America, Father Skeris was president of the association from 1996-2004 and edited the continuing series, *Musicae Sacrae Meletemata.* He was invited to teach master classes and summer courses in Portugal, Hungary, and Lithuania. He was one of the chairmen of the Fifth International Church Music Congress in Chicago and Milwaukee (1966) and the Sixth International Church Music Congress in Salzburg, Austria (1974), both under the sponsorship of the *Consociatio Internationalis Musicae Sacrae.*

Acknowledgments

As the editor of this book, I am indebted first of all to its author, Monsignor Richard J. Schuler. In re-reading the essays that he published in *Sacred Music*, the journal of the Church Music Association of America, when he was its editor, with the intention of explaining the meaning and importance of the documents of the Second Vatican Council on sacred music and the liturgy to its readers, I was inspired to re-publish those essays in one place now in order to offer them to a new generation. Monsignor Schuler understood those documents and their relationship to the rich traditions, history, and doctrine of the Catholic Church. He also understood how Vatican II had been misinterpreted by some in an effort to change the Church.

On a most practical level, I wish to thank and acknowledge Cindy Paslawski, who edited *To Sing with the Angels*, and without whom this book would never have been completed. She knows the subject matter and also the practical details of publishing a book. I also thank Rhonda Klein of Evergreen Press for the cover and interior design. My gratitude to John Paul Sonnen for his encouragement and recommending me and this book to Arouca Press.

Of course, I wish to thank all who have contributed to putting Monsignor Schuler's essays in a contemporary context. I thank William Mahrt, president of CMAA and editor of *Sacred Music* for his introduction and his wise advice, and John DeJak for the prologue which puts everything in context. And I thank Paul LeVoir, Father John Paul Erickson, Jennifer Donelson-Nowicka and Father Mark Moriarty for their contemporary commentaries based on their current experience. I am also most grateful for the permission of Father Skeris, Father Sanderson and Charles Nelson to re-publish their previously published essays on Monsignor Schuler. I thank Diane Foote, the widow of the talented artist Christopher Foote for permission to use his portrait of Monsignor Schuler as the cover of this book. My gratitude to all who have supplied pictures and especially to Neal Abbott whose pictures and practical help have been essential.

Finally, I send warm thanks to my family and friends for always understanding and encouraging me in this endeavor.

Index

www.ingramcontent.com/pod-product-compliance
Lightning Source LLC
Chambersburg PA
CBHW051254120626
46547CB00014B/1943